Thinking Through Science

Arthur Cheney
Howard Flavell
Chris Harrison
George Hurst
Carolyn Yates

Series editor: Chris Harrison

**HODDER
MURRAY**

The cover image shows a section through the shell of a Nautilus. It is sometimes called a *chamber snail*. As the animal grows, new chambers are added one at a time to its shell. The Nautilus is a marine mollusc, and resembles a squid with its many tentacles that surround its mouth.

© Arthur Cheney, Howard Flavell, Chris Harrison, George Hurst, Carolyn Yates 2002

First published in 2002
by Hodder Murray, an imprint of Hodder Education, a member
of the Hodder Headline Group.
338 Euston Road
London NW1 3BH

Reprinted 2002, 2004, 2005

Layouts by Stephen Rowling/springworks
Artwork by Oxford Designers & Illustrators Ltd

Typeset in 11/13pt Lucida by Wearset Ltd, Boldon, Tyne and Wear
Printed in Dubai

A catalogue entry for this title is available from the British Library

ISBN 0 7195 7851 5
Teacher's Book 1 0 7195 7852 3
CD-ROM 1 0 7195 7853 1

Contents

Acknowledgements

Source acknowledgements
The following are sources from which artwork and text have been taken:

p.45 'The Otter' from *Lupercal*, by Ted Hughes. Faber and Faber Ltd
p.71 *b* from *Physics for Life*, by Peter Warren, with permission
p.230 Dave Keeling and Tim Whorf, Scripps Institution of Oceangraphy
p.237 from the Science and Technology in Society (SATIS) Atlas, the Association for Science Education

Photo credits
Thanks are due to the following for permission to reproduce copyright photographs:

Cover Martin Bond/Science Photo Library; **p.1** *tl* Science Photo Library/Sinclair Stammers, *bl* Science Photo Library/ Matt Meadows, *bc* Oxford Scientific Films, *r* Science Photo Library/Ed Young; **p.5** John Townson/Creation; **p.18** John Townson/Creation; **p.19** Andrew Lambert; **p.26** Oxford Scientific Films; **p.40** *tl* Science Photo Library/Alfred Pasieka, *tc* Oxford Scientific Films, *tr* Science Photo Library/ John Heseltine, *cl* Science Photo Library/Gregory Ochocki, *c* Oxford Scientific Films, *cr* Science Photo Library/Maximillian Stock, *cb* Bubbles, *br* Science Photo Library/Dr Morley Read; **p.46** Oxford Scientific Films; **p.47** Oxford Scientific Films; **p.51** Ronald Grant Archive; **p.58** John Townson/Creation; **p.60** John Townson/Creation; **p.64** Courtesy of Black & Decker; **p.68** *l* Mary Evans Picture Library, *r* John Townson/ Creation; **p.72** Science Photo Library/Chris Knapton; **p.75** Andrew Lambert; **p.76** *t* Science Photo Library/Chris Knapton, *b* Science Photo Library; **p.79** *t* John Townson/ Creation, *b* Courtesy of Express Dairies; **p.80** Science Photo Library/Matthew Oldfield/Scubazoo; **p.81** John Townson/ Creation; **p.88** Andrew Lambert; **p.90** *l* Science Photo Library, *r* John Townson/Creation; **p.91** Andrew Lambert; **p.92** Andrew Lambert; **p.93** **Roger Scruton**; **p.94** John Townson/Creation; **p.100** John Townson/Creation; **p.101** John Townson/Creation; **p.103** John Townson/Creation; **p.104** Colorsport; **p.105** *l* Robert Harding Picture Library, *c* Empics, *r* John Townson/Creation; **p.106** Mary Evans Picture Library; **p.108** MIRA; **p.115** Robert Harding Picture Library; **p.117** John Townson/Creation; **p.121** Science Photo Library; **p.123** Andrew Lambert; **p.128** *l* Mary Evans Picture Library, *tr* Empics, *br* Mary Evans Picture Library; **p.129** Robert Harding Picture Library; **p.132** *t* Science Photo Library/ Dr Jeremy Burgess, *b* Science Photo Library/Astrid & Hans-Frieder Michler; **p.133** *t* Science Photo Library/Biophoto Associates, *b* Science Photo Library/A B Dowsett; **p.141** *l* & *r* Science Photo Library/Dr Gopal Murti; **p.148** *tl* Science Photo Library/Marilyn Schaller, *tr* Science Photo Library/ David Hall, *b* Science Photo Library/CNRI; **p.152** *t* Science Photo Library/Don Fawcett, *bl* Science Photo Library/Petit Format/Nestle, *br* Bubbles; **p.160** *t* Natural Visions, *bl* Natural Visions, *br* Bruce Coleman; **p.162** Science Photo Library/ Alex Bartel; **p.172** John Townson/Creation; **p.175** John Townson/Creation; **p.183** *t* Science Photo Library/Peter Menzel, *bl* Roger Scruton, *br* John Townson/Creation; **p.185** Science Photo Library/Novosti Press Agency; **p.186** Science Photo Library/Charles D Winters; **p.193** Ancient Art & Architecture; **p.194** Science Photo Library/ESA; **p.198** *l* Oxford Scientific Films, *c* Science Photo Library/Dennis Potokar, *tr* Science Photo Library/Francoise Sauze, *br* Science photo Library/Martin Bond. **p.199** NHPA; **p.201** Science Photo Library; **p.202** Oxford Scientific Films; **p.203** *t* Science photo Library/Frank Zullo, *b* Science Photo Library/Rev. Ronald Royer; **p.204** Mary Evans Picture Library; **p.206** *tl* Science Photo Library/Jerry Lodriques, *tr* Ancient Art & Architecture, *b* Science Photo Library/ Francois Goher; **p.208** *l* Science Photo Library/Fred Espenak, *r* Science photo Library/Celestial Image Picture Co; **p.210** John Townson/Creation; **p.211** John Townson/ Creation; **p.214** Popperfoto; **p.215** John Townson/Creation; **p.216** Science Photo Library/Adam Hart-Davis; **p.218** John Townson/Creation; **p.220** Oxford Scientific Films; **p.221** Mary Evans Picture Library; **p.225** Science Photo Library; **p. 234** John Townson/Creation; **p.236** *t* Science Photo Library/Crown Copyright/Health & Safety Laboratory, *b* Science Photo Library/Richard Folwell; **p.240** *tl* Oxford Scientific Films, *tr* Roger Scruton, *cl* Science Photo Library/ Martin Bond, *cr* Science Photo Library/Martin Bond, *bl* Oxford Scientific Films, *bc* Robert Harding Picture Library, *br* Oxford Scientific Films; **p.246** John Townson/Creation.

l = left, *r* = right, *t* = top, *b* = bottom, *c* = centre

The publishers have made every effort to contact copyright holders. If any have been overlooked, they will be pleased to make the necessary arrangements at the earliest opportunity.

Introduction

→ Scientists at work

Scientists do many types of work. Some monitor the world around us to find how the environment is changing. Others carry out tests in hospitals and factories to check things are working properly. Some scientists work on new inventions and technologies, or search for cures to diseases. Other scientists seek explanations for ideas that we cannot yet understand.

DNA fingerprinting.

Identifying bacteria.

Estimating populations.

Experimenting.

→ Science in schools

The science that you learn in school introduces you to many ideas that scientists have worked out over the centuries. New ideas and theories are being worked out all the time and so there will always be new things to learn in science, even when you are an adult.

Understanding scientific ideas helps you make sense of the world and many of the experiences in your life. If you have tests at a hospital you will be able to discuss the results with the doctor or nurse. When you read magazine articles about new materials or new processes, you will be able to judge how useful this will be to you and your society. If issues arise, such as the government asking which types of fuels should be used in power stations in future years, you will be able to understand the arguments of the different groups involved and reach an informed decision.

Part of your science work in school will give you opportunities to investigate ideas. This often involves practical work. You will make predictions, test ideas, collect and interpret data and evaluate your work. Some of these skills need to be developed before you try out a full investigation; others will improve through attempting a whole investigation.

Thinking is an important part of the work you will do in science. It helps you link ideas together, to form explanations and understand theories. Asking **questions** has an essential role to play as this promotes thinking. **Discussing** ideas, **checking** findings and **communicating** with others in your group also helps. This will help you make your own ideas clear, and listening to what others have to say sometimes challenges your thinking. So, be prepared to ask questions both of yourself and others!

Working safely

It is important to work safely in a science laboratory. Look at the picture below that shows an unsafe school laboratory.

1 Can you list eight or more dangers in this laboratory?
2 If you had to decide on six safety rules for the school in the picture, what would they be?
3 How do your rules compare with others in your group?
4 How do your rules compare with your school laboratory rules?

Creative thinking *Safety*

Try one of the following:

1 Write a short story about a dangerous school laboratory.

2 Write a poem about being safe in a school laboratory.

3 Draw a poster for the laboratory safety rule that you think is most important.

Variables, values and relationships

Key words
* variable
* value
* relationship
* prediction

Science often looks at how some things are different and others are the same. In science we call the differences **variables**.

Look at the books below. They have many differences.

They are different sizes. They have different numbers of pages. They have different coloured covers. Some are fiction and some are non-fiction. The variables for these books are:

size
number of pages
cover colour
type.

The colour of the covers could be red, blue, yellow, brown or green. Scientists call these **values**.

The variable 'size' might have values of big, medium and small, or actual measurements could be given. The variable 'number of pages' will have numbers as the values. For the variable 'type', it will simply be fiction and non-fiction.

Variable	Value
size	big, medium, small
number of pages	up to 100, 101–500, 501–1000, over 1000
cover colour	red, blue, yellow, brown, green
type	fiction, non-fiction

Scientists are interested to see if any variables are linked to one another. If they are this is called a **relationship**. With the books, we might look at how heavy the books are. This would be related to the size of the book. Big books are heavy and small books are light. The bigger the book, the heavier it should be. If we came across a new book and saw that it was big, then we would not need to weigh it. We would know that it was heavy. Relationships help scientists make **predictions**.

Information processing

Variables

Look at these shapes.

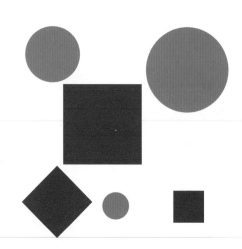

1 What are the variables for the shapes shown right?

2 What are the values for each variable?

3 Which variables are linked?

4 What is the relationship between these two variables?

5 If you had a circle diagram, what colour would it be?

6 If you had a red diagram, what shape would it be?

7 If you had a large, green diagram, what shape would it be? What helped you decide?

Look at the three sets of pictures below.

£ 725   £ 1125   £ 315   £ 75

Range Rover 2500 cc/130 m.p.h.

racing car 4000 cc/200 m.p.h.

Fiesta 1100 cc/80 m.p.h.

moped 50 cc/40 m.p.h.

8 What are the variables?

9 What are the relationships in each set?

Here are some relationships that you will already have come across in science.

> The more powerful the battery, the brighter the bulb.
> The warmer the water, the faster sugar will dissolve.
> The nearer a star is to Earth, the brighter it looks.

10 What are the variables in each of these relationships?

11 What are the values for each of these variables?

12 What predictions can you make with these relationships?

Input and outcome variables

Key words
* input variable
* outcome variable
* fixed variable

In science investigations, we can change a variable and see what this does to another variable. We might move a plant nearer to a window and measure how much more it grows. We decide how near to the window to place the plant. In science we call this type of variable an **input variable**. The plant growth that we measure is called the **outcome variable**.

Distance is the input variable and growth is the outcome variable.

This investigation would only work if all the other variables were kept the same. These are called **fixed variables**. So the amount of water that both plants gets must be the same. The amount of fertiliser that each gets must also be the same.

Identifying variables

Hannah and Faye made some 'krispy cakes'.

Last week they made some and they were delicious. Today they made some and they were horrible. Hannah thought that it might be the type of chocolate that they used. Last week they used milk chocolate and today they used dark chocolate.

Both girls were keen to investigate if Hannah was correct. They decided that the outcome variable would be taste.

1 What would be the values for the outcome variable?

2 What would be the input variable?

3 If Hannah was correct, what would the relationship be?

4 What would be the fixed variables in this investigation?

David and Connor were investigating how good paper towels were at mopping up water. They had three types of paper towel – thin towels, thick towels and extra thick towels. They took a metre length of each towel and dipped it in 600 ml of water. They took out the towel and measured how much water was left in the bucket. Their results were:

Type of towel	Water left in bucket
thin towel	500 ml
thick towel	350 ml
extra thick towel	175 ml

5 What is the input variable?

6 What is the outcome variable?

7 What would be the values for the outcome variable?

8 What are the fixed variables in this investigation?

9 What is the relationship?

Using graphs and charts

Identifying variables and finding relationships helps you make sense of things. Sometimes it is easy to see a relationship, but often you need to sort out the information first.

Mr Bertolli owned a sweet shop and his most popular sweets were 'fruity bon-bons'. These sweets were lemon, lime, orange or strawberry flavoured. Mr Bertolli topped up the fruity bon-bons jar every night with the different flavours. Many customers asked Mr Bertolli to put extra of their favourite flavour into their bag. Mr Bertolli wanted to find out which flavours were most popular.

For one week he counted the number of each flavour every night and then topped up the jar so that there were 200 of each flavour for the following day. Here are his results. They show the number of sweets left at the end of each day.

Day	Lemon	Lime	Orange	Strawberry
1	45	97	126	54
2	51	99	111	70
3	50	116	95	64
4	27	95	92	25
5	34	89	58	26
6	82	108	110	70
7	61	96	108	41

It is difficult for Mr Bertolli to see which flavour is most popular from the table. He has to work out how many of each flavour are eaten each day and then compare that with the figures for all the other days. We can help Mr Bertolli by presenting the results in a pie chart.

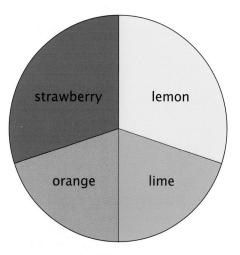

Mr Bertolli can then easily see that lemon and strawberry flavour are equally popular. He can also see that both lemon and strawberry are more popular than lime or orange.

We could also have presented these data as a bar chart for Mr Bertolli to find the answer to his question. Then he could see the exact numbers sold for each flavour.

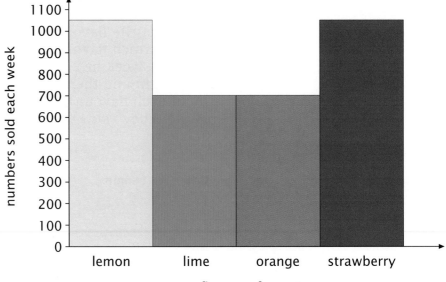

In science, you will often have to decide what is the best way to present your results. Getting a good table design is a start. You then need to think – What is the problem that I am trying to sort out? Would a pie chart or a bar chart or a line graph be the best way of presenting the data?

Information processing *Finding information*

Look at the data below.

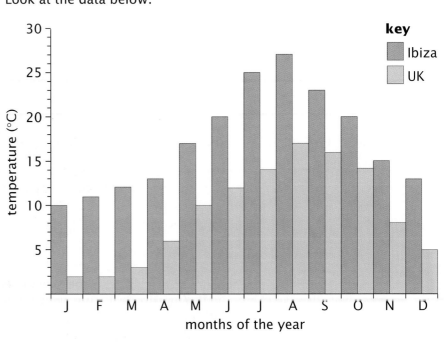

1 What was the temperature in Ibiza and the UK in June?

2 When was the temperature in Ibiza 10°C higher than the UK?

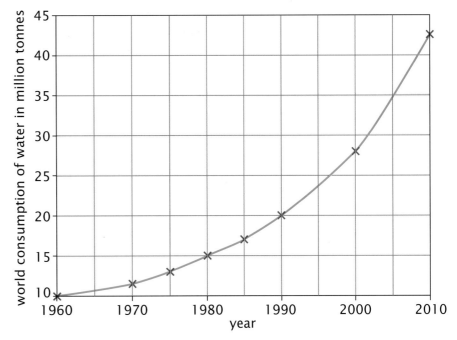

3 What was the world water consumption in 1985?

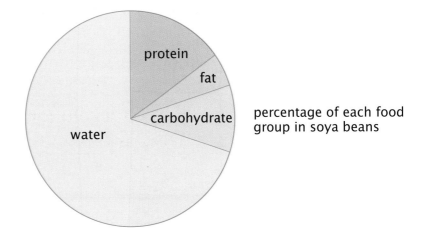

percentage of each food group in soya beans

4 What is the percentage of protein in soya beans?

5 Why have each of these sets of data been presented in this way?

6 Can any of these sets of data be presented in another way and still be useful? Can you answer questions 1–4 if the data are presented differently? What type of value do the horizontal axes have to be for a line graph?

7 How would you present the following sets of data:
  a) average number of hours of daylight over a year
  b) the average shoe size of year 7 pupils compared to other year groups
  c) the growth of a baby over the first 6 months
  d) the amount of different types of plant growing on the school field
  e) your pulse rate after a race until it returns to normal?

Problem solving

Science is often about solving problems. Working in groups of three or four, try to solve the following problem.

Reasoning   ## Mystery photograph

Miss Smith was woken up by a noise in her study. The next day she set up her camera in the study to take photographs at various times during the night. When she got the photographs back from the shop, she found that she had six photographs, but the camera had only taken five snaps. One snap must be a mystery photograph. Find the mystery photograph for Miss Smith and be prepared to explain to her how you made your decision.

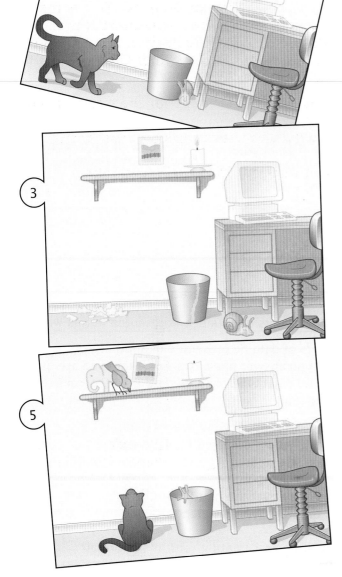

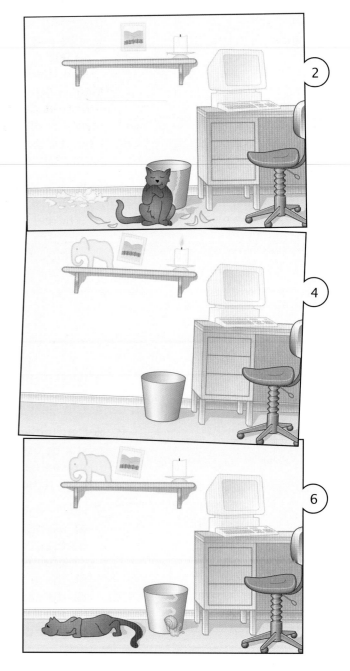

1 How did you start to sort out the problem?

2 Were any clues more important than others?

3 Which was the mystery photograph?

4 Did you do any checks to see if you had selected the correct number for the mystery photograph?

5 What was likely to be making the noise that woke up Miss Smith on the first night?

Anomalous results

Key words
* 'line of best fit'
* anomalous result

Sometimes we get a mystery result in a set of data. This experiment is looking at how much a spring stretches when a load is attached to it.

Putting the results in a table or plotting the results on a graph helps us see the odd result. It is seen even more clearly when we draw on the '**line of best fit**'. This is the line that passes through most points. Sometimes it is a straight line like this one but sometimes it can be a curved line. The odd result does not fit on the line. The odd result is called an **anomalous result**.

Mass (g)	Stretch of spring (cm)
0	0
100	3
200	6
300	9
400	10
500	15

5 What do you think the correct result for the stretch from a 400 g load should be?
6 What information did you use to work out your answer to question 5?
7 What else can you work out from the line graph?

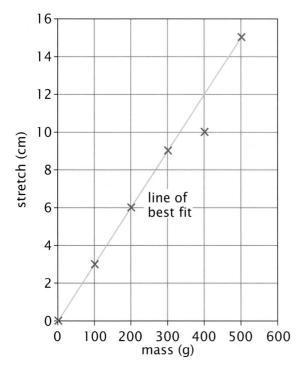

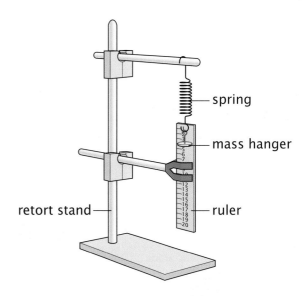

Concept maps

Concept maps help you link ideas together. Here is a concept map about school.

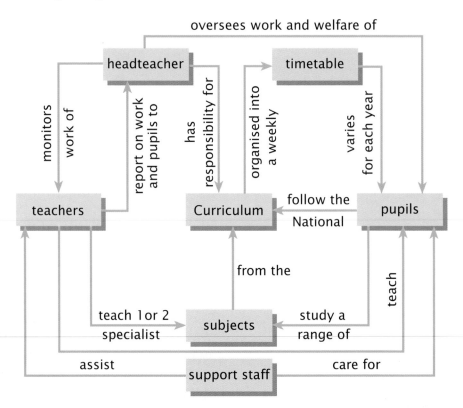

The boxes contain the key words for the main parts of a school. The lines that join them provide the link between the two boxes. It really is simply a way of putting together all the sentences that you might write to describe a school.

Here is the start of a concept map for plants.

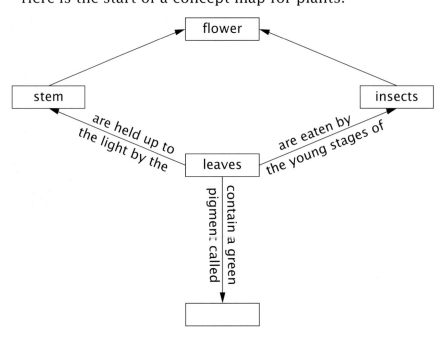

8 What would you write on the line that links flower and insects?

9 What would you write on the line that links flower and stem?

10 What is the missing word in the box linked to leaves?

11 What other boxes and linking lines could you add?

Models

Sometimes scientists use models to help explain scientific ideas and theories. This involves using another system that someone understands to explain how a second system works. You could explain the way that your school works using the model of the army.

The general would be the headteacher.
The majors would be the deputy heads.
The sergeants would be the teachers.
Corporals would be prefects, and soldiers would be pupils.

Using the army model may not explain perfectly how a school works. However, it does give some idea of the different levels of organisation in the school and the number in each group. You have one general and one headteacher but hundreds of soldiers and pupils.

Sometimes a model is a physical model. Here is a model to help us understand how we breathe. It is a model of the chest region.

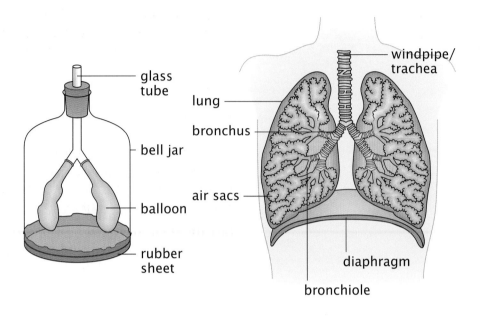

12 Which part of the model represents the lungs?
13 Which part of the model represents the windpipe?
14 Which part of the chest is represented by the rubber sheet?
15 Which part of the chest is represented by the bell jar?
16 Which parts of the model are very similar to the real chest region?
17 Which parts of the model are different from the real chest region?
18 Do you think this is a good model to show the parts of the breathing system or a poor one? Why?

This model is used to demonstrate how the lungs fill with air. By pushing the rubber sheet up and then letting it come back down, air enters the balloons. So, it helps show how the breathing system works but it is not very much like the real parts.

Getting started

In this book, we will help you:

- identify variables and values
- find relationships between variables
- present data in a useful way
- read and interpret data
- recognise anomalous results
- draw line graphs
- find the 'line of best fit' on line graphs
- solve problems
- share ideas with others
- learn and use key words
- link ideas using concept maps
- use models to help scientific understanding

but most of all, we will help you THINK!

1

Environment and feeding relationships

In this chapter you will learn:

→ **how habitats vary but have similar parts**
→ **how some plants and animals are adapted to live in a particular place**
→ **that some animals are adapted for feeding**
→ **the direction of energy flow in a food chain**
→ **how the organisms in a food chain are linked together**
→ **how food chains can link to form food webs**

You will also develop your skills in:

→ **observing and interpreting information**
→ **interpreting data from bar charts, line graphs, tables and datalogging read-outs**
→ **identifying variables**
→ **deciding on sample size**
→ **working out proportionality**

→ → → WHAT DO YOU KNOW?

Here is a section of a school's grounds. This area of land has been specially altered so that it can be used for sport and so that the grass can be easily cut.

1 How many different animals and plants can you see?

2 Can you group the animals into two or three different groups and describe what each group has in common?

3 Can you construct a key to help someone identify at least six animals in the picture?

4 Can you construct a key to identify at least four plants in the picture?

5 Can you write two to three sentences that explain any links between the living things in this picture? You might want to explain what they eat or where they live.

There is a wood a short distance away from the school. This is how the school grounds would look if they had not been altered and the grass was not regularly cut and walked on.

6 Which of the animals and plants that you named in question 1 can also be seen in the wood?

7 Which different animals and plants can be seen in the wood?

8 Why is there a difference in the type and number of animals and plants in the wood from in the school grounds?

9 There is only one fox in each area. Have you any ideas why that should be?

10 Grey squirrels can live in school grounds but you often find many more living in woods. Can you suggest reasons why this might be?

11 Ants live in the school grounds and in the wood. First imagine that you are an ant in the school grounds and describe your typical day. Where do you get your food? What dangers are there for you? How do you recognise these dangers? How do you escape problems? What are the good or difficult parts of your day? Then write the story for your cousin, the woodland ant. Will life be very different or much the same?

Observing and counting

Key words
* habitat
* sampling
* quadrat
* percentage cover
* sample
* reliable

A **habitat** is an area where particular animals and plants live. There are grassland habitats, woodland habitats, rocky shore habitats, rain forest habitats and many others, and each has its own special set of animals and plants. It is not an easy task to work out the type and number of animals and plants in an area. Animals rarely wait around to be identified and counted, and plants tend to be so numerous that it becomes an impossible task to count them all. To overcome these problems, scientists use **sampling**.

1 Look at the picture. These are all samples. Why do manufacturers produce samples of their products? How similar and how different are these samples to the real thing?

To sample plants in an area, scientists often use a **quadrat**. They can estimate how many of each plant type there is inside the area of the quadrat. Scientists can then work out the **percentage cover** of each plant and how many different types of plant can be found in the area being sampled.

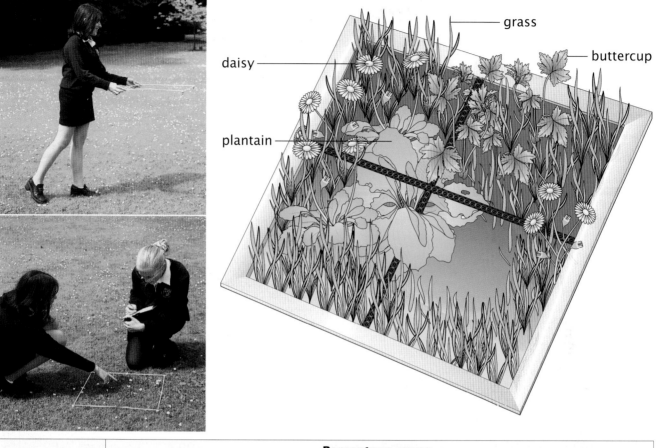

Name of plant	Percentage cover				
	1	2	3	4	Total
grass					
daisy					
plantain					
buttercup					
clover					
other plants					

This quadrat may be a true **sample** of what the plant cover is in the whole field or it might be in an area that attracted the scientists' attention because it had colourful flowers in it. To collect a **reliable** picture of the plant cover in the field the scientists would collect data from many more quadrats, perhaps 25 or 100.

The scientists would also try to do this in a random way. Sometimes this is done by someone throwing the quadrat over their shoulder so that they cannot pick out an area in advance. Scientists also use random number tables (these are tables of numbers generated by a computer which have no patterns in them) but the same can be done by simply taking the birthdays (day and month) of your class and then using these numbers in pairs to locate a spot.

Reasoning *Taking samples*

Look at the data below.

	1	2	3	4	5	6	7	8	9	10	11	12
Grass	50	75	90	50	70	75	80	90	50	70	90	80
Daisy	10	–	–	20	10	–	10	–	10	–	5	10
Plantain	25	–	–	–	10	25	10	–	10	20	5	5
Buttercup	10	10	–	–	10	–	–	–	20	–	–	5
Clover	–	10	–	20	–	–	–	–	10	–	5	–
Other plants	–	–	–	10	–	–	5	–	–	–	5	–
Bare ground	10	5	10	–	5	–	5	10	–	10	–	–

1 Why were 12 different quadrat samples taken?

2 Sometimes the total percentage cover in one quadrat adds up to over a hundred. Why do you think that this sometimes happens?

3 Why do you think the scientists who collected these data did not list each of the types of plant in the 'other plants' row?

You can draw bar charts of the data. Here are the bar charts for quadrat 1, quadrats 1–6, quadrats 1–12 and data from a larger study where 100 quadrats of data were taken.

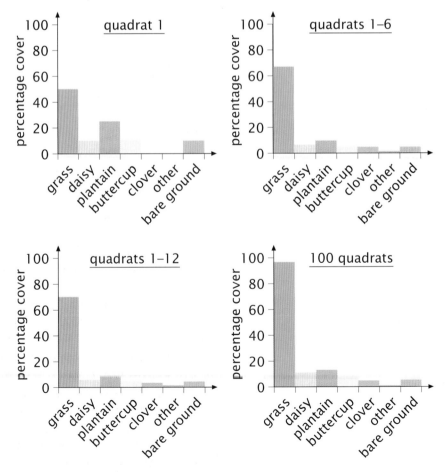

4 Why was taking 12 quadrats a good sample size to take in this study?

What do you think?

→ *Estimating*

Key words
* estimate
* population
* 'mark and recapture'
* extinction

Counting animals in a habitat is difficult because they move around and are very good at hiding. Many animals such as slugs, owls, bats and moths are rarely seen during the day because the active part of their lives happens during the night. Instead of counting the number of animals, scientists **estimate** the size of animal **populations** in a habitat. This usually requires either long periods of observation or a method called '**mark and recapture**'.

Mark and recapture involves trapping and marking the animals in some way and then releasing them into the habitat and setting up a second trapping exercise at a later date. Birds are sometimes caught and ringed. This involves putting a metal band with a number or code around the bird's leg. The birds can then be released unharmed into the habitat. If the nets are put up a second time the scientists can look at the number of ringed birds and the number of unringed birds. They can then use the ratio of ringed:unringed birds to estimate the total bird population in the habitat.

Other animal populations can be estimated in a similar way. Mice, rabbits or voles might have a tiny piece of fur shaved off to mark them. Woodlice, beetles or ants might have a tiny spot of paint put on their body.

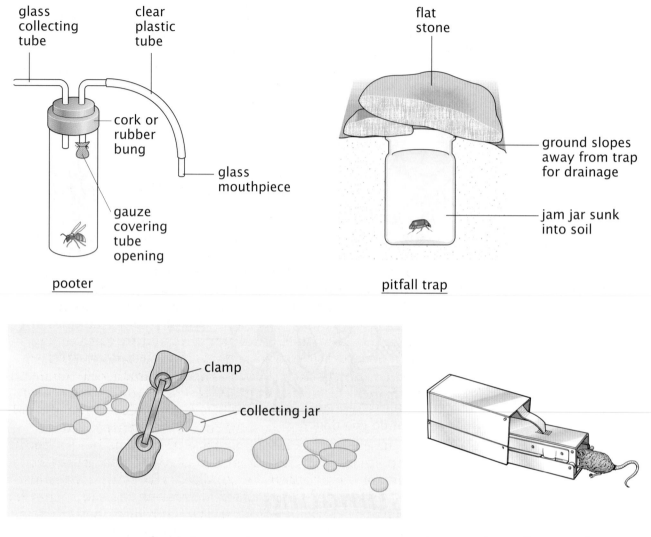

glass collecting tube

clear plastic tube

cork or rubber bung

glass mouthpiece

gauze covering tube opening

pooter

flat stone

ground slopes away from trap for drainage

jam jar sunk into soil

pitfall trap

clamp

collecting jar

fixed stream net

Longworth small mammal trap

All of these can be used to trap animals safely so that they can be returned to the wild later.

Population size

The population size will always be an estimate because animals die and others are born. Also some animals move into the habitat while others move out. It is a part of science where it is difficult to give an exact number. However, this skill can be used to help scientists find out important information about our planet. For example, Chinese scientists needed to estimate the population of giant pandas to help save them from **extinction**. In China, the number of giant pandas has greatly reduced over the last 50 years. Giant pandas have a diet almost entirely of bamboo. National Parks have been created for pandas, with enough areas of bamboo to provide the current population of giant pandas with plenty of their favourite food.

1 Why is it difficult for scientists to give an exact figure for population size?
2 How was the estimate of the number of pandas in China used to save them from extinction?

The Sumatran tiger is the most endangered member of the cat family with only about 20 adults living in the wild. Many zoos are creating breeding programmes to try and increase the numbers of the Sumatran tiger, but it is expected to become extinct like the Caspian tiger, which died out in the 1970s, and the Bali tiger, which became extinct in the 1940s.

Daily and seasonal changes

Key words
* environment
* nocturnal
* migrate
* hibernate

Animals and plants react to their surroundings – the **environment** around them. Plants usually grow better where there is plenty of sunlight and in soil that has lots of water. So the amount of light energy and the amount of water are important variables for plant growth.

Most animals have body temperatures that change with the temperature of their surroundings. For example, on cold days animals like worms, ants and frogs have low body temperatures and so they move and do everything slowly. In very hot countries, many animals only come out at night to find food when their surroundings are cooler, and during the day they hide away in holes in the ground or caves. These animals are called **nocturnal** animals.

Mammals like mice, squirrels and humans have a body temperature that is always at a steady temperature and does not change with the outside temperature. Birds also have a steady temperature that remains the same whether it is hot or cold outside. Mammals and birds have special systems in their bodies to help keep their body temperatures steady. These animals also have many special behaviours to help them warm up or avoid very cold conditions. Birds **migrate** to warmer countries when it gets too cold. Many mammals **hibernate** in the winter.

Animals react to all types of variables in the environment. Temperature is one variable but amount of food is another. Animals might be nocturnal because it is safer to find their food in the dark. They might be nocturnal because the animals they eat only come out at night.

Research   Check the dictionary definitions for these words:

migration
hibernation
nocturnal

and then do some research to find examples of animals that migrate, animals that hibernate and animals that are nocturnal. Name two to three animals for each group.

Information processing *Bird watching*

The table below shows the data collected at a nature reserve showing their bird visitors over the year.

Birds	Months											
	J	**F**	**M**	**A**	**M**	**J**	**J**	**A**	**S**	**O**	**N**	**D**
grey heron	18	12	7	14	15	19	17	18	12	20	15	16
common shelduck	10	8	6	0	0	0	2	6	8	10	9	8
Canada goose	46	42	39	47	40	51	50	38	42	44	47	40
mallard	62	61	70	69	62	68	75	61	60	54	69	63
goldeneye	8	10	2	2	0	0	0	0	2	4	4	6
avocet	0	0	0	2	1	0	2	0	0	0	0	0
coot	8	10	8	12	8	8	10	11	10	12	8	9
teal	26	29	11	4	5	7	6	29	21	26	30	20
redshank	18	19	15	16	8	6	8	9	12	19	18	20

1 Use the data to make four posters that could be put up in the nature reserve for each season – spring, summer, autumn and winter, to tell the human visitors which birds to look for.

A group of bird-watchers collected the data in a notebook on the right.

Monthly Count

Grey Heron	ЖН ЖН IIII
Canada Goose	ЖН ЖН ЖН ЖН ЖН ЖН ЖН ЖН ЖН II
Mallard	ЖН ЖН ЖН ЖН ЖН ЖН ЖН ЖН ЖН ЖН ЖН ЖН ЖН IIII
Goldeneye	II
Avocet	II
Coot	ЖН ЖН II
Teal	IIII
Redshank	ЖН ЖН ЖН I

2 What is the input variable?

3 What is the outcome variable?

4 At which time of year do you think these records were made? Explain your choice.

5 If the bird-watchers had to put a table of results in an official report, how would it look different to their notebook table?

Information processing ## *Changing seasons*

The graphs below show the changes in temperature in the wood over 24 hours at four different times of the year.

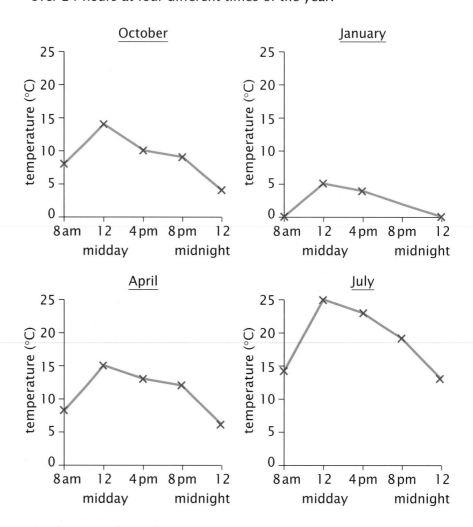

1 When was the highest temperature recorded in the wood?

2 When was the lowest temperature recorded in the wood?

3 What was the temperature at midday on each of the days that readings were taken?

4 For each day that readings were taken, imagine what the surroundings would look like. Draw a picture of the surroundings at midday for each of these days.

5 What was the approximate temperature at midnight on each of the days that readings were taken?

6 For each day that readings were taken, imagine that you are a squirrel and describe three different activities that you might do and when you might do them.

7 For each day that readings were taken, imagine that you are a slug and describe three different activities that you might do and when you might do them.

➡ *The stream environment*

Many small animals live in streams and can be affected by the speed of the water flow, the temperature of the water, the type of soil and rocks in the water and many other variables. Scientists wanted to investigate how the number of freshwater shrimps changed over 18 hours and what variable was affecting the difference.

Every hour the scientists used nets to sample how many shrimps were present in a small area of a stream. They spent 2 minutes kicking the stream bed to knock the shrimps off the stony bottom and catch them in their nets. After each count they carefully put the shrimps back into the stream. They used a flowmeter, which was a small paddle like a water wheel connected to a counter, to measure the speed of the water. They also used dataloggers and probes to measure other variables over the 18 hours of the investigation.

Information processing ## Stream investigation

The print out below shows the datalogger readings using light, sound and temperature probes in a stream. The flow rate is also given. The table shows the shrimp catches.

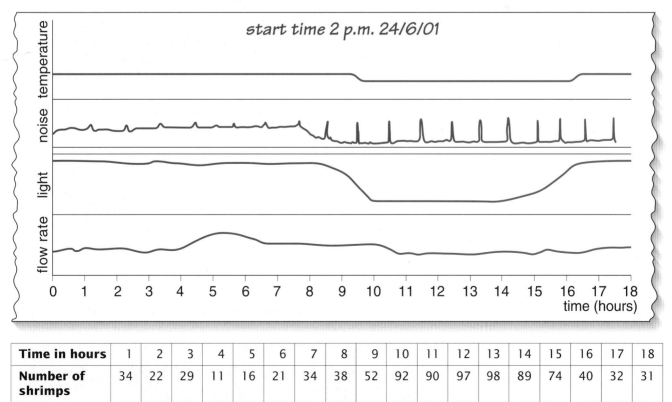

start time 2 p.m. 24/6/01

Time in hours	1	2	3	4	5	6	7	8	9	10	11	12	13	14	15	16	17	18
Number of shrimps	34	22	29	11	16	21	34	38	52	92	90	97	98	89	74	40	32	31

1 When was the shrimp count highest?

2 When was the shrimp count lowest?

3 How did the shrimp count change over the 18-hour period of the investigation?

4 There was a heavy rainstorm 4 hours after the start of the investigation. Which variable did this affect? How and why did this affect the shrimp count?

5 How did the light change over the 18 hours of the investigation? When was it night? When was it daytime?

6 How did the water temperature change over the 18 hours of the investigation?

7 Why do you think the scientists took sound readings?

8 What was the outcome variable in this investigation? What were the input variables?

9 From the results, which variable seems to have the most effect on the number of shrimps? Can you explain this relationship?

10 What other variables might affect the number of shrimps in the stream? How would you try and measure these variables?

Who eats who?

Key words
* energy
* food chain

Thrushes eat snails. Worms eat dead leaves. Ants eat any small plant scraps. Foxes eat most smaller animals. Squirrels eat plants, especially fruits such as acorns. Blackbirds and robins eat worms. Snails eat leaves and young plants. When an animal eats a plant or another animal, it uses its food as fuel for its own body and for growth. The animal gets the **energy** it needs to live from the animal or plant that it eats. The path of the energy is called a **food chain**.

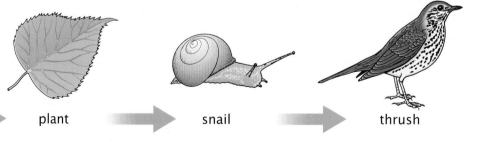

Sun   plant   snail   thrush

This is a simple food chain. The plant takes in energy from the Sun. The snail eats the plant and the energy gets passed on. Then the thrush eats the snail and again the energy passes on. So the energy that the thrush gains came originally from the Sun. The arrows in the food chain show the direction in which the energy flows.

Food chains have two, three, four and sometimes more plants and animals in them. The food chain shown on page 27 could be made longer if it also included the fox. Foxes eat thrushes. The energy from the thrush will pass on to the fox. The arrow in the food chain would go from the thrush to the fox.

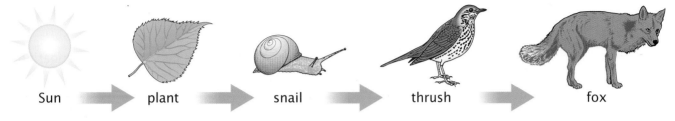

Sun ➤ plant ➤ snail ➤ thrush ➤ fox

Information processing ## Food chains

Look back at the animals and plants that you found in the school grounds and wood pictures. Read again the start of this section.

1 Draw a food chain that has worms and at least one other animal in it.

2 Draw a food chain that has a squirrel and at least one other animal in it.

3 Draw two more food chains for either the wood or the school grounds.

Check your arrows are in the right direction.

4 For one food chain, write an explanation in one or two sentences of what the food chain shows. You might start with:
This food chain shows how energy from the. . . .

➤ # Your place in the chain

Key words
* chlorophyll
* photosynthesis
* producer
* consumer
* herbivore
* carnivore
* predator
* prey

Plants can convert sunlight energy into a food source because they contain a special chemical called **chlorophyll**. This chemical is found in most plant cells and makes the plant green. When sunlight hits the green plant, **photosynthesis** starts. The plant cells start making sugars driven by the energy from the sunlight. Green plants produce sugars and other foods and so are called **producers**.

Animals are called **consumers** because they eat the food that plants produce. Animals that eat only plants are called **herbivores**. Sheep, cows, horses, mice, grasshoppers and most snails are herbivores. Eating plants is a difficult job because plant cells have a tough wall that the herbivore has to chew or grind away. Herbivores have special teeth or mouthparts to break open plant cells.

Animals that eat other animals are called **carnivores**. Cats, dogs, owls, thrushes, frogs and spiders are carnivores. Carnivores have to catch their food and kill it.

Carnivores have special teeth or mouthparts to pierce and hold their food. Carnivores that hunt for their food are called **predators**. Often predators will have adaptations for hunting such as claws or the ability to sprint. The animal that is hunted is called the **prey**. Bears are predators and, in the springtime, their favourite prey is salmon.

Word play   Copy the word spiral and use the clues to complete it.

1 Producers (5, 6)
2 Hunter (8)
3 Energy input (3)
4 Carnivore (4, 5)
5 Food _____ (5)

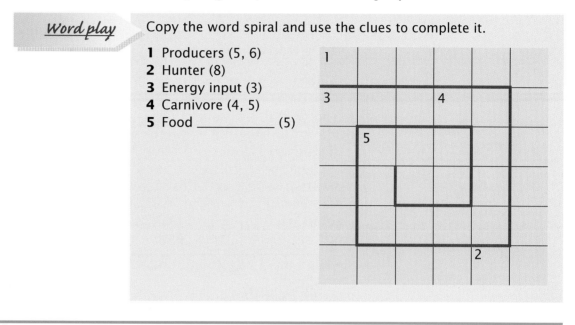

Information processing   ## Investigating the compost heap

Look at these plants growing on the edge of an open compost heap.

1 List all the plants that you can see growing by the compost heap.

2 Draw three food chains that you can see in the picture.

3 Plants are called producers when they appear in a food chain. Explain what the word producer means.

4 What pattern can you see in your food chains about carnivores, producers and herbivores?

5 Caterpillars develop into butterflies or moths. They have a different diet from the adult. Caterpillars usually feed on leaves, and adults feed on flower nectar. In terms of survival, why is it an advantage for the young and adult of an animal to have different diets?

What is adaptation?

Key word
* adaptation

Over millions of years animals and plants have developed a range of different features. Those features that help the animal or plant survive in a particular environment get passed on to the next generation. We call these useful features **adaptations**.

Adaptations evolve over a long, long time and result in animals or plants living successfully in a particular set of conditions. Most living things have adaptations that help them to live in a particular environment. For example, the polar bear has layers of fat and a thick fur coat that stop it from losing heat energy in the cold of the Arctic. These adaptations would not help polar bears survive if they lived in a desert. They would overheat and die.

The adaptations described below help these animals and plants live successfully. Can you work out why these features help their survival? You may find it useful to think about what life would be like for that animal or plant if it did not have its special adaptation.

- Bats have developed sonar to help them hunt for insects at night.
- Cacti have leaves that are spikes to cut down water loss in the desert. They also have swollen stems to store water.
- African elephants have large ears which allow them to lose heat and so cool down.
- Giraffes have long necks which allow them to reach leaves in trees in an area where there is a shortage of food.
- Desert rats produce urine which is solid. This helps them to save water.
- Scorpions have a poison gland on their tail which kills the smaller animals that they eat.
- Venus flytraps have triggered traps which catch flies. These plants are then able to get nitrates from the dead flies to help them make proteins.

Many adaptations are less dramatic.

Sheep have teeth that keep growing which is useful because their teeth grind down as they chew their food. Brambles have thorns which help them climb trees towards the light. Honey bees have tiny dents in their back legs where they carry pollen. Bluebells flower early in spring before the trees spread their leaves and block out most of the light energy. The bluebell stores energy in a bulb ready to flower early again the next spring.

Animals also react to their environment. If a woodlouse walks into soil that is dry it finds it uncomfortable and moves away to find wetter soil. Woodlice also are happier in dark places. So it is not surprising that you usually find woodlice under stones or in leaf litter. To detect light and dampness, woodlice have sense organs. Having special sense organs is another way in which animals are adapted to a particular habitat.

You might see foxes in your garden in the evening. Many foxes live in towns today and are called urban foxes. There are still quite a number of foxes living in woods and on heaths, which is their natural environment. Here foxes eat rabbits and other small animals. The fox is a carnivore and a predator. The rabbit is a herbivore and the prey. Both animals have adaptations. The fox has adaptations which allow it to hunt and eat the rabbit. The rabbit has adaptations for eating grass. It also has adaptations which help it detect an approaching fox and run away.

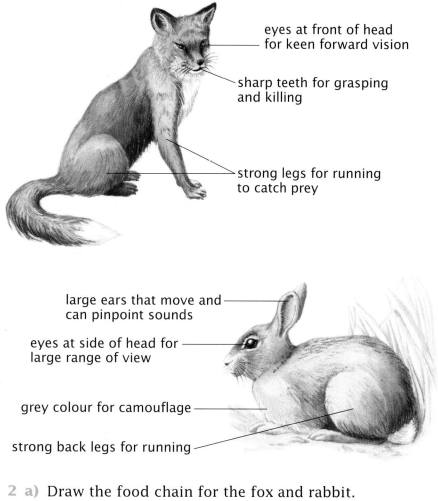

eyes at front of head for keen forward vision

sharp teeth for grasping and killing

strong legs for running to catch prey

large ears that move and can pinpoint sounds

eyes at side of head for large range of view

grey colour for camouflage

strong back legs for running

2 a) Draw the food chain for the fox and rabbit.
   b) Describe how the fox is adapted for hunting the rabbit.
   c) Describe how the fox is adapted for eating the rabbit.
   d) Explain what the word prey means.
   e) Explain how the rabbit might detect a fox creeping towards it.

3 Look back at the picture of the animals and plants in a woodland. Select three or four of these and explain how they have adaptations that help them live successfully in the wood.

Time to think

1 It is very easy to set up an aquarium tank or a pond if you know where the animals and plants like to live and what they feed on. The table below gives some information on living things that you might find in an aquarium or pond:

Waterflea	feeds on floating algae	swims in mid and surface water
Watersnail	feeds on algae on rocks and tank walls	moves on solid surfaces. Can float to surface
Water scorpion	feeds on smaller insects	lives in and on water surface
Pond skater	feeds on smaller insects	lives on water surface
Tadpole	feeds on plants and later on younger tadpoles and other smaller animals	swims midwater
Water boatman	feeds on algae and small plants	swims on surface and midwater

Amoeba	feeds on algae in mud	oozes across bottom
Phytoplankton (single-celled, filamentous algae)	photosynthesises	floats on surface and midwater. Some stick to rocks and tank sides
Stickleback	feeds on algae and small plants	swims midwater
Duckweed	photosynthesises	floats on surface

   a) Create a new table to show all the producers, herbivores and carnivores.
   b) Draw three food chains that you are likely to find in a pond.
   c) Describe how two of the carnivores are adapted for feeding.
   d) Describe how two of the animals are adapted for breathing air but living in water.
   e) Explain how the fish is adapted to living in water.

2 Invent a predator that lives in wet, muddy conditions in dark caves and feeds on moths and flies. Draw the animal and make notes to show its adaptations.

3 Imagine that you are writing a science fiction story and you land on a planet similar to Earth except that it has very long nights of around 48 hours and short days of around 2 hours. Imagine that you find two animals that you suspect are a predator and its prey. What evidence would you look for, apart from directly seeing the predator eat the prey, to check whether they were predator and prey?

   What adaptations do each have to:
- this long night/short day planet
- help them feed
- prevent them from being eaten?

→ How much to eat?

Key words
* proportionality
* pyramid of numbers

When people who have pets go on holiday, they often ask a friend or relative to look after their pet. When they deliver their pet, they take with it the supply of food for the time that they are away. They can work out how many dishes of seeds the gerbil needs or how many tins of food the cat needs. In a similar way we can work out how to change recipes to suit the number of people eating a meal. This is because we use **proportionality** to work out the amounts.

Reasoning   *Party time*

Look at the recipe below for tangy fruit salad.

Recipe for

Tangy Fruit Salad

Serves 2

Ingredients
2 satsumas
1 mango
1 pawpaw
1 thick slice of pineapple
8–10 black grapes
100 ml orange juice
50 ml lemon or lime juice

Method
- Peel and chop the satsumas, mango, pawpaw and pineapple into chunks, and place into a large serving bowl.
- Cut the grapes in half and remove the pips.
- Add the grapes to the chopped fruit.
- Pour in the orange and lemon (or lime) juice.
- Mix the contents of the bowl and chill for 1–3 hours before serving.

---

1 Imagine you were going to make this recipe for a party of 20 people. How much of each ingredient would you need?

2 On the day, your aunt, uncle and three cousins cannot come and so you need to alter the recipe for 15 people. How much of each ingredient would you need?

3 How did you work out the number of grapes for 20 people? For 15 people? What would it be for 50 people?

4 Talk to others and see if they use the same method for working out the number of grapes. Can you see how their method works and how it is similar to yours?

Just like getting the right amount of ingredients for a recipe, you can look at the amounts of food in a food chain.

12 lettuce leaves → 3 snails → 1 thrush

This food chain works. There is enough energy in the 12 lettuce leaves to keep the three snails alive for a day or so. A thrush can survive on the energy that it gets from three snails.

4 How many lettuce leaves would it need to keep five thrushes alive?

5 How many thrushes could be supported by 90 leaves of lettuce?

6 A hawk would need about two thrushes a day to keep alive. How many snails and lettuce leaves would this require? What would be the totals for each organism for a week's worth of food?

Scientists sometimes represent the numbers in a food chain like this.

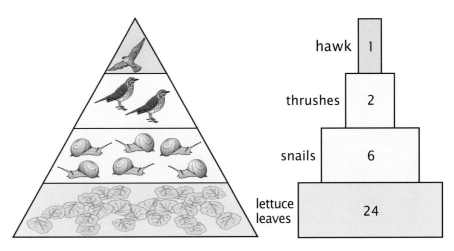

hawk 1
thrushes 2
snails 6
lettuce leaves 24

It is called a **pyramid of numbers**.

7 Try and work out a pyramid of numbers for one of the food chains that you have looked at.

DID YOU KNOW?

The most greedy insect is the desert locust. These animals do not have enzymes to break open the cells in the plant food that they eat and so most of the food just passes out as faeces. Sometimes desert locusts form a swarm of millions of locusts and these eat all the plants in their path causing starvation for the people in that area. In one day a locust swarm could eat enough food to provide for 500 people for a whole year!

→ *Food webs*

Key words
* food web

Some food chains have the same animal or plant in them. Look at the three food chains below. You can see that two of them contain wheat and two of them contain a chicken.

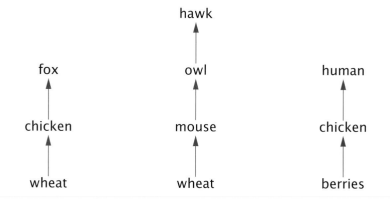

hawk
↑
fox   owl   human
↑   ↑   ↑
chicken   mouse   chicken
↑   ↑   ↑
wheat   wheat   berries

If we link the food chains together they form a **food web**.

algae and plankton

A food web for a rocky shore is shown opposite. A rocky shore is a difficult place to live. For part of the day the animals and plants are under water, then some of the animals and plants become stranded away from water and are easily seen by the animals that eat them. Out of the water, many animals and plants would dry up if they did not have special adaptations to prevent this. As the tide returns, the waves come crashing across the rocks. The animals and plants hold on tight to the rocks or find somewhere to hide.

8 Identify all the possible food chains from the food web.

9 Which are the producers on the rocky shore?

10 Name three herbivores in this food web.

11 Construct a table to show the producers, herbivores and carnivores on the rocky shore.

12 What are conditions like for the animals and plants
   a) when the sea covers the rocky shore
   b) when the tide goes out
   c) when the tide returns to the rocky shore?

13 Which animals and plants remain on the rocky shore when the tides go out?

14 What adaptations do the producers have to help them live on a rocky shore?

15 What adaptations do the herbivores have to help them live on the rocky shore?

16 Explain how the crab is a well-adapted carnivore.

17 Choose another carnivore from this food web and find out how it is adapted for feeding and for living in this habitat.

18 Imagine that another carnivore was added to the food web that ate the same animals as the crab. What effect might this have on
   • crabs
   • dogwhelks
   • seagulls
   • other animals in the food web?

19 Imagine that a disease has killed off most of the snails that are herbivores. What effect might this have on
   • the seaweed
   • the dogwhelks
   • other animals in the food web?

Time to think   Look back at the key word lists. For each group of key words use the words to write two or three sentences to explain the main ideas in that section. Then use these sentences to make either:

▪ a written summary of this topic

or

▪ a concept map that links the words together and shows their meaning.

2 Variation and classification

> **In this chapter you will learn:**
>
> → about variation within and between species
> → why classification is important and how animals are classified scientifically
> → how the environment can cause variation, as well as inheritance
> → what a mutation is
> → about the usefulness of statistics in finding out how populations vary
>
> **You will also develop your skills in:**
>
> → data analysis
> → classifying
> → interpreting information and drawing conclusions from graphs, tables and spreadsheets
> → investigating correlation patterns
> → understanding the importance of sample size
> → calculating averages of different kinds

WHAT DO YOU KNOW?

Key words
* vertebrate
* invertebrate

All of the animals in the picture opposite have backbones. They are examples of different kinds of **vertebrates**. There are five groups of vertebrates.

1 Name the five vertebrate groups and match the names with their correct description below:

Bodies are slimy, live on land and in water, lay eggs in water
Swim, walk or hop

Bodies have hair, young develop inside the mother and are fed on milk after birth, live on land, in water and in the air
Walk, swim or fly

Bodies covered in scales, live in water, swim
Lay eggs in water, have gills to breathe

Bodies are covered in feathers, have wings, live on land and in the air
Lay hard-shelled eggs

Bodies have dry waterproof skin with scales, most live on land, some can swim
Some have legs and some slide along the ground
Lay soft-shelled eggs on land

2 This picture shows some **invertebrates**. These are animals without backbones. Can you spot them and name them all? There are eight different types.

3 Draw a picture called 'under the sea'. Populate your scene with these invertebrates: a crab, a star fish, a mussel, a squid (or octopus if you prefer), a jellyfish and some coral. Also add at least one vertebrate you would find in the sea.

4 The invertebrates in the garden scene on page 39 can be grouped as worms, insects, arachnids (animals with eight jointed legs), or molluscs (animals with shells). Note down the group name, then list all the animals in the pictures that are in each group.

5 Sometimes it is hard to tell if an organism is a plant or an animal. How does your group decide if a living thing is a plant or an animal? What do you think each of the organisms in the pictures below are, plant or animal? How did you decide?

Microscopic viruses and bacteria live in air, water, soil and inside organisms.

Sundews grow in bogs where soil is poor in minerals. They have sticky hairs on their leaves to catch insects, and absorb nitrates from the decaying bodies.

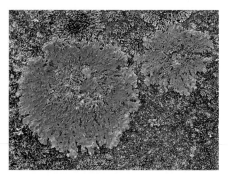

Lichen grow on rock surfaces. They are often bright yellow or orange.

Sea anemones fasten to rocks in rock pools. They feed on small shrimps and fishes captured by their tentacles and put into their central hole. They can be various colours.

Sparrows eat grass seeds and small insects. They live in gardens and nest in hedges.

Daisies grow in fields. They have green leaves and white flowers.

Children eat meat, fruit and vegetables. They go to school and live in houses.

Bats live under roof eaves. They fly at night fall and eat insects. They have a furry body.

6 Make a key (decision tree) to help other groups decide which is a plant and which an animal. (To see an example of a decision tree, turn to page 43.)

The seven characteristics of living things

All living things carry out all of these processes: **respiration**, **feeding**, **excretion**, **movement**, showing **sensitivity**, **growing** and **reproduction**. These are known as the characteristics of living things.

All living things need energy to live. Most plants get this from the Sun which is used to make food in the leaves that can be used by the whole plant. Animals feed on plants and other animals. Both plants and animals get energy from food when they respire.

1 Check you know what each of these seven characteristics of living things means by copying and completing the sentences in this paragraph:

All living things are made up of microscopic units called cells. You will learn more about these in chapter 7. Lots of chemical reactions take place inside cells to keep the organism alive. Substances are constantly broken down or built up to make structures like muscle or roots. Some of the chemicals that are produced by these chemical reactions are poisonous and must be got rid of. This process is called _____. Living things need _____ to move, grow and replace the worn out bits of their bodies. This is gained from _____. Animals eat food but plants make food using the Sun's energy. Oxygen from the air is needed to help release energy from food through a process called _____. As plants and animals develop they get larger and heavier, they _____. Plants and animals also respond to the world around them, for example they can sense changes in temperature, light and heat. They are _____. Often this is shown by the way they respond. Animals will move towards or away from a stimulus, plants may grow or bend towards light or moisture. All living things can make new plants and animals; this is called _____.

Sorting things out

There are about two million different types of plants and animals alive today. With so many plants and animals, scientists need to have some kind of sorting system or **classification** system that divides animals and plants into groups. The smallest division of a group of organisms is known as a **species**. You belong in the human species and humans are in a group of animals with backbones known as mammals. Animals with backbones are grouped together and called vertebrates. Animals without backbones are invertebrates. Living things can be grouped in many different ways. For example, they can be grouped by the way they look, how they feed or reproduce, where they live or how they behave. No single method is correct because grouping is done for different purposes by biologists.

Reasoning Can you 'sort it'?

Look at the cartoon. The twins' room is a real mess! Mum and Dad have decided to put up six shelves that everything must be tidied on to. Make some labels for each shelf, to give the twins some rules for what they can store on each shelf.

1 What criteria did you use to decide what could go on each shelf?

2 Did anyone else in your class use the same classifying system as you? Find out how they made their decisions.

3 Are some classifying systems better than others for sorting out the twins' room? Explain your answer.

DID YOU KNOW?

The Greek philosopher Aristotle grouped living things into plants and animals and he further divided animals into three groups and plants into three groups. The animals were divided up according to where they lived: on land, in the air or in water. The plants were divided up into groups defined by their types of stem.

→ What is an insect?

Key words
* antennae
* thorax
* abdomen
* segmented

Look at this drawing of a typical insect. It is drawn much larger than life so that you can see its body parts.

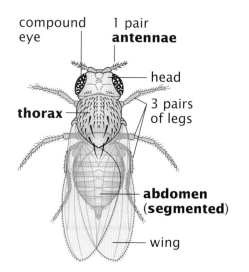

2 Which large group do insects belong in, invertebrates or vertebrates? Why?

3 How many legs does an insect have?

Reasoning *Identifying invertebrates*

1 Here is a key (decision tree) and some drawings of lots of 'creepy crawlies'. See if you can identify **A**, **B**, **C**, **D**, **E**, **F** and **G**.

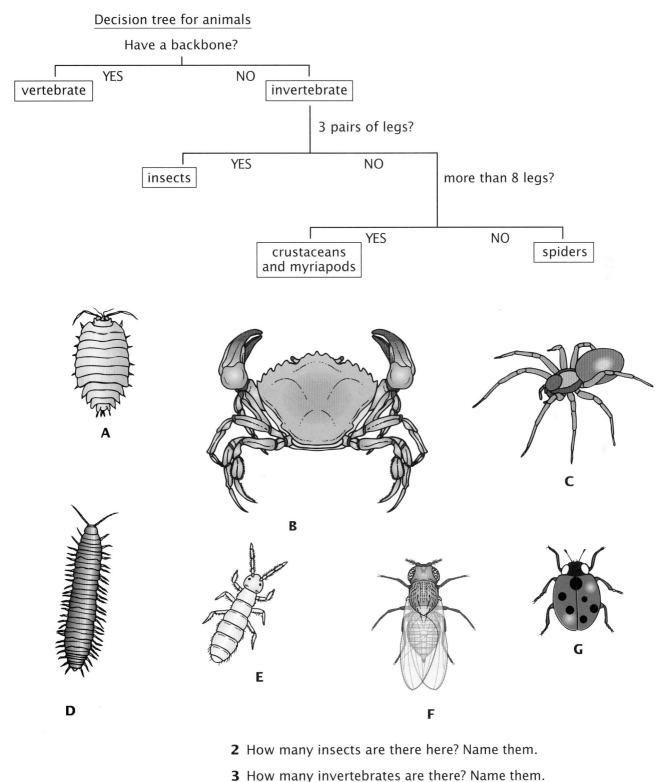

2 How many insects are there here? Name them.

3 How many invertebrates are there? Name them.

4 How many animals have wings? Are they all insects?

→ *The scientific classification of living things*

This is the way most scientists agree to classify living things today – but it may change in the future.

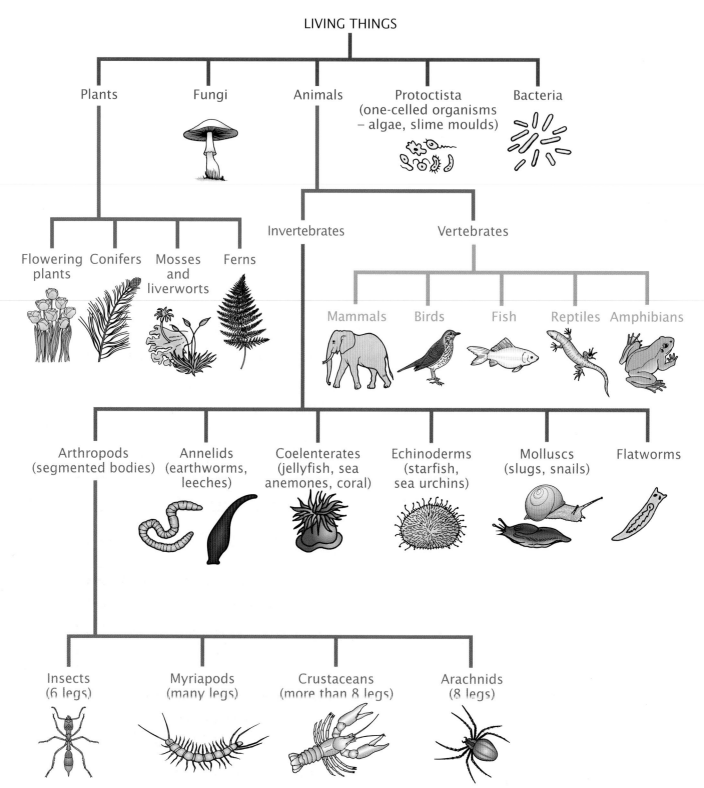

LIVING THINGS

Plants   Fungi   Animals   Protoctista (one-celled organisms – algae, slime moulds)   Bacteria

Plants:
Flowering plants   Conifers   Mosses and liverworts   Ferns

Animals:
Invertebrates   Vertebrates

Vertebrates:
Mammals   Birds   Fish   Reptiles   Amphibians

Invertebrates:
Arthropods (segmented bodies)   Annelids (earthworms, leeches)   Coelenterates (jellyfish, sea anemones, coral)   Echinoderms (starfish, sea urchins)   Molluscs (slugs, snails)   Flatworms

Arthropods:
Insects (6 legs)   Myriapods (many legs)   Crustaceans (more than 8 legs)   Arachnids (8 legs)

There are five main groups of vertebrates. They are reptiles, amphibians, fish, birds and mammals. (Look back at page 39 if you need help with the characteristics of each group.)

4 Why do you think a frog is classified as an amphibian and not a fish? What are the characteristics of birds?
5 A bat is classified as a mammal, not a bird. Why?
6 Name two animals that are reptiles.
7 Construct a key (decision tree) showing how living things are divided into two groups, plants and animals, how animals are divided into invertebrates and vertebrates, and how vertebrates are divided into five groups.

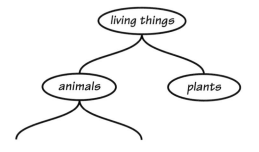

Information processing *The otter*

Read an extract from a poem by Ted Hughes and the section taken from a reference book.

> Underwater eyes, an eel's
> Oil of water body, neither fish nor beast is the otter:
> Four-legged yet water gifted, to outfish fish;
> With webbed feet and long ruddering tail
> And a round head like an old tomcat.
>
> ....
>
> The hunt's lost him. Pads on mud,
> Among sedges, nostrils a surface bead,
> The otter remains, hours. The air,
> Circling the globe, tainted and necessary,
>
> Mingling tobacco smoke, hounds and parsley,
> Comes carefully to the sunken lungs.
> So the self under the eye lies,
> Attendant and withdrawn. The otter belongs
>
> In double robbery and concealment –
> From water that nourishes and drowns, and from land
> That gave him his length and the mouth of the hound.
> ....
>
> *'An Otter' by Ted Hughes.*

The otter, scientific name *Lutra lutra*.

Otter cubs are very small at birth, their body being only 5–6 cm in length, with a tail of about the same length. At about 3 months old they take their first swim. Up to this time they have been suckled by their mother, and are brought fish.

Adult otters seize their prey from underneath with their front feet, and kill it before swimming to the bank or to shallow water to eat it. The otter's fur is closely set and waterproof, while air, trapped in the fur, acts as an insulating layer. They use regular feeding places. They eat crayfish, frogs, voles and birds, as well as fish. These can be found by looking for their droppings or 'spraints'. These are distinctive being black, slimy and oily-smelling. They use their droppings to mark their territory. The male otter is called a dog and the female is a bitch. They construct shelters called 'holts' under the roots of trees or large stones on the banks of rivers, lakes or the sea. They leave distinctive paw marks, showing five toes with a web between them. Tail marks are often seen between the paw marks. Otters are playful and often make slides down banks of mud or snow into water. Otters may be spotted at dusk swimming on the surface of the water, although they are shy and easily scared away by humans.

Extract based on *The Country Life Book of the Natural History of the British Isles*. Otters, which at the turn of the century were widespread and common, have declined in numbers. The otter is now protected by law, under the Wildlife and Countryside Act 1981.

1 How would you classify this animal?

2 If you were trying to identify the animal, which description would you find most helpful, the poem or the reference book?

3 If you were asked to say how the animal was adapted to moving and eating, which description would you find most helpful?

4 Choose an animal or plant you know well and write a poem based on its appearance or its behaviour.

The Linnean system of taxonomy

Carl Linnaeus lived from 1707–1778. He is often called the 'father of **taxonomy**'. His system for naming, ranking and classifying organisms is still in wide use today (with many changes). His ideas on classification have influenced generations of biologists during and after his own lifetime. Born in southern Sweden, Carl showed a deep love of plants and a fascination with their names from a very early age. He went to university to study medicine. At the time, training in botany (the study of plants) was part of the medical curriculum, as every doctor had to prepare and prescribe drugs derived from medicinal plants. However, he spent more of his time collecting and studying plants than studying medicine. In 1735 he published the first edition of his classification of living things, the *Systema Naturae*. Linnaeus based his plant classification system on the number and arrangement of their reproductive organs.

After he became a Professor, he sent many of his students out on trade and exploration voyages to different parts of the world. Perhaps his most famous student was Daniel Solander, the naturalist on Captain James Cook's first round-the-world voyage, who brought back the first plant collections from Australia and the South Pacific to Europe. What has survived of the Linnean system is its method of dividing groups into smaller and smaller sub-groups and the system of 'binomial' naming. Linnaeus made naming simpler by choosing one Latin name to indicate the genus, and one as a 'shorthand' name for the species. The two names make up the binomial ('two names') species. Before Linnaeus invented this system, scientists used many different names for the same organism; often inventing their own long Latin names which only they used. Biologists are still trying to make better systems for sorting living things into groups.

An example of the Linnean sequence used to classify a rhinoceros:

Phylum: Chordata (vertebrates)
  Class: Mammalia (mammals)
    Order: Perissodactyla (horse type)
      Family: Rhinocerotidea (rhinos)
        Genus: *Rhinoceros*
          Species: *Rhinoceros uniconis* (the Indian rhino – one horned)

1 Find out what 'taxonomy' means. You can use a dictionary.
2 What problems do you think there were with the way plants and animals were named before Linnaeus created his system?
3 Why do you think we still use Latin names rather than English names for classifying organisms?
4 Which people once spoke Latin as their main, everyday language? (This is a history question!)
5 Invent your own classification system for a human, using the rhinoceros as an example of how to go from one very big group (animals) down to the species *Homo sapiens* (*Homo* meaning mankind and *sapiens* meaning wise).

Key words
* taxonomy
* phylum
* class
* order
* family
* genus
* species

Time to think

Look back at what you have done so far in this chapter. Divide a page of your exercise book into four sections. Select one of the key ideas from the chapter and explain it in one of the sections. Do the same for three other key ideas. Compare what you have written with others in your group.

Variation and inheritance

Key words
* variation
* characteristics
* unique
* offspring
* inherited
* environment

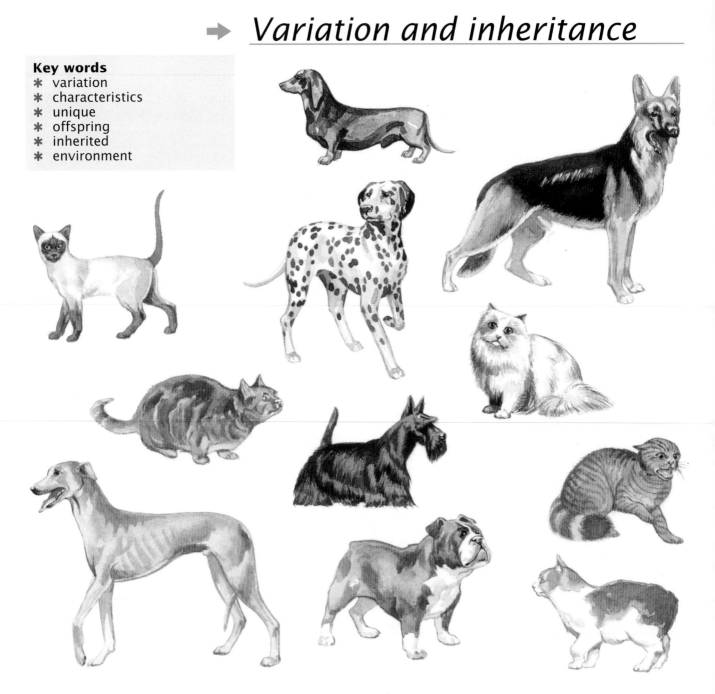

8 How do you tell the difference between cats and dogs? Make a list of the characteristics that show the differences between cats and dogs.

Organisms that have lots of features in common with each other are classed together as a species. Not all individuals of the same species are identical to each other. Look around the classroom, you are all human beings yet there is lots of **variation** in the way you each look. You have different features or **characteristics**. These variations identify individuals within a species.

9 Look again at the cats in the picture. How is each cat different from the others?

10 List three ways in which the people in your class vary from each other. List three ways in which you are all the same.
11 What characteristics do you think are unique to you?

Rajid says that he has noticed that some people of his age are tall and some are short. He has also noticed that many of his friends look a bit like their parents.

12 Why do you think most people look a bit like their parents?
13 What features do you think you have inherited from your parents? If you have brothers or sisters, have they inherited the same sort of characteristics?
14 What do you think might be the causes for variation in the height of people?

These two things (sharing some characteristics and having others that are **unique**) occur because all organisms reproduce their own kind. Cats have kittens, dogs have puppies, humans have children, and acorns grow into oak trees. **Offspring** look like their parents in some ways because they have **inherited** certain characteristics, but they can grow up to be quite different due to their **environment**.

15 Look at the picture of trees growing on a mountainside. What do you notice about the ones at the top compared with the ones at the bottom?
16 What do you think causes this difference, inheritance or environment? Why?
17 Think of some examples where variation is probably due to inheritance and some where it is caused by the environment.

What is responsible for inheritance?

Key words
* gene
* chromosomes
* organism
* model
* analogy

A **gene** is the basic unit of inheritance. Genes are responsible for the characteristics that each person has (like eye colour, facial features, and many health conditions). Genes are grouped together on **chromosomes**. You could imagine that genes are like letters that make up chromosomes which are like words, and they act together to tell a story. The story is about what an **organism** will look like. However, what you are is not just a matter of your inheritance. You are also influenced by your experience and environment. The idea of genes being letters, chromosomes being words, and a whole organism being a story is a **model** or an **analogy** (you may have come across this word in your English lessons). The model explains something by describing its similarities to something else. Scientists use models to understand the world around them. A very useful way of thinking up your own model is to say: 'This is like that; what other things is it like?'.

Genes are a bit like the letters of the alphabet

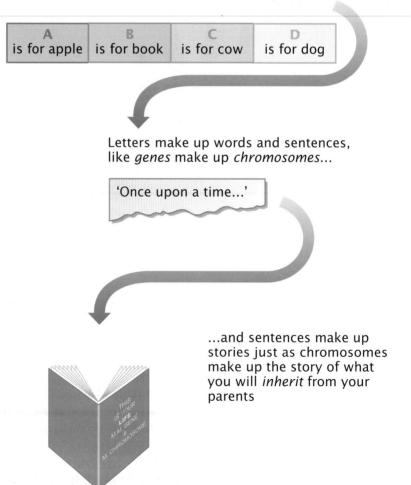

A	B	C	D
is for apple	is for book	is for cow	is for dog

Letters make up words and sentences, like *genes* make up *chromosomes*...

'Once upon a time...'

...and sentences make up stories just as chromosomes make up the story of what you will *inherit* from your parents

An analogy for inheritance.

Mutations

Key word
* mutation

Occasionally a change can occur in an individual plant or animal unexpectedly. The feature does not seem to be inherited from either parent. It may have been caused by a **mutation**. You may have heard the word mutant in films or on TV.

The film, X-men shows mutants born with strange and amazing powers.

A mutation is a change in a gene or chromosome. When sex cells are being made (see chapter 8), chromosomes are copied. If the chromosomes are not copied exactly a mutation occurs. It is a bit like you making a spelling mistake when you are copying down notes from a book. This can occur naturally for no reason but it is known that radiation, temperature extremes and some chemicals increase the chances of mutations.

Sometimes a mutation causes new characteristics that help the organism to survive. For example, plants become resistant to drought or moths are hatched with a darker colour that helps camouflage them. In these cases the mutated organisms live more successfully than the rest of their generation.

18 What is a mutation?
19 Why do you think camouflage helps a moth survive?

Genetic modification

Key word
* modify

To **modify** something means to change it. Scientists have discovered how to change genes and chromosomes so that the organisms made from these modified cells have different characteristics. Some people are concerned that genetically-modified foods might be dangerous to eat. There is no evidence from science to suggest that they are. However, some supermarkets were so worried that customers might not buy these foods that they stopped selling them.

THE DAILY NEWS

Thursday, October 12 2000

GM farmer is determined to fight on

The Norborough farmer whose trial genetically-modified maize crop was trashed by environmental campaigners says he is determined to fight on despite a setback in the courts. Last month 21 environmental protesters, who destroyed the farmer's crop, were cleared of criminal damage by a jury at Norchester Crown Court, because they were acting in what they believed was a socially responsible way.

The protesters explain why they destroyed the crop: 'The process of civilisation is about changing the law. Sending children up chimneys was legal once – people stopping that would have been criminals in their day, now we see them as heroes. We think GM crops should be illegal, we are protecting the future of mankind from Frankenstein-type horrors'. The farmer says, 'The destruction of my livelihood has had a bad effect on me and my family. I have lost money. I suppose farmers have to be optimists, we put seed in the ground and work hard hoping it will be a good crop. If the protesters think they can frighten me they have picked the wrong person.'

A spokesperson for the company who contracted the farmer to test their genetically-modified maize seeds described his reaction: 'Depression. What upsets me is that there are so many mistruths about GM crops. It is all more emotional than it needs to be. We need scientific facts.'

Read the newspaper article.

20 What do you think about the jury's view of the 'crime'?
21 Who do you think is right, the company or the protesters? Why?
22 Do you think scientists could give more facts to change people's views about genetically-modified foods? Explain your answer.

Research 'Designer babies' is a term used by journalists, not scientists, to describe several reproductive technologies which give parents more control over what their offspring will be like. Find examples of where journalists have used the term designer babies. What do you think about our ability to influence inheritance?

DID YOU KNOW?

In 1791 an American farmer called Seth Wright was the first person to deliberately breed his animals for favourable characteristics. He mated short-legged sheep together so that the lambs had even shorter legs. This prevented them jumping over his fences and escaping!

➡ *Measuring variation*

Key words
* trends
* data
* statistics

Scientists often want to look at whole populations of organisms to see how they live. It is useful for them to know what features or behaviours are part of the characteristics for that population and what are individual differences. This means that they look for **trends** or patterns in **data**. To do this they do some maths called **statistics**.

Information processing   *Average sizes*

Here are two graphs showing the average weight and height for a sample of boys and girls aged from 0–18 years old.

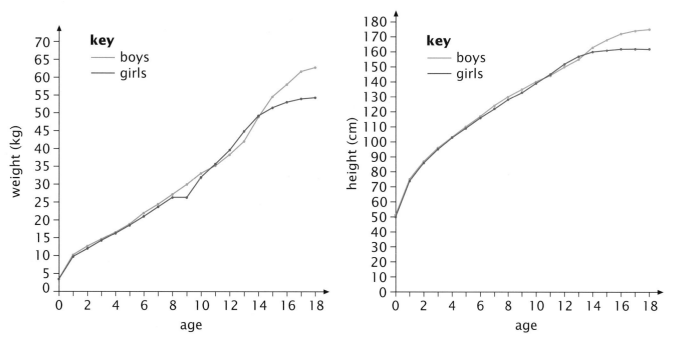

1 What does the word 'average' mean?

2 What does the word 'sample' mean?

3 How many girls and boys do you think have been 'sampled' to provide the data for average weight and height – three of each gender, five of each, twenty-five of each, or more? If you think more, how many more? How did you decide?

4 What differences do you notice between the boys' and the girls' graphs?

5 At what age are girls taller than boys on average, and at what age is the reverse true?

6 When do boys stop growing?

7 Where do you fit on these graphs?

8 What causes these differences between the growth of boys and girls: the environment, inheritance or both?

Different kinds of averages

In science we use different types of averages.

There is the **mean**. This is calculated by adding up all the individual numbers and dividing by the number of individuals, for example all the heights of seven 11-year-old girls and dividing by seven. In the example on the right the mean is 139 cm.

Name	Girl's height (cm)
Sue	140
Daisy	138
Frederica	135
Veena	138
Shona	141
Molly	142
Lorraine	138

There is the **mode**, which is the most common or popular measurement. In the example the mode is 138 cm.

Finally, there is the **median**. This is the middle measurement. First you need to put all the height readings given in this example in order from the tallest to the shortest (ranking). Then find the height that is in the middle. Can you work out the median for the example above?

Key words
* mean
* mode
* median

Correlation

Let's look at shoe size to see if the height of a person is linked to the size of their shoes. We could **predict** that tall people have bigger shoe sizes than short people, at the same age. We are assuming a **correlation** between shoe size and height. That is, we think these two variables might be linked together in some way. To test this idea we need to draw a **scatter graph**.

Key words
* predict
* correlation
* scatter graph

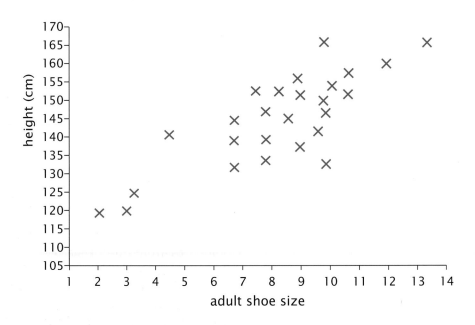

23 Is our prediction correct? How did you decide?

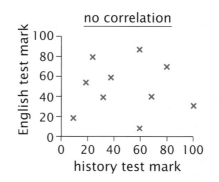

Above is another scatter graph. The plots do not make a straight line. This means there is no relationship between the input variable (history test mark) and the outcome variable (English test mark). In other words being good at history does not mean a person is good at English. You cannot make any predictions from a graph like this.

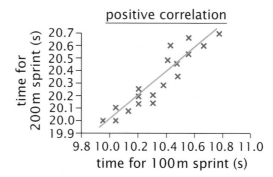

Here you can see that a straight line can be drawn through the plots diagonally from left to right. This shows that the time for sprinting 100 metres is related to the time for running 200 metres. There is a relationship between the two variables. This graph can be used to make predictions.

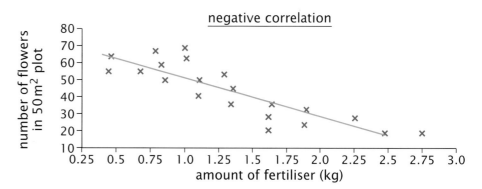

A straight line can be drawn from top left to bottom right on this graph. This shows that the variables are related. The more fertiliser, the fewer the flowers. The input variable (fertiliser) seems to have a negative effect on flower growth (outcome variable). You can make predictions about the amount of fertiliser and the number of flowers that might grow.

Information processing   *Winter holly*

Here are two more graphs about the number of berries on 12 holly bushes and the lowest winter temperature over the last 10 years.

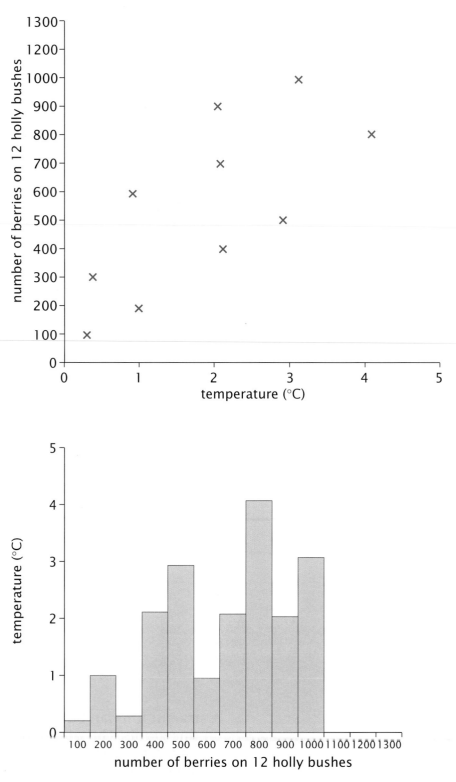

1 One of these graphs is the wrong one to draw for this kind of data. Which is the wrong graph? Why?

Looking at the correct graph, answer these questions:

2 Do colder winters produce more holly berries for all the holly bushes?

3 How many berries do you think will be produced on average by 12 holly bushes if next winter the temperature drops down to −2 °C?

4 How did you come to this conclusion?

5 Are the variations in the numbers of holly berries due to the environment or inheritance? What made you decide on your answer?

Word play

Make a list of all the new words you have learnt in this chapter. Put them in alphabetical order and write down what each one means in your own words.

Time to think

Think back over the facts and activities you have done in this chapter. What has been the most interesting part of the chapter for you? Why?

3 Electricity

In this chapter you will learn:

→ the names of the components shown in the picture below
→ how circuits containing switches, fuses and buzzers operate
→ how to construct series and parallel circuits and be able to explain how they work
→ the relationship between current and resistance in a circuit
→ how a variable resistor works
→ how to represent circuits using circuit diagrams
→ the difference between electric current and energy transfer in electric circuits
→ the effect on current of increasing voltage

You will also develop your skills in:

→ presenting data in a table
→ interpreting data gathered from an experiment
→ recognising anomalous results
→ drawing conclusions from experimental results
→ identifying variables
→ using models

➡ ➡ ➡ WHAT DO YOU KNOW?

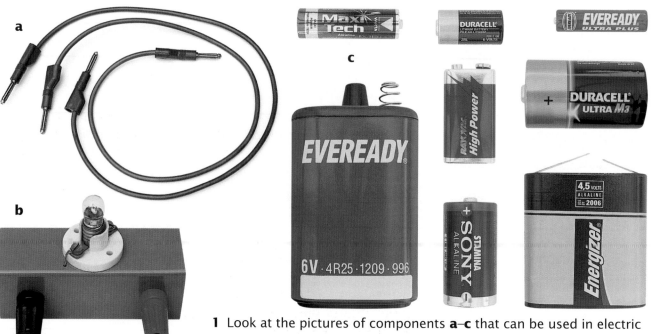

1 Look at the pictures of components **a–c** that can be used in electric circuits. Make sure that you know what each one is called.

2 Look at the picture showing a battery which needs to be connected to a 'festoon' bulb.

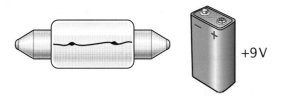

Discuss with your partner how you would connect them so that the bulb lights up. On a piece of paper draw how you would connect them. Show the path taken by the electricity round the circuit.

3 Look at the next set of drawings. Explain whether or not the bulb lights and why.

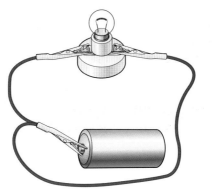

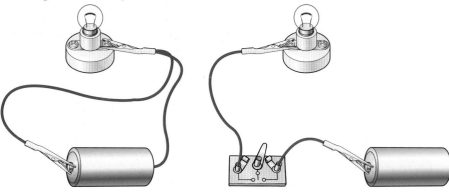

4 Look at these two circuits.

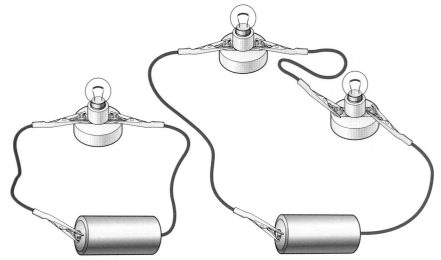

In the circuit on the left the single cell lights the bulb normally. In the circuit on the right an extra bulb has been included. Do you think the bulbs will shine more brightly or less brightly? Why?

➡ *Safety!*

Usually electrical appliances work either from the **mains** or from batteries. Mains electricity can be dangerous, and when you do experiments you usually use batteries because they are less powerful.

Key words
* mains

SAFETY! **You should never connect circuits to the mains.**

Circuits

➜

Key words
* cell
* positive
* negative
* circuit
* component
* terminals

Sometimes we talk about batteries and sometimes we use the word **cell**. A battery is made up of several cells. A car battery is made up of six cells. When we use several cells in a circuit, then we need to be careful to connect them correctly with the **positive** end of one connected to the **negative** end of the next cell.

The energy is stored as chemicals in the battery. The diagram on the right shows an SP2 dry cell.

The electricity transfers the energy to the bulbs to light them. For a bulb to light, there must be a complete path through which the electricity can flow between the two ends of the cell. This is called a **circuit**.

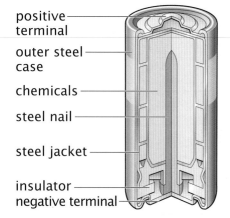

positive terminal
outer steel case
chemicals
steel nail
steel jacket
insulator
negative terminal

We connect various things into our circuits. These include bulbs (which we sometimes call lamps), switches, buzzers, resistors and motors. These are all **components** of the circuit. There must always be a component like a lamp or a buzzer in the circuit. If just a wire joins the two ends of the battery it is called a short circuit. When there is a short circuit there is a large flow of electricity from the battery and either it is damaged or it goes 'flat'. You must always avoid a short circuit.

So far we have shown a drawing or a picture of components used in electrical circuits. But scientists and engineers have developed a shorthand way of showing these as symbols. The table opposite shows each component with a picture and its symbol.

Name	Picture	Symbol
lamp (bulb)		
switch		
cell		
battery		
ammeter		
voltmeter		
connecting wire		
diode		
two-way switch		
fuse		
resistor		

Name	Picture	Symbol
light dependent resistor (LDR)		
loudspeaker		
buzzer		
bell		
push-to-make switch		
open terminals		
motor		
variable resistor		
light emitting diode (LED)		
potentiometer		

When the components are joined together they make an electric circuit. A circuit is a complete path between the two ends of the cell (or battery). Remember batteries have two **terminals** which are labelled + and − (not north and south!). The components generally have two connections. The electricity goes IN at one and OUT at the other.

1 Look at the circuits at the bottom of page 59 and on a piece of paper draw circuit diagrams using the correct symbols.
2 You may remember building electric circuits before in science lessons and also drawing circuit diagrams of the circuits you have built. Look at the following circuit diagrams. All the bulbs and cells are identical. In the diagrams, where bulb **a** is connected to one cell it is at normal brightness. Decide for each bulb (**b**–**h**), whether it is out, dim, normal or brighter than normal.

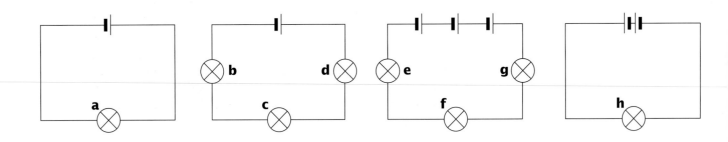

3 In circuits **A** and **B**, the switch is open. What happens when it is closed?

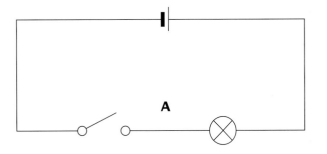

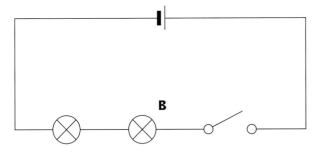

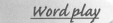 *Word play*   The word 'circuit' has a very specific meaning in science. How is this meaning similar to or different from the use of the word in

1 a motor racing circuit?
2 a theatre circuit?
3 How are these words linked to the word circuit:
circus, circumference, circle?

➡ *Series and parallel circuits*

Look at the two circuits shown:

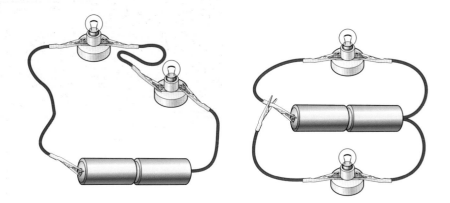

You may have set up these circuits or seen them demonstrated. Notice the brightness of the bulbs in the first circuit. If one bulb is unscrewed the other bulb goes out. In the second picture, the bulbs are brighter than the bulbs in the first picture. If you unscrewed one bulb, the other bulb stays on. The diagram on the left shows a **series** circuit, and the diagram on the right shows a **parallel** circuit.

4 The circuit diagrams for the two circuits shown above are drawn below. Do you think the bulbs will be dim or bright in each of these circuits?

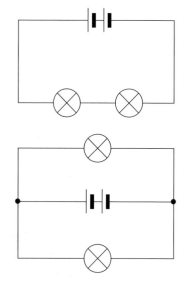

Sometimes we connect things up in series circuits and sometimes in parallel. In your house the room lights are connected in parallel. If they were connected in series, can you think of any problems this may cause?

➔ *Two switch circuits*

Sometimes we have safety circuits that have two switches in them.

The saw shown above is easier to switch OFF than ON. For safety reasons, machines are often controlled by two switches. To start the machine *both* switches must be turned ON, but to stop it you only have to turn OFF one of the switches.

Another type of circuit that has two switches is one to control the light at the top and bottom of the stairs in a house. This is so that you can switch the light ON and OFF at either switch.

5 The circuit diagram for a two-way switching circuit is shown. Can you explain how the circuit works?

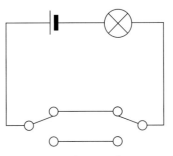

6 Look at the cross section through a torch and explain how the various parts work.

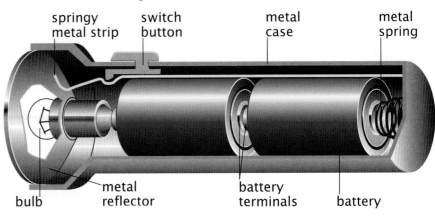

springy metal strip   switch button   metal case   metal spring

bulb   metal reflector   battery terminals   battery

7 Here are some more circuits with cells and lamps. Lamp **a** is connected to one cell and is at normal brightness. Decide for each lamp (**b**–**l**) whether it is out, dim, normal or brighter than normal.

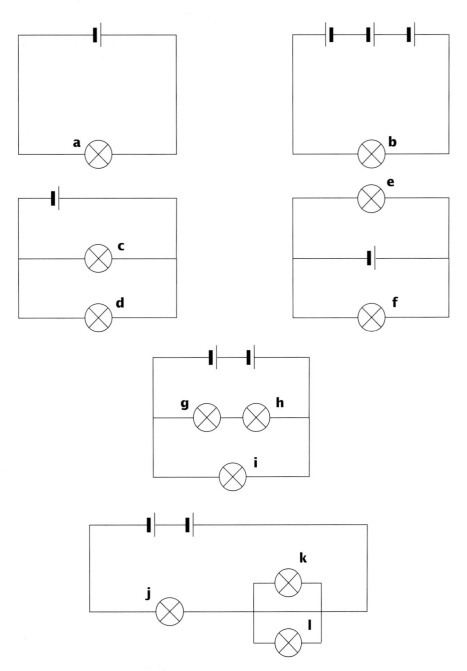

Draw a table similar to the one shown below and enter your results into it.

Lamp	State
lamp a	normal

8 In circuits **A**, **B** and **C** the switch is open. What happens when it is closed?

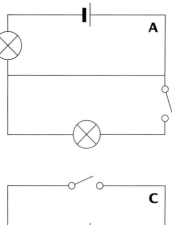
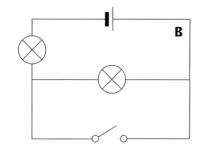
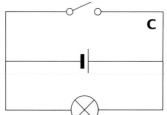

9 Why should you never connect up circuit **C**?

➡ *Large and small units used in science*

Getting bigger:

Number	Name	Symbol
1000	kilo	k
1 000 000	mega	M
1 000 000 000	giga	G
1 000 000 000 000	tera	T

Getting smaller:

Number	Name	Symbol
0.1 or $\frac{1}{10}$	deci	d
0.01 or $\frac{1}{100}$	centi	c
0.001 or $\frac{1}{1000}$	milli	m
0.000 001 or $\frac{1}{1000000}$	micro	μ
0.000 000 001 or $\frac{1}{1000000000}$	nano	n

You will see that the symbol for mega is written with a capital M, whereas milli is a small m. Note also that kilo is the only one of the 'getting bigger' multipliers that is written with a small letter (k).

Examples where the names and symbols shown opposite are used are: kilometre (km), microamp (μA), millimetre (mm), gigawatt (GW).

Volume can be measured in cubic metres (m³) sometimes cubic decimetres (dm³) or sometimes litres (l).

$$1\,l = 1\,dm^3$$

Small volumes are measured in cubic centimetres (cm³) or millilitres (ml).

$$1\,cm^3 = 1\,ml$$

The unit for measuring area is the hectare (ha). A square field 100 m long by 100 m wide would have an area of 1 ha. So 1 ha = 10 000 square metres. However, many people still stick to the old unit, acres, for measuring land.

➡ *Measuring electric current*

Key words
* particle
* electron
* charge
* amp
* milliamp
* microamp
* ammeter
* digital
* analogue

Electric current cannot be seen, so it can be difficult to explain. Earlier in this chapter we talked about the flow of electricity round a circuit. We call this an electric current. It is a flow of tiny **particles** called **electrons**. These particles have an electric **charge**. An electric current is a continuous flow of charged particles from one battery terminal, round the circuit and back to the other battery terminal. Electric current is measured in amperes which is shortened to **amps** (A). If the current is small it is measured in **milliamps** (mA).

$$1000\,mA = 1\,A$$

Another way of saying this is

$$1\,mA = \frac{1}{1000}A$$

If the current is very small it is measured in **microamps** (μA).

$$1\,000\,000\,\mu A = 1\,A, \text{ or } 1\,\mu A = \frac{1}{1\,000\,000}A$$

An electric current of 1 A means that 6 240 000 000 000 000 000 electrons pass by a given point of the circuit every second!

We measure electric current with an **ammeter**. Nowadays most ammeters are **digital**, but sometimes you will still find the older **analogue** meters. Instead of giving the reading directly in numbers on a display, a needle moves across a dial and you have to interpret the reading.

Ammeters need to be connected the correct way round in the circuit. The red terminal is connected to the wires that lead to the positive terminal of the battery or power pack.

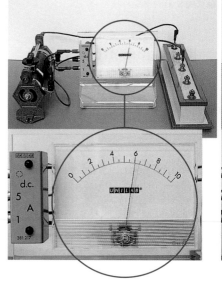
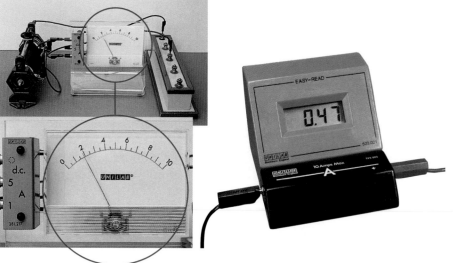

10 Look at the dials on the analogue meters above and decide what each one reads.
11 There are analogue and digital clocks. Can you think of an advantage of using a digital clock? When would an analogue clock be more useful?
12 Comparing analogue and digital ammeters, list the advantages and disadvantages of each type of ammeter.

Time to think | List all the key words in the topic so far. Select three words and use them to write a few sentences to explain one thing that you have learnt about electricity. Ask others in your group if they agree with what you have written. Do you agree with what they have written? Try to use several explanations to write a longer piece about electricity for an encyclopaedia.

→ *Thinking about models in electricity*

Key words
* model
* analogy

Models are often used in science to help our understanding of a topic. These models are used to try to explain ideas, for example the flow of electric current. The model is not the same as electric current, but will have similar features and mimic important properties of the electric circuit. This is sometimes called an **analogy**. Here is a model that helps us think about electricity.

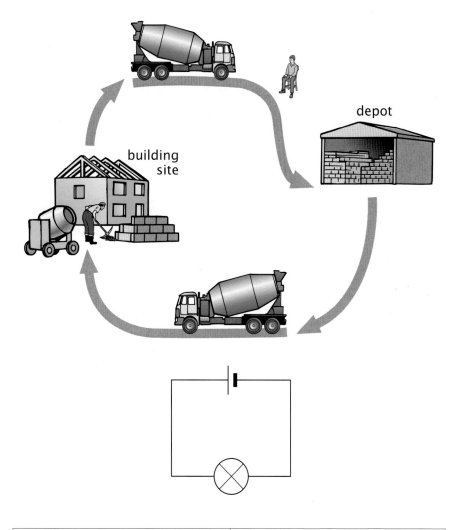

electricity	lorries
battery	depot
wire	road
moving charge	lorry
energy	concrete
bulb	building site

The charged particles move round the wires. They represent the electric current. They gain energy going through the battery. They transfer this energy as they pass through the bulb. All the charged particles return to the battery where they gain more energy. The lorries are travelling from the depot to the building site. They collect their concrete at the depot and transfer it to the building site. Then they all travel along another road back to the depot where they collect more concrete. A person sitting by the side of the road could count the rate at which the lorries pass. In a similar way, an ammeter measures the rate of flow of charge.

Here is another model.

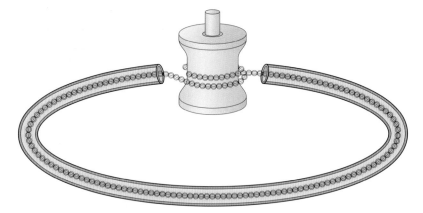

electricity	chain
wire	
current	
battery	

13 What do you think represents the wire, current and battery in this model?

Creative thinking ## Using models

There are many other models that are used to explain electric current:

water pumped around plastic tubes
cross-country runners
central heating systems in a home.

Can you draw these or think up one of your own to explain the electric current flowing round a circuit to light a lamp?

➡ Using ammeters in circuits

This picture shows two ammeters ready to be connected up in a series circuit. Note that once the crocodile clip is attached to the cell the current will flow through the ammeters and each of the bulbs.

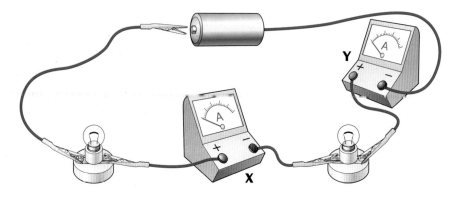

14 Thinking back to our models, what can you say about the readings on ammeters **X** and **Y** once the circuit is connected up? Will they be the same, or will **Y** be more or less?

This picture shows a parallel circuit.

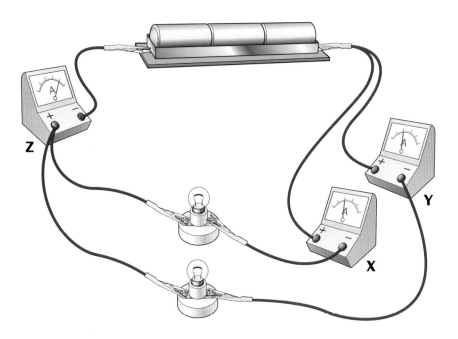

A model for part of this circuit is shown below.

15 Can you use the picture to explain the current readings on the ammeters at **X**, **Y** and **Z**?

In a series circuit the electric current is the same all round the circuit. The reading on the ammeter is the same at the start of the circuit as it is at the end. In a parallel circuit, the current splits, some goes through one bulb and the rest goes through the other. If the bulbs are identical (exactly the same) the split will be half through each bulb.

16 In the circuit shown, the ammeter in position **1** reads 0.5 A. If the ammeter was placed in each of the positions **2**, **3** and **4** what would it read?

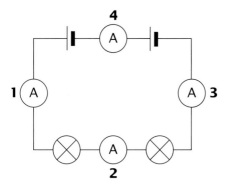

17 a) In the circuit shown, which of the ammeters in positions **2**, **3** or **4** would read the same as the ammeter in position **1**?
  b) In which two positions are the readings smallest?
  c) In which two positions are the readings largest?

→ # *Resistance and fuses*

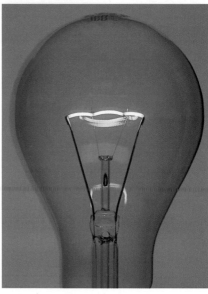

The current in a circuit depends on the components connected in the circuit. Look at the two circuit diagrams.

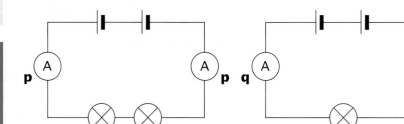

The current through the **p** ammeters is less than that through the **q** ammeters. Because there are two bulbs, there is a greater **resistance** to the flow of the electric current. The greater the resistance, the less the flow of electric current. Resistance opposes (tries to stop) the flow of current. The electricity cannot flow so easily through the very fine wire in the bulb. The bulb resists the flow of electricity through it. The bulb has an electrical resistance. In our lorries model resistance would be road works. Road works would affect the rate at which lorries travel along the road.

You know that things that allow electricity to flow through them are called **conductors** and those that will not allow electricity to flow through them are called **insulators**.

18 Copy and complete this table and add a further eight objects to it.

Object	Material	Conductor or insulator
comb	plastic	insulator
spoon	silver	conductor

Evaluation ## *Changing current*

Natasha and Alastair performed an experiment using a pencil 'lead' to vary the current in a circuit. These are the results written down by Alastair.

Length of pencil lead in cm	Current in amps
9	0.10
0	0.50
2	0.25
4	0.67
6	0.13
1	0.30

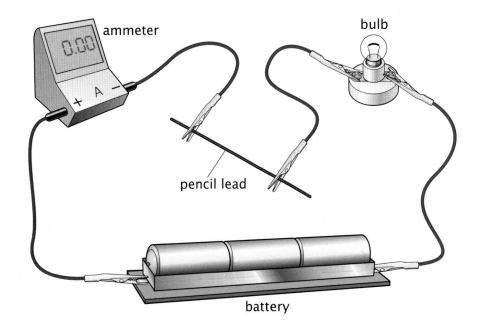

ammeter · bulb · pencil lead · battery

1 If you had done the experiment, could you have presented the results in the table in a better way?

2 Alastair has written one of the results down incorrectly. Which one do you think it is?

3 In this experiment which is the input variable and which is the outcome variable? (Remember: the input variable is 'what we changed' and the outcome variable is 'what we measured'.)

Natasha plotted a graph of the results. This is shown below. The axes have not been labelled.

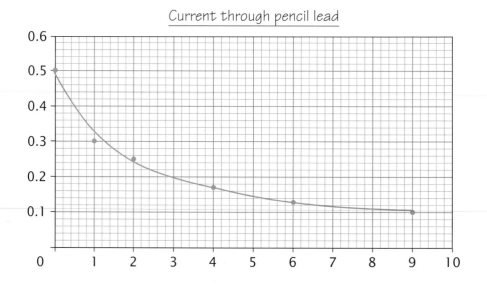

Current through pencil lead

4 What should have been written on the vertical axis, and what should have been written on the horizontal axis for this experiment? (Remember: 'what we changed' tells us what to write along the bottom and 'what we measured' should be written up the side.)

Natasha correctly plotted all the points. She drew the line of best fit. The line of best fit does not have to join up each dot, or be a straight line. It starts at the first reading, which might not be at the bottom corner (the origin). Any point that is 'out' is easy to see because it does not fall on the line. Such a point is called an anomalous result (see chapter 1).

This is what Alastair wrote:

'From my results I noticed that the current changed when the length of the lead was changed. I expected this because the pencil lead is not such a good conductor.'

5 Can you write a better conclusion than Alastair's to explain how the size of the current changes with the length of the 'lead' in the pencil?

6 What do you think would be the effect of connecting two pencil 'leads' side by side (in parallel) in the circuit? How would the current change? Why?

→ *Altering the current in a circuit*

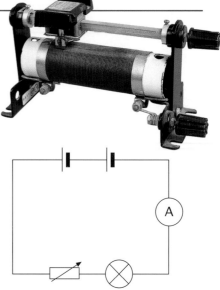

This diagram shows a **variable resistor**.

This works rather like the pencil 'lead' in the previous experiment. As you slide the knob a sliding contact moves along the coil of wire. This varies the amount of the material that is connected in the circuit.

The circuit diagram shows a variable resistor connected in a circuit to a bulb and an ammeter. As the resistance is increased, the current gets less and the lamp gets dimmer.

Some houses have dimmer switches for the room lights. These use a variable resistor. By turning the knob on the dimmer switch you lower the current reaching the light so it shines less brightly.

→ *Voltage*

There is another way we can alter the current in a circuit. This is to increase the number of cells. This increases the **voltage**. Voltage is measured in **volts** (V). Look at these two diagrams.

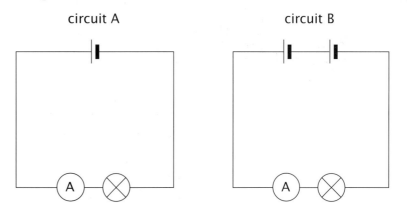

In circuit B the number of cells has been increased and the current reading is greater. Also the bulb is brighter. If one cell is 1.5 V, two cells is 3 V and three cells would be 4.5 V.

Increasing the voltage increases the current. It also increases the amount of energy transferred from the battery.

Thinking back to our lorries model, not only is the amount of concrete carried by the lorries more, but the rate at which the lorries are filled at the depot is greater.

Fuses

Key word
* fuse

Sometimes we want to protect a circuit to stop the current getting too great. To do this, we use a **fuse**. This is a fine length of wire often in a glass cylinder.

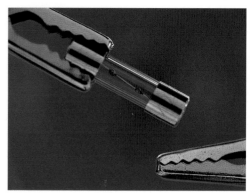

When the current becomes too great, the fuse wire is designed to melt. This causes a break in the circuit. The whole circuit is now 'dead'.

Plugs contain fuses. A hairdryer plug has a 5 A fuse. If the current from the mains electricity is higher than 5 A then the fuse melts and the hairdryer switches off.

19 A kettle has a 13 A fuse. Can you explain how this fuse is a safety device for the kettle?

Luigi Galvani and Alessandro Volta

Both the development of modern electric batteries and also electrophysiology can be attributed to Luigi Galvani, an Italian scientist who was born in 1737 and died in 1798.

In our bodies messages are sent along nerve cells as electrical impulses. This allows us to respond to things around us. The change in voltage makes our muscles contract. Our heart maintains its rhythmic beat because of regular electrical pulses. These cause the walls of the heart to contract and push the blood around the body.

Electrocardiographs (ECGs) are machines that record these electrical pulses. To do this electrodes (metal discs) are attached to the body. A study of the trace that is produced allows doctors to diagnose heart disease.

Artificial pacemakers have been developed that stimulate the nerves of the heart muscle. This work follows on from the pioneering work of Luigi Galvani, who discovered that dead frogs' legs would twitch and kick. He hung the legs by a copper hook on the balcony of his house and when the breeze caused the legs to make contact with the iron railings, the legs were seen to twitch. He mistakenly thought that the nerves in the leg were the source of electricity. However a fellow countryman, Alessandro Volta, challenged Galvani's conclusions. He thought that the electricity was produced because the two different types of metal, together with the salty liquid inside the frog, produced the electricity. Volta went on to make the first electric cell using acid instead of salt water. Today's modern dry cells are a development from this early work.

1 Which of the scientists has a unit of electricity named after him?
2 Where in the human body does electricity play an important role?
3 What is an electrocardiograph (ECG) used for?
4 What would be the reason for fitting someone with a pacemaker?
5 How did Galvani and Volta interpret the observation of the twitching frog's leg differently?
6 Explain the reason for the frog's leg twitching. What was the source of electricity?
7 What three substances were needed to make the first electric cell (battery)?

Research Find out what is used to make dry batteries today. What are the different sizes of batteries that you can buy and what are they used for?

Time to think Write a series of questions and answers for an electrical quizboard. The picture shows an example of a quizboard.

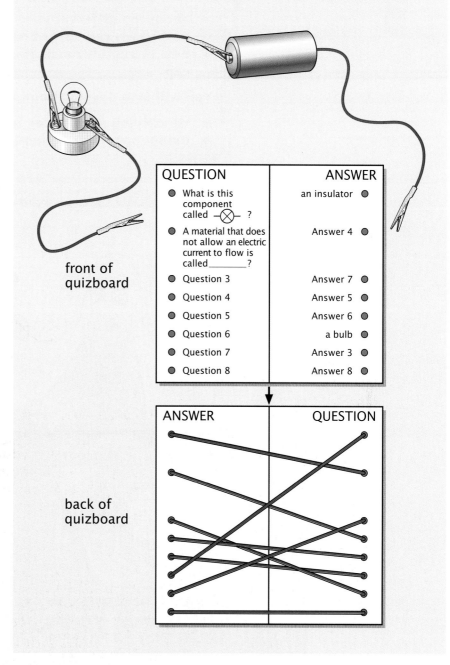

front of quizboard

QUESTION · ANSWER

- What is this component called ─⊗─ ? · an insulator ●
- A material that does not allow an electric current to flow is called _____ ? · Answer 4 ●
- Question 3 · Answer 7 ●
- Question 4 · Answer 5 ●
- Question 5 · Answer 6 ●
- Question 6 · a bulb ●
- Question 7 · Answer 3 ●
- Question 8 · Answer 8 ●

back of quizboard

ANSWER · QUESTION

4 Solids, liquids and gases

In this chapter you will learn:

➡ about the different uses of solids, liquids and gases
➡ how gases can spread out for miles around
➡ how incredibly small air particles can crush a metal can

You will also develop your skills in:

➡ classifying substances by using and changing a key
➡ using models to explain observations

➡ ➡ ➡ WHAT DO YOU KNOW?

Everything around us is made from matter. There are three states of matter: solids, liquids and gases.

Look at the picture above and see if you can find three examples of a solid, a liquid and a gas.

The table below lists three things you can try to do to solids, liquids and gases. Copy out the table. Working in a group, discuss (which you think you can do) and complete the table by marking each box with a tick (✓) or cross (✗).

Property	Solid	Liquid	Gas
keeps its shape?			
easy to squash?			
easy to pour?			

→ Uses of solids, liquids and gases

The uses of solids, liquids and gases are linked to their different **properties**.

Solids

Stone pillars are used in churches because they keep their shape, even though the weight of the roof is pressing down on them.

Liquids

Milk from a farm is poured from a churn into a tanker to transport it to the dairy. At the dairy, the milk is pumped out of the tanker. The milk takes up the shape of any container that it occupies. The milk cannot be squashed to make more fit into the tanker.

Gases

Scuba divers often do dives that last for an hour or more. A scuba diver breathes in about 3000 dm³ of air per hour but the volume of the air cylinder is only about 6 dm³. This is possible because the air is **compressed**. The air is fed through a tube from the cylinder to the breathing mask. A gas can be squashed, and it takes up the shape of the container that it occupies. It can also be poured and pumped.

1 The tyres of early bicycles were solid.
   a) What is the main advantage of a modern, air-filled tyre?
   b) What is the main disadvantage of an air-filled tyre?

2 This question concerns the materials used in a car. Copy out the table and complete it by thinking of one solid, one liquid and one gas used in a car. One example has already been done to give you some idea of what to do.

State	Material	Use	Reasons for use
liquid	oil	to lubricate moving parts	it is runny, it takes up the shape of its container
solid			
liquid			
gas			

Classifying solids, liquids and gases

Key words
∗ key
∗ classify
∗ characteristic

Property	Solid	Liquid	Gas
keeps its shape?	yes	no	no
easy to squash?	no	no	yes
easy to pour?	no	yes	yes

Scientists use a **key** to **classify** things into different groups. A key can be created by taking some **characteristics** of the different classifying groups, and asking simple questions that require yes or no answers. A simple key (decision tree) to classify things into the three states of matter is shown on page 81.

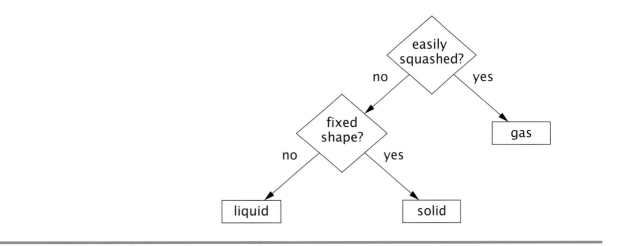

Reasoning ## What is it?

1 Use the key (decision tree) to classify the following five things as a solid, liquid or gas.

2 Some of the things may have surprised you with their classification.
   a) Which things were a surprise?
   b) Explain why they were a surprise.

3 Can you change the key so that it gives the 'expected' classification results?

It is sometimes an advantage if a solid behaves like a liquid. Sometimes soft toys are filled with small pieces of foam rather than a solid piece. This makes the toy more flexible as the pieces of foam can pour over one another when the toy is squashed or hugged.

At other times, if a solid behaves as a liquid, it can cause problems. Quicksand behaves like a liquid rather than a solid. If someone falls into quicksand they sink as the tiny particles of quicksand slide past them.

4 Some coal–fired power stations grind up the coal into a powder and blow air through it to make it behave like a liquid.
   a) What is an advantage of making the powder behave like a liquid?
   b) There is another advantage in using powdered coal rather than lumps of coal. What is it?

5 Michelle and Gaku investigated how easy it was to squash different material using the set-up shown on the right. They tested water, sand, flour, wood, juice and air.

Each time they filled the plastic tube to the 10 cm mark, and then put the airtight, moveable stopper on top before adding the 100 g mass to try to squash the material. They then measured the new height. Here are their results.

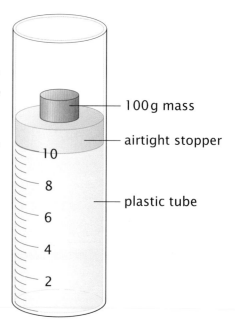

100 g mass

airtight stopper

plastic tube

water	9.9 cm
sand	9.8 cm
flour	9.2 cm
wood	10.0 cm
juice	9.9 cm
air	6.0 cm

a) What do their results tell us about the 'squashability' of solids, liquids and gases?

b) Can you explain the 'unexpected' result for flour?

→ *The particle theory*

Key words
* particle
* theory
* model
* Brownian motion
* kinetic theory

If you had an amazingly powerful microscope, you would see that all matter is made up of incredibly small **particles**. The particles are arranged in different ways in solids, liquids and gases. This basic **theory** can be used to produce detailed **models** that help to explain the different properties of solids, liquids and gases. Scientists call this the 'particle theory' or 'kinetic theory'.

Brownian motion and the kinetic theory

In 1827, a Scottish scientist called Robert Brown was looking at microscopic pollen grains taken from a flower. He noticed that when they were put in water, the grains moved from side to side and he believed that they were living. He then examined the pollen from a plant that had been dead for over 100 years and was astonished to see that these grains also moved around in the water. Further study showed that even particles of smoke showed similar movement. This observation of moving particles was called '**Brownian motion**'.

Scientists tried to explain the movement by saying that it was due to currents in the water carrying the pollen grains as it warmed up. However, this idea was proved wrong when it was pointed out that the pollen grains moved randomly in different directions.

1 Why was Robert Brown astonished to see that the pollen from a dead plant also moved around in the water?
2 What would you have expected to see if the movement of the pollen was due to heat currents in the water?

In the 1870s, some scientists came up with a new theory (the '**kinetic theory**') that liquids and gases were made up of particles that were constantly moving around and bouncing off each other. So, the pollen grains that Robert Brown saw were being moved by tiny, moving water particles bouncing against them. The theory could not be proved because the particles were so small that they could not be seen, even with the most powerful microscope at that time.

In 1889, a scientist carried out a fair test investigation on Brownian motion in liquids. He found that the motion was faster if the pollen grains were smaller and if the liquid was more runny. This was the first evidence to prove that the kinetic theory was correct because it was able to explain Brownian motion.

3 Name the input and outcome variables mentioned in the 1889 fair test investigation.
4 How did the results of this investigation help to explain how Brownian motion happens?

→ *The 'particles in a box' model*

Today we use the 'particles in a box' model to help us explain the different ways in which solids, liquids and gases act.

The following three diagrams show the particles (greatly magnified) in a box containing a solid, a liquid and a gas.

A solid has particles that are packed closely together so that each particle touches its neighbours. This arrangement means that solids keep their shape even when squashed. The particles are held in this packed arrangement by strong attractions. The particles in a solid cannot move around so solids do not pour easily. Solid particles can only vibrate from side to side.

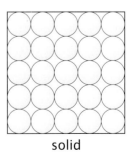
solid

A liquid has particles that are slightly more spaced than solids and these particles can move past each other. This is why liquids are easy to pour. However, the particles are attracted to each other by forces which stop them spreading out more widely.

Gas particles are very widely spaced and have very little attraction for one another. They move freely, colliding with each other and everything around them. Gas particles can escape from containers because they have lots of energy to move around.

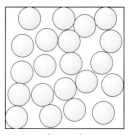

liquid

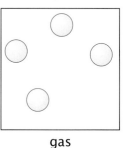

gas

Reasoning   ## Using models

1 Use the model to explain why:
  a) a solid keeps its shape
  b) a liquid takes up the shape of its container
  c) a gas is easily squashed
  d) a liquid is easy to pour but a solid is not
  e) the smell of frying onions quickly spreads across a room.

2 Read the following comments of three students.

Tom:
> A liquid is much more like a gas than a solid because you can pour it.

Mario:
> A liquid is halfway between a gas and a solid because you can pour a liquid but you can't squash it.

Jill:
> A liquid is much more like a solid than a gas because you can't squash it.

  a) Decide who you think is right and explain why. Try to list more evidence using your knowledge about the properties of gases, liquids and solids.
  b) Use your knowledge of the particle theory to back up your answer to part **a**.

DID YOU KNOW?

All gases are mainly made of space. The volume of the particles is extremely small compared with the volume that the gas occupies. This is because the gas particles are whizzing about at great speeds covering large distances for their tiny size.

Changing state

Imagine what happens to the particles in ice as it melts.

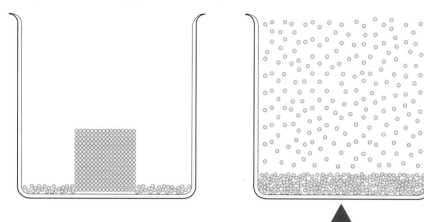

heat

Ice is a solid. Its particles are closely packed together and can only move by vibrating. When the ice particles gain energy from the surroundings they start to vibrate more. Eventually they can break away from other particles in the ice and move around as water particles.

The heat energy from the Bunsen burner provides enough energy for the water particles to move around rapidly. Eventually some break free as water vapour (steam).

Time to think

A balloon was blown up with camping gas. A very small volume of liquid camping gas produced enough gas to fill a large balloon.

Pupils were asked to explain why the volume of the gas is much larger than the volume of liquid. Here are some of their answers.

Tom:
> When a liquid turns into a gas, the particles get bigger and lighter and fill a larger volume.

Mira:
> There are lots of air particles in between the camping gas particles, so the volume is bigger.

Rashid:
> There are dust particles in between the camping gas particles giving a larger volume.

Natasha:
> There is nothing in between the camping gas particles. They are much further apart than when it is a liquid.

Neil:
> When a liquid turns into a gas, it just grows bigger.

Read through and evaluate the answers and:
1 decide which one is the most correct
2 explain why you think each of the other answers is wrong.

➡ Diffusion in liquids and gases

Freezer factory panic!

Hundreds of people were evacuated from their homes yesterday when ammonia gas leaked from a frozen food factory. The gas quickly spread through the surrounding area, causing stinging eyes and coughing fits.

Looking at the above examples, you can see that gas particles move around quite quickly. This happens even if there is no breeze. The movement of particles by themselves is called **diffusion**. Particles spread out as they diffuse.

Reasoning **Why does this happen?**

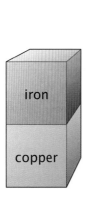

iron

copper

The cube of iron does not mix with the cube of copper.

water

orange

The layer of orange squash slowly mixes with the water over a period of a few days.

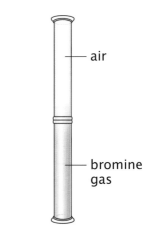

air

bromine gas

The brown bromine gas quickly mixes with the air to give a pale brown mixture.

Iron does not mix with copper because the particles in a solid are held close together and cannot move past each other.

1 Use your knowledge of the particle theory to explain the results of the other two experiments.

It is possible to remove all the air from a sealed container. This leaves a **vacuum**. There is nothing in a vacuum. All the particles have been removed.

Bromine gas is brown. It is sealed in a round flask and connected by a tube to the flask that has had the air removed. The connecting tube is closed off with a tap.

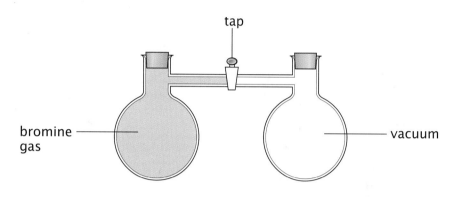

When the tap is opened, the brown colour becomes evenly spread through the two flasks in a fraction of a second.

In a second experiment the bromine flask is connected to a flask containing air.

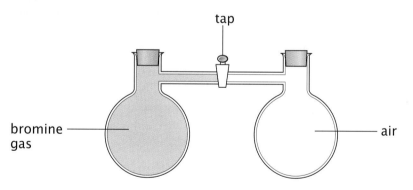

When the tap is opened, the brown colour becomes evenly spread through the two flasks after an hour.

2 Use your knowledge of the particle theory to explain the above two results. Why does it take longer for the bromine to move into the air flask than the vacuum flask?

3 Imagine that you are a particle of 'fried onions smell'. Write a story called *From the frying pan into a dark hole* which describes what the particle sees and feels in its journey from the frying pan to being 'sniffed' into a person's nose.

Gas pressure

Air is all around us but we don't notice it because we can't see it. The particles of air are bumping into each other and everything around them. When they **collide** with something, they push against it causing pressure and then bounce off. This is called **air pressure**.

3 Can you think of any simple pieces of evidence that prove that air is all around us?

DID YOU KNOW?

The particles of nitrogen and oxygen in the air around you are travelling at about 1100 m.p.h. It is estimated that a particle of air has about one hundred million collisions per second at atmospheric pressure.

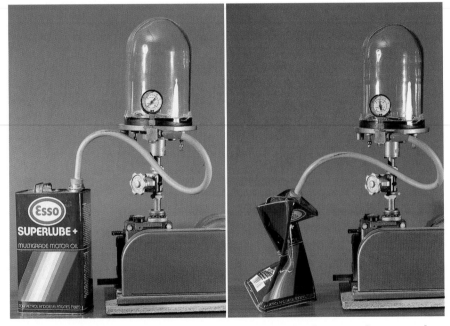

When there is air inside the can, air particles are hitting the inside and the outside of the can. When the air is removed from the can, the air particles are only hitting the outside of the can, causing it to collapse.

Word play

Some words have different meanings in science and everyday language:

particle
pressure
model

For each word:
1 write a sentence as it is used in everyday language
2 write a sentence as it is used in scientific language
3 explain the different meanings of the two uses.

Time to think

Look at the following questions and see if you can answer them using your understanding of the particle theory.

- If some lemonade is poured into a glass, it takes up the shape of the glass. If an ice cube is placed into the glass, it keeps the same shape. Why can a liquid easily change shape but a solid cannot?
- A large volume of nitrogen gas is stored as a small volume of liquid in a metal cylinder. Why is the volume of the liquid much smaller than the volume of the gas?
- In a darkened classroom, dust particles can be seen in the beam of light from an overhead projector. Why are the particles 'dancing around' in all directions?
- In preparation for a party, some balloons were blown up and hung outside the house on a cold day. After an hour, the balloons were found to be much smaller and softer than when they were first put outside. What happened to the particles inside the balloon?

5 Acids and alkalis

In this chapter you will learn:

➜ that acids and alkalis are chemical opposites
➜ to understand the terms concentrated and dilute and know the difference between strong and weak acids and alkalis
➜ to use indicators to tell acids and alkalis apart
➜ how to use the pH scale
➜ about neutralisation and how we use this important reaction
➜ to investigate everyday uses of acids and alkalis
➜ to develop techniques to use acids and alkalis safely

You will also develop your skills in:

➜ planning experiments and constructing variables tables for fair testing
➜ using models to explain key ideas
➜ choosing the range of data
➜ analysing data
➜ suggesting improvements to investigations
➜ constructing and interpreting graphs

➜➜➜ WHAT DO YOU KNOW?

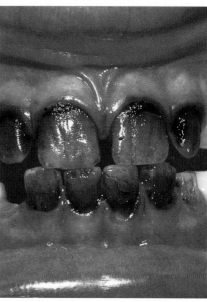

This child has been taking part in a lesson about healthy teeth. The staining shows how plaque builds up on your teeth.

A selection of common acids.

1 How many acids can you name in the display opposite?

2 In groups or with a partner make a list of as many facts as you can about the acids you have named. You need to think carefully about the properties of each of the acids. Compare your list with others in your class.

3 Plaque contains acid. What effect does it have on your teeth? How is plaque formed?

4 Some people say that chewing sugar-free gum is actually good for you. Why do you think this is?

Acids

Key words
* acid
* sour
* corrosive
* hazard

You might think that all **acids** are dangerous, but they have many different uses. Many fruit juices contain citric acid, and an acid is also used in car batteries. Ethanoic acid is the acid that gives vinegar its **sour** taste. Vinegar means 'sour wine'. Food can be pickled in vinegar to stop it going rotten. Methanoic (formic) acid is a highly irritating acid that is found in nettle stings. It is painful for humans but useful for the nettle plant. All of these acids are very different. Some can be eaten but others would harm you. They are **corrosive**. Many acids used in the laboratory or industry have the **hazard** warning sign shown on the container on the right.

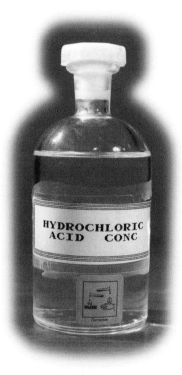

HYDROCHLORIC ACID CONC

DID YOU KNOW? Knowing about acids could make you very rich! A contestant on *Who wants to be a Millionaire?* was asked 'Which animal lives in a formicary?' He knew that ant stings contain formic acid and won the round.

Word play   What other words could you use to help explain the meaning of corrosive? Make a list of these words and use them to explain what the hazard word 'corrosive' means on a bottle of acid.

Evaluation ## Testing different liquids on limestone

Paul and Ali tested different liquids on limestone to see which ones were the most corrosive. They put five drops of each liquid onto a piece of limestone. Here is their table of results:

Name of liquid	Effect on limestone
vinegar	a number of bubbles are observed
pure water	no bubbles observed
orange juice	a few small bubbles are observed
white wine	some bubbles were observed
stomach acid	lots of fizzing, limestone dissolves
rainwater	liquid soaks in, one or two bubbles

1 What was the input variable and outcome variable in this experiment?

2 What are the fixed variables in this experiment?

3 What would Paul and Ali have done to carry out these tests safely?

4 Why did they try rainwater? Is this result surprising? Why?

5 Place the liquids in order with the most corrosive first. Are there any liquids that are difficult to place?

6 Ali suggested carrying out the experiment again in order to get more reliable results. How could they improve their method in order to collect more accurate data?

Laboratory acids

You have probably seen these acids in the laboratory. These liquids are in fact solutions of pure chemicals in water. **Concentrated** acids must be handled very carefully because they are very corrosive. They can eat away most materials including metals and skin! If the concentrated acids are mixed with more water they can be described as **dilute**. Acids that are very corrosive are described as **strong** acids. Acids that are not so corrosive, even if they are concentrated, are called **weak** acids.

Key words
* concentrated
* dilute
* strong
* weak

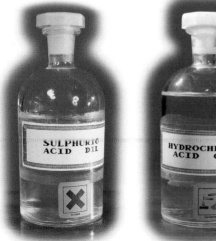

1 Which of the acids on the left would cause damage to your clothes?
2 Which of the acids in Paul and Ali's experiment are weak acids?

999: An emergency

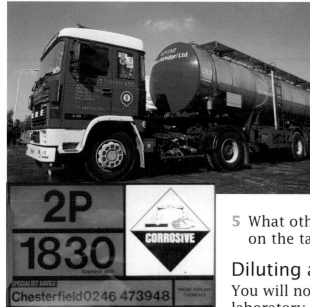

Chemicals have to be transported all over the country by road and rail. Acids that are transported are very concentrated.

This tanker is carrying **sulphuric acid**. It has a hazard warning which tells the emergency services how to deal with any spillage.

3 What does the hazard sign tell you about this chemical?
4 Can you think of any advantages of carrying highly concentrated chemicals to the customers?
5 What other sorts of chemicals might require hazard signs on the tanker carrying them?

Diluting acids

You will normally only use very dilute acids in the laboratory. Before the acid reaches you it will have been diluted so it is safe for you to use. Acids are diluted by mixing them with water but there is a correct way of doing this and a dangerous way.

You always start by measuring the correct volume of water then adding the acid very slowly and then stirring frequently. The mixture can get very hot so the acid *must* be added slowly. When water is added to concentrated acid the heat generated can turn the water into steam which could spray into your face. So NEVER add water to concentrated acid! It is usual to cool the mixture as well – why do you think this is?

6 Make a list of safety precautions that must be used when diluting a concentrated acid.
7 What other rules should you be aware of when using acids in the laboratory?
8 What must we do when somebody does get acid into their eyes? Look up the safety sheet for sulphuric acid and explain what has to be done.
9 All concentrated acids can be diluted by mixing them with water. Try to explain the difference between dilute and concentrated acid by using the idea of particles (see chapter 4).

Draw two beakers in your book. Make sure they are equal sizes. Draw one beaker with a concentrated solution of hydrochloric acid and the other with a dilute solution of hydrochloric acid. The different particles should be represented as shown in the diagram right.

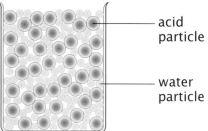

acid particle

water particle

Alkalis

Alkalis are the opposite of acids in many reactions. They can dissolve your skin and produce a soapy feeling. Two fingers covered in an alkali solution will feel slippery when rubbed together. Alkalis can be strong enough to burn your skin just like strong acids.

Sodium hydroxide is an alkali that is also known as **caustic** soda. The word caustic means 'burning'. This means that strong alkalis, like strong acids, are very corrosive and must be handled carefully. The alkalis that you are likely to find at home are bleach, indigestion tablets and many household cleaning fluids. The ones you will meet in the laboratory are sodium hydroxide and calcium hydroxide.

Look at the alkalis in the photographs and decide which ones are strong alkalis and which are weak.

The modern chemical industry began over 200 years ago and started with the manufacture of alkalis. The word alkali is the Arabic for ashes. Long ago people burned plants and used the ashes, which were alkaline, to make soap. The Egyptians probably made the first soap from goat's fat and beechwood ashes.

Time to think

Check how many of these questions you:
- are confident with already
- need to look back at the text
- need help from your friends or teacher.

1 Name three laboratory acids.
2 What are the main uses of alkalis in the home? Name three and give their uses.
3 Describe what is meant by a corrosive chemical?
4 Why are Student Safety Sheets (or Hazcards) useful? What information do they contain?
5 When people use oven cleaners the label tells them to be sure to use oven gloves. Give reasons why. What type of warning sign would you expect to see on the packet or canister?
6 Patients with indigestion are given **antacids** (alkalis). Do you think these alkalis are strong or weak? Explain your choice.
7 You have to dispose of an old leaky car battery. How would you make the battery acid safe?

Research

1 Name the acid found in the following liquids:
   a) tea
   b) wine
   c) sour milk
   d) tired muscles
   e) unripe fruit.
2 How is soap manufactured today? Use the internet to find out what chemicals are used in the modern soap-making industry.

Indicators

Key word
∗ indicator

Most acids and alkalis are clear, colourless liquids just like water. It is important to identify acids and alkalis with a simple test. So far we have learnt that acids are corrosive and alkalis dissolve your skin. So we need a safe way to test and identify them.

Indicators are very useful chemicals that turn different colours in acids and alkalis. The indicator that is most often used is litmus paper. This turns red in acid and blue in alkali. There are other natural indicators that can be extracted from plants.

DID YOU KNOW?

Litmus is an indicator that has been around for over 400 years and is made from lichens. Some lichens are also pollution indicators, because they will not grow in areas where there is high acid pollution in the air.

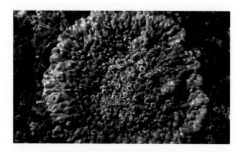

Reasoning ## Plant indicators

Hannah and Carlos made an indicator by boiling red cabbage in a small amount of water. They then tested their 'cabbage indicator' on a number of different liquids.

Liquid	Colour change
lemon juice	purple→red
water	stayed purple
hydrochloric acid	purple→red
lemon squash	purple→red
bathroom cleaner	purple→green
milk	stayed purple
sour milk	purple→red
toothpaste	purple→green/yellow

1 Describe how the cabbage indicator reacts in acid and in alkali.

2 What does the experiment tell us about milk?

Evaluation ## Orange indicator

Read this account of a pupil's method for extracting the juice from orange peel. They wanted to test the juice to see if it would make a useful indicator.

> We took four big pieces of orange peel and put them into 200 ml of cold water. We stirred the mixture for 10 minutes and then poured the juice into a beaker ready to test on our acids and alkalis.
>
> Results
> We found that our juice seemed very weak. We found it hard to see any colour changes.

Split into groups and discuss how you could improve the method so that they get a more concentrated juice.

Agree on a step-by-step method you would use. Include all the apparatus you would need.

Comparing different indicators

The table shows the results for a number of plant extracts.

Plant material	Usual colour	Colour in acid	Colour in alkali
red cabbage	purple	red	green/yellow
rose	pink	pink	yellow
fuchsia	purple	red	orange/yellow
blackberry	black	red	green
blackcurrant jam	dark red	red	green
bilberries	dark red	red	green
hydrangea	purple	pink	yellow
strawberries	red	red	green/yellow
marigold	orange	orange	orange

10 Which of the plant extracts would not make a good indicator?

11 Choose three plant materials that would make useful indicators.

12 Can you think of any problems with using plant extracts as indicators in the laboratory?

13 Blackberry indicator was used to test the following liquids. What colour would you expect to see when you tested each of them?
   a) Vinegar
   b) Lemon juice
   c) Oven cleaner
   d) Water
   e) Liquid from car batteries

Universal indicator

This is a mixture or blend of indicators. It has a wide range of colours depending on how strong the acid or alkali is. It can be used as a solution or soaked into paper. You will see that each colour also has a number. This is called the **pH scale**, and each number describes how acidic or alkaline a substance is.

On this scale:

- an acidic solution has a pH less than 7
- an alkaline solution has a pH greater than 7

Solutions that are neither acid nor alkali have a pH of exactly 7. These are called **neutral** solutions. Pure water is a neutral liquid.

Key words
* pH scale
* neutral

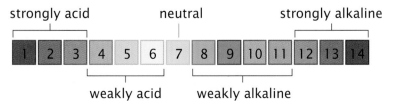

Word play

In this chapter the word neutral means a liquid that is neither acid nor alkali. The word is used in many other ways.

1 In a car, the gear stick must be in neutral when the engine is turned on.
2 In a plug there is a neutral wire.
3 People often say they are going to stay neutral in an argument.
4 Some colours, such as cream or beige, are called neutral.

Discuss in pairs these different uses of the word neutral. Try and explain what the word means in each case. Are any of the explanations similar to the meaning that it has in chemistry?

14 Five solutions have been labelled A, B, C, D and E. They have all been tested with universal indicator paper and recorded in a table.

Solution	pH number
A	11
B	2
C	6
D	14
E	7

a) Which liquid is neutral?
b) Which liquid must have been yellow after the test?
c) Which is the most acidic liquid?
d) Which liquid could be sour milk?
e) How many acids have been tested?

15 The following table shows how different plants prefer different types of soil.

Plant	pH value of soil	Acid or alkaline soil
potato	4.0–5.0	
rhubarb	5.5–7.0	
radish	6.0–7.0	
hydrangea (pink)	7.0–8.0	

a) Copy and complete the table.
b) Which plants would you grow if you had a soil pH of
   i) 7.5
   ii) 5–5.5?
c) Hydrangea petals can be different colours, blue or pink, depending on the pH of the soil. What type of chemical do you think can be extracted from hydrangeas?

Time to think A key idea in this chapter is the pH scale. Copy the pH scale onto the centre of a full page. Make the pH scale into a concept map using as many of your key words as possible. Compare your concept map with at least two other people and check where your ideas are the same and where they are different. Discuss why and how you made the decisions you did.

Enquiry **Testing acid**

You have learnt that the best way to make an acid safe is to dilute it by adding it to lots of water. Therefore, we can have different concentrations of the same acid.

Some pupils investigated whether the pH of an acid changes when it is diluted by mixing the acid with different volumes of water. They drew up the variables table below to help them set up a fair test.

Variable – what will change	Type of variable – input, outcome, fixed	Values
concentration of acid		strong, medium, dilute
volume of acid tested		$50 \, cm^3$
pH of acid tested		between 1 and 6

1 Copy and complete the 'type of variable' column.

2 How will the team measure the pH of the diluted acid?

The table below shows how the pupils diluted their acid.

3 Another team wanted to repeat this investigation but decided they needed more than four readings. What other readings for the volumes of acid and water should they take? Copy and complete this table to include the extra readings.

Volume of acid (cm^3)	Volume of water (cm^3)	Total volume (cm^3)
50	0	50
40	10	50
30	20	50
20	30	50

4 Why did each team need to have a total volume of $50 \, cm^3$ each time?

5 Describe a safe way to mix the acid and water each time.

→ *Making use of acids and alkalis*

Key word
* neutralisation

If you add just the right amount of alkali to an acid, you will make the liquid neutral. This type of chemical reaction is called **neutralisation**. Remember that in this topic neutral means neither acid nor alkali.

Gardeners and farmers often need to change the pH of their soil in order for their crops and flowers to grow.

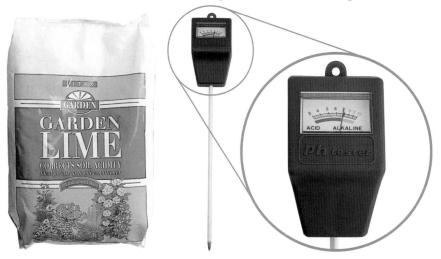

Lots of plants will not grow in acid conditions, but by adding lime to the soil the pH of the soil is increased, making it less acidic.

16 What sort of chemical is lime? Do you think it is acid or alkali?

Tooth decay is caused by acid.

The acid that causes tooth decay is made by bacteria that live off the little bits of food which are left behind when you don't clean your teeth properly. Toothpaste contains calcium carbonate, which is used as an abrasive. This means it cleans and polishes your teeth. It has another very important property. It is an antacid.

17 What effect would an antacid have on an acid?

18 Why is it very important to have antacid in toothpaste?

19 Paul and Rosie wanted to compare the pH values of well-known brands of toothpaste. They were told to draw up a variables table to help them set up a fair test. Make up your own variables table, making sure you include fixed variables as well as the input and outcome variables. Suggest suitable values for each variable.

Antacids are also used to cure acid indigestion. Your stomach contains hydrochloric acid that has a pH of 1 or 2. This acid stops harmful microbes from making you ill, and it helps to create the right conditions to digest all that food you eat! Sometimes we eat too much or we rush our food and too much stomach acid is produced. This is called acid indigestion, or heartburn. The acid doesn't touch the heart but squirts into the oesophagus that runs behind the heart, burning the lining of this food tube.

20 Is stomach acid strong or weak? Explain your answer.

21 Indigestion cures usually have a pH of about 9. Are they strong or weak alkalis?

22 Why is sodium hydroxide not used as an acid cure?

23 What happens to the acid in your stomach when you take indigestion tablets?

24 Why do people say that they have heartburn after a large or spicy meal?

Our skin is weakly acidic (a pH of about 5.5). More and more soaps, shampoos and other skin products advertise their pH value. Remember soaps tend to be alkaline and can dry our skin. This is very true for young babies, and therefore parents have to be very careful what sort of shampoos, bubble bath and creams they use on their children.

25 Discuss the advantages of using skin products that are pH 5.5 and produce a leaflet for new parents.

Creative thinking Neutralisation

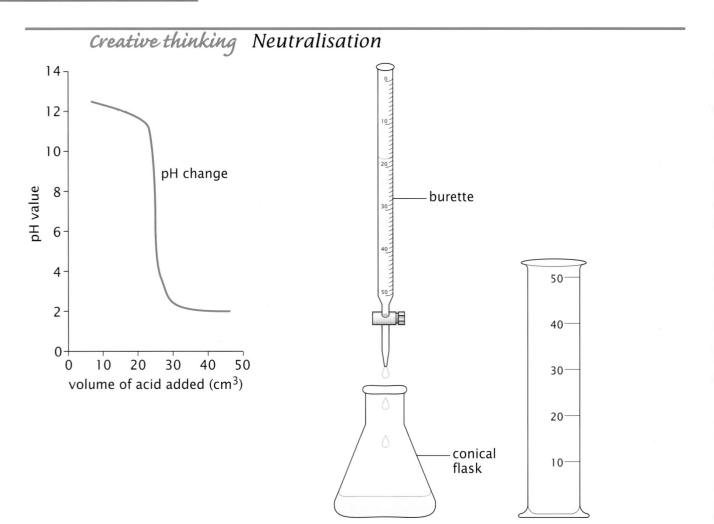

A burette helps you make an accurate measurement of the volume of acid.

1 The pH of the liquid in the flask was tested at regular intervals. Look at the graph showing the pH changes during the neutralisation reaction. What would the pH be of a neutral solution?

2 How much acid was needed to make the alkali neutral?

3 What type of solution is in the flask at the start of the experiment? Choose from the following:
  ▪ acid or alkali
  ▪ strong or weak.

4 Imagine you are inside a pH probe and you can see the acid and alkali particles. Describe what happens as the acid is slowly added to the alkali in the flask. Remember to tell the story carefully and mention all the changes in pH.

5 The acid and alkali in this reaction are colourless. You can't see anything happening when they are added together. What information on the graph suggests a reaction has taken place?

6 A burette makes this experiment more accurate. Why is the burette more accurate than the measuring cylinder?

More about neutralisation

Key word
* salt

When an alkali is exactly neutralised by an acid, a new chemical called a **salt** is made. When *sodium* hydroxide is mixed with hydro*chloric* acid the result is the most famous salt of all – common salt (table salt) or to give it its chemical name, *sodium chloride*. You will learn how to prepare common salt from rock salt in chapter 9.

Salts are present in all of these everyday products.

Besides flavouring your food, salt is used to preserve food. Most tinned vegetables are stored in brine (salt solution). There are many more salts such as bath salts, liver salts and salts are also used as medicines, fertilisers and even explosives.

Here is a table with some common salts and their uses.

Chemical name	Common name	Uses
sodium carbonate	washing soda	water softener
sodium sulphate	Glauber's salts	mild laxative
copper chloride	fungicide	cures fish fungus
calcium sulphate	plaster of Paris	plaster casts

Time to think

1 Make a complete list of all the key words you have learnt in this chapter. Arrange them in alphabetical order. Try to give an example or a definition of each word without looking back at the chapter. Now make two lists — key words you are sure about and those that you need to work on. Decide on the best way to learn and remember *all* the key words and their definitions.

2 Make up your own domino game to include neutralisation, indicators, using acids safely.

6 Forces and their effects

In this chapter you will learn:

→ that forces can:
  make an object start to move
  make an object slow down or speed up
  make an object change its direction of movement
  change the shape of something
→ that some forces attract and other forces repel
→ that the stopping distance of a vehicle depends on a number of factors including the driver's reaction time and the speed
→ that forces are measured in newtons
→ that forces are measured using a forcemeter
→ that speed is

$$\frac{\text{distance moved}}{\text{time taken}}$$

→ that density is

$$\frac{\text{mass}}{\text{volume}}$$

You will also develop your skills in:

→ identifying variables
→ reading and interpreting line graphs
→ drawing line graphs and bar charts
→ presenting and interpreting data in tables
→ making predictions
→ drawing conclusions

→ → → WHAT DO YOU KNOW?

Look at the following five pictures showing forces.

Special shoes worn for curling have one sole made from Teflon and the other from rubber. The curler can then slide easily on one shoe and grip when necessary with the other.

1 In pairs decide what picture 1 is showing. Can you explain how the large granite curling stone is moving? What can you say about the forces acting on it? Try to use the word friction in your answer.

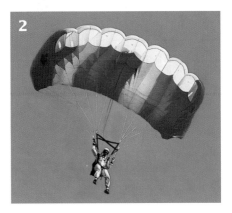

2 Look at picture 2 of the parachutist. How do you think the motion would have been different if the parachute had failed to open? What could the parachutist have done to make sure that she fell more slowly? What do you think would happen to astronauts landing on the moon if they had tried to use parachutes?

3 Picture 3 shows a football that has just been kicked by the footballer. What are the forces acting on the football? On a piece of paper draw the ball and draw arrows to show all the forces. Use a different colour to draw an arrow to show the direction in which the football is moving.

4 Explain what picture 4 is measuring. The reading on the scale is '7.2'. How do you think this reading would change if the equipment was taken to the Moon? Would the number be the same, more or less on the Moon? In science we give a special name to the meter shown in the picture that measures weight. It is called a forcemeter.

5 Look at picture 5. What forces act on the duck? The duck is made of plastic. Why is it not made out of iron? What other materials could be used to make it?

The units of science

Key words
* metre
* second
* kilogram
* ampere
* newton
* watt
* joule

The system we have adopted is the Système International d'Unités (SI units). It is based on seven units.

You have already met many of these special units that we use to measure in science:

metre	unit of length	symbol is 'm'
second	unit of time	symbol is 's'
kilogram	unit of mass	symbol is 'kg'
ampere	unit of electric current	symbol is 'A'

When a unit is named after someone, the name is not written with a capital letter, but the symbol for the unit is given as a capital letter. For example, force is measured in **newtons**, and the symbol is 'N'.

Sir Isaac Newton was a famous English scientist born in 1642 in Lincolnshire. He died in 1727. The story goes that, as a young man, he discovered the law of universal gravitation when he observed an apple fall to the ground. He also wrote a book on optics and invented the reflecting telescope.

You will meet many other units that are named after scientists such as the unit for power, the **watt**. This is named after James Watt and the symbol is 'W'. Another is the unit for energy, the **joule**. This is named after James Prescott Joule. The ampere (or amp for short) is named after the French physicist, André Marie Ampère.

André Marie Ampère.

Sir Isaac Newton.

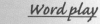

Word play — Some words have different meanings when used in science compared to their use in everyday language. An example is the word force. In everyday language we may say, 'when I was young my mother forced me to eat up all my cabbage'.

As we shall see, when we use the word force in science it has a much more precise meaning. Can you write two sentences, one where the word force is used in everyday language; and one where the word force is used scientifically?

→ *Forces, forces everywhere*

Key words
* attractive
* repel
* electrostatic force
* non-contact force
* twist
* deform

We come across forces all the time and we use different words to describe them. You may have met the words 'push' and 'pull' to describe a force. To open a drawer you have to pull on the handle.

You give someone a push on a swing to make them go higher and faster.

Sometimes forces are **attractive**. An example is a magnet picking up a paper clip. The paper clip is attracted to the magnet. To remove the paper clip we have to pull it off. We also have forces that **repel**. You may have seen two ring magnets set up like this:

If you try to push them together they repel one another and are pushed apart again.

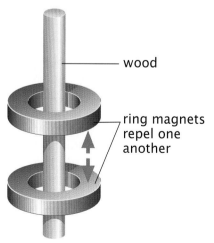

wood

ring magnets repel one another

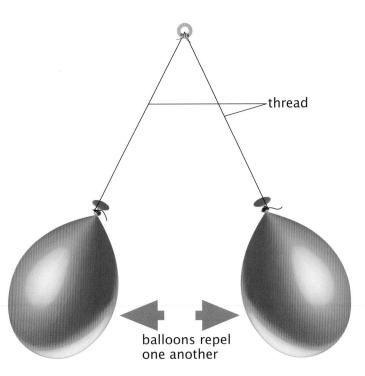

thread

balloons repel
one another

Someone gave the balloons an electric charge by rubbing them on their jumper. As you can see the effect is to make them dangle at an angle. The **electrostatic forces** are acting at a distance and pushing them apart. The balloons are not in contact with one another. These are called **non-contact forces**.

1 We met an example of another non-contact force earlier in this section. What was it?

To open many bottles of lemonade we need to give the cap a **twist**. This is another way in which we use a force.

If you push your thumb into some plasticine, you will make a dent in it. You have permanently changed its shape. Forces can change the shape (or **deform**) an object.

Time to think

So far in this chapter we have talked about types of forces and their effects. Make a table of the types of forces and what they do. Are they contact or non-contact forces? The headings for your table could be: type of force; effect; contact.

Showing forces

Key words
* represent
* resultant
* exerted
* balanced
* gravity

In science we try to explain the action of forces by using diagrams. In these diagrams we draw an arrow to **represent** the force. The direction of the arrow shows the direction of the force. The width of the arrow represents the size of the force. In the picture below the force shown is the pull of the dog on the girl's hand.

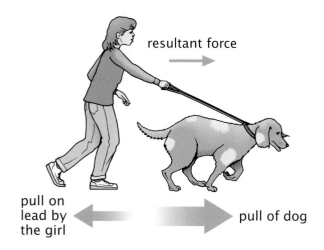

resultant force

pull on lead by the girl

pull of dog

This is a strong dog and the **resultant** effect is that the dog starts to pull the girl along. The force of the dog is greater than the force **exerted** by the girl. There is a resultant force in the direction shown by the arrow.

Look at Jack holding a bucket of water. You can see two forces shown. They are equal in size but act in opposite directions. The force pulling up is the same size as the force acting down. The forces are **balanced**. There is no resultant force acting, and so the bucket remains stationary.

This next drawing shows a football hitting the back of a net. Here the force shown is making the football slow down.

2 What would happen if there were no net? What would happen if there was a brick wall there instead?

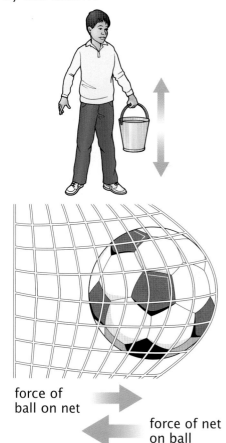

force of ball on net

force of net on ball

There is another force acting on the football, which should have been shown. This is the force of **gravity**. Scientists call the force that pulls an object towards the centre of the Earth the force of gravity.

3 Forces can have the following effects:
  • they can make something move
  • they can make something speed up
  • they can make a moving object slow down
  • they can make a moving object change direction
  • they can change the shape of an object.
Give an example of each of these effects of forces.

Information processing   *Reaction time*

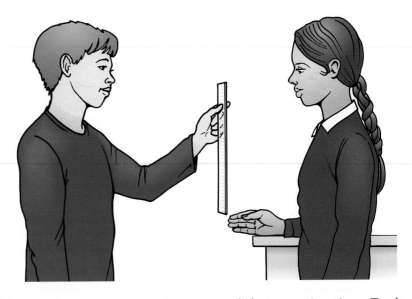

In this experiment some people measured their reaction time. To do this they tried to catch a ruler that was dropped by a friend. They measured how far it had fallen. Their results are shown in the table.

Name	Age	Right hand (distance in cm) Experiment					Left hand (distance in cm) Experiment				
		1	2	3	4	Average	1	2	3	4	Average
Debbie	15	19	18	18	17		26	22	16	16	
Howard	54	14	13	17	16		15	13	14	14	
Lesley	53	9	18	8	9		13	13	13	13	
William	41	25	27	22	22		27	10	13	14	
Vesna	40	36	22	34	20		24	28	15	39	
Caroline	13	31	26	21	18		28	31	23	22	
Laurène	10	24	19	14	15		25	19	23	23	
Nathalie	40	16	16	9	11		13	13	10	14	
Zorica	65	32	23	26	27		23	24	31	27	
Daniel	47	15	17	13	15		13	10	7.5	11	

The results in the column labelled 'average' have not been worked out. For Caroline the mean or average is $(31 + 26 + 21 + 18)$ divided by 4; which equals 24.

$$\text{Average} = \frac{31 + 26 + 21 + 18}{4} = 24$$

If you record these results in a spreadsheet such as Excel, you can get the spreadsheet to calculate the average automatically for you.

After doing the experiment and calculating the average distance, they then used the graph below to interpret their results and find out their reaction time. Look at the graph. You can use it to work out your own reaction time.

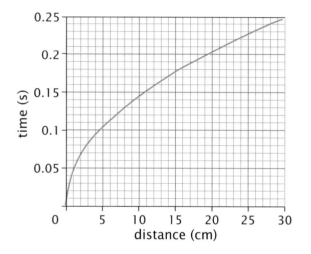

Suppose you do the experiment and the distance fallen is 25 cm. Go up to the graph from 25 on the distance axis, then go across and read off the time on the vertical time axis. You will see that it is between 0.2 and 0.25. It is about 0.225 s. Check this out to see if you agree. Now use the graph to find your own reaction time. You will need to do this with a partner. What equipment will you need?

1 What was the reaction time of Laurène with her right hand?

2 Who had the slowest reaction time with their right hand? What was it?

3 Overall, who had the fastest reaction time?

4 Was there any difference between people's reaction time with their right and left hands? Can you think why this may be?

5 If you had a reaction time of 0.2 s how far would the ruler drop?

6 If you had a reaction time of 0.1 s how far would it fall?

7 A £10 note is 14 cm long. If you held it vertically and asked someone to catch it, what would his or her reaction time need to be to be certain of catching it? Which of the people in the experiment would have caught the £10 note?

8 Why do you think the readings were taken four times?

➡ ## *Road safety*

Key words
✳ thinking distance

In the activity to measure our reaction time, we saw that there is always a time delay. The reason we have this delay, between seeing the ruler move and catching it, is because it takes time for the signal from our eye to travel to our brain and for our brain to then send a message through our nerves down our arm to our hand. In a similar way if someone is driving a car, they have a reaction time between seeing, say, a dog run onto the road in front of them and putting their foot on the brake. The signal this time has to go from their eye to their brain and down to their foot. While this is happening the car is still moving forward at the same speed. The distance it travels before the brake is applied is called the **thinking distance**. As you saw, different people have different reaction times. Other factors that can slow down reaction time are alcoholic drink or drugs.

4 There are several factors that affect the stopping distance of a car. How many can you think of? Some ideas are given in the list below. What effect do you think each of these factors would have on the stopping distance of a car?
- thinking time
- type of car
- weight of car
- weather
- speed of car
- type of road surface

One of the factors is the speed of the car. The speed of a car is often measured in miles per hour (sometimes abbreviated to m.p.h.). So the top speed of a car may be 120 m.p.h. This means that if the car moved continuously at this speed, it would travel 120 miles in one hour. Of course, not only is this illegal, but the car would not be able to move at a steady speed on a normal road because of other traffic, traffic islands and other obstacles. Many modern cars have a computer which calculates the average speed during a journey.

In Britain the speed limit on motorways is 70 m.p.h. In France the speed is measured in kilometres per hour (km/h). The maximum speed allowed on French motorways is 130 km/h. This is not the same speed limit as in Britain.

5 Work out what the equivalent speed of 70 m.p.h. is in km/h. A distance of 5 miles is about the same as a distance of 8 km.

As you can see it may be confusing if different units are used in different countries. In the same way, it is difficult to compare the cost of something when it is priced in dollars or pounds or euro. In science, we try to be consistent with our units. This is why we use SI units. The most common units used in science to measure speed are metres per second (m/s). If a long-distance runner is moving at 3 metres per second (3 m/s), they would go 180 metres in 1 minute, or 10 800 metres in 1 hour (10.8 km/h). This is about 6.5 m.p.h.

➡ # *Calculating speed*

Key words
✱ axes/axis

To work out the speed of something we need to know two measurements: the distance travelled and the time taken to go this distance.

Look at the following example.

A hedgehog travels across a road 10 m wide in 5 s. How fast is it going?

distance travelled = 10 m; time taken = 5 s

$$\text{speed} = \frac{\text{distance travelled}}{\text{time taken}}$$

$$= \frac{10 \, \text{m}}{5 \, \text{s}}$$

$$= 2 \, \text{m/s}$$

A fox smells the hedgehog and crosses the 10 m road in 2.5 s.

distance travelled = 10 m; time taken = 2.5 s

$$\text{speed} = \frac{\text{distance travelled}}{\text{time taken}}$$

$$= \frac{10 \, \text{m}}{2.5 \, \text{s}}$$

$$= 4 \, \text{m/s}$$

Research

How long is a marathon in kilometres? What is the record time for completing a marathon? What was the winner's average speed in km/h?

Information processing *Animal speed*

The table shows the maximum speed that different animals can reach.

Animal	Speed (km/h)
antelope	89
brown hare	72
cheetah	105
eider duck	113
greyhound	68
horse	69
gazelle	80
tuna fish	70
swift	171
tiger shark	53

This information is also shown in the bar chart below. You could use a spreadsheet such as Excel to produce the bar chart. Remember the rules for producing a chart: 'What we change' (input variable) and 'what we measure' (outcome variable) are the headings for both the results table and for the **axes** of the graph. The names of the animals go along the bottom line. The scale, going up the vertical **axis**, needs to be just bigger than the largest reading.

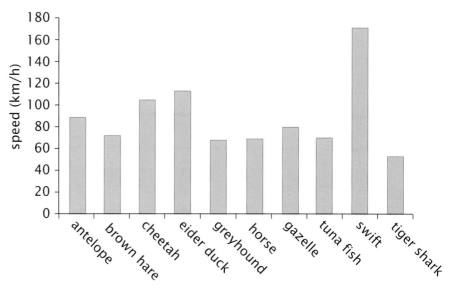

1 What is the input variable?

2 What is the outcome variable?

3 Which is the fastest animal?

4 Which is the slowest?

5 How many animals have a speed greater than 80 km/h?

The Japanese Shinkansen bullet train moves really fast. With a top speed of 186 m.p.h., it travels at an average of 162 m.p.h. between Hiroshima and Kokura stations. Not to be outdone, the French are working on a new TGV line that will top the 200 m.p.h. barrier. Then you will be able to see the sights of Paris and Marseille in one day.

Reasoning   ## Train travel

We can represent a lot of information in a graph, but we need to be able to understand and interpret this information. Look at the distance–time graph below. It shows a French TGV train travelling at a steady speed of 300 km/h between Lyon and Lille in France.

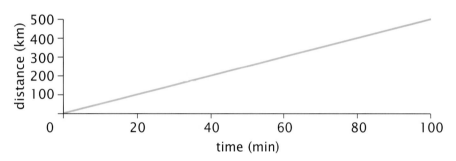

In the second graph a train is now travelling between Folkestone and London.

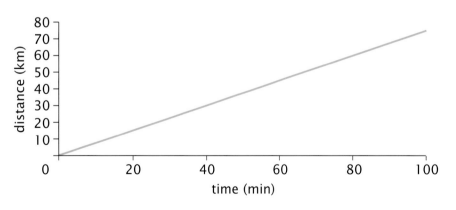

1 How far does the train go in 1 h in England?

2 How long does the TGV train take to go 100 km in France?

3 How long would the English train take to go the same distance?

4 There are a number of reasons why the shape of the graph does not give the true picture of the journey. Can you think of any reasons why it may not be truthful?

The next graph shows the distance–time graph for the Midland Metro tram from Wolverhampton to Birmingham. This graph has been split up into sections. At A the tram is moving; at B it stops to pick up passengers for 2 minutes and then it travels 0.5 km before stopping again for passengers.

5 Which are the sections in which the tram is moving?

6 How many times does it stop to pick up passengers?

7 For how long is it moving?

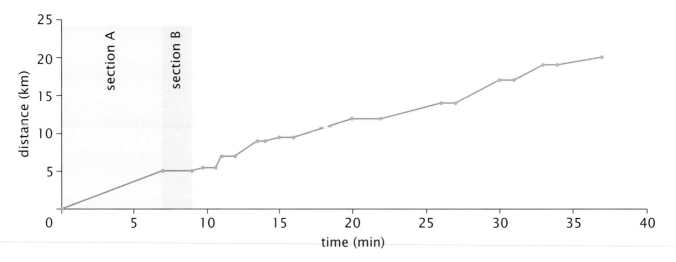

Look at the next graph. This shows a lift travelling up from the ground floor to the top floor of a tower block of flats.

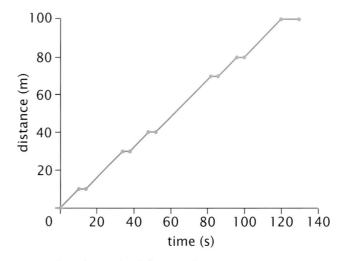

8 Can you explain how the lift travels?

9 Does it stop at every floor?

10 Do you know how many floors there are in the block?

11 Suppose the lift now returns to the ground floor without stopping. What would the graph look like?

12 With a partner see if you can explain different sorts of distance–time graphs. For example, you could sketch out a graph for walking to school or for the bus or car journey to school.

You may have a motion sensor in your school. This plots a graph on the computer screen as you move towards or away from the sensor. The picture shows someone using a motion sensor and also the graph that they obtain. Can you explain how the person moved?

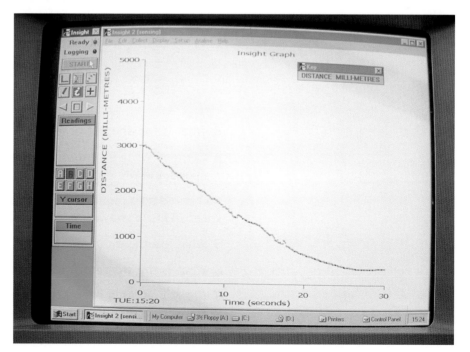

Information processing *Road safety*

We have already looked at factors that affect the stopping distance of a car. The spreadsheet below is similar to the one in the Highway Code but the data have been converted to km/h and m.

Speed (km/h)	Thinking distance (m)	Braking distance (m)	Overall stopping distance (m)
0	0	0	0
30	6	6	12
50	10	17	27
70	14	33	47
90	18	54	72
110	22	81	103
130	26	113	139

1 What do we mean by the thinking distance?

2 What do we mean by braking distance?

We could use a spreadsheet to plot a graph of thinking distance against speed. Remember when we plot a graph we put what we change (the input variable) along the horizontal (*x*) axis and what is measured (the outcome variable) along the vertical (*y*) axis. Either use a computer or graph paper to plot this graph.

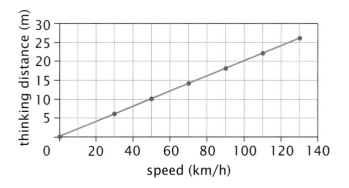

3 What is the shape of the graph?

4 Can you write a sentence to explain the relationship between the speed and the thinking distance?

You could also plot a second graph to show braking distance against speed. This is shown on the opposite page.

5 What are the input and outcome variables?

6 What is the shape of this graph?

7 Can you write a sentence to explain the relationship between the speed and the braking distance?

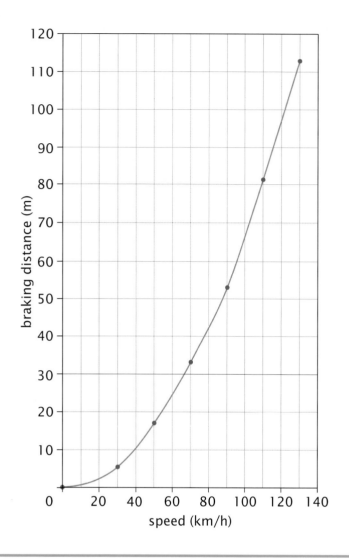

Time to think Split into groups and discuss one of the following:

1 Should there be speed limits on the roads and if so what should they be?
2 Should people be allowed to drink any alcohol and drive a car?
3 Should the age at which you can drive a car in the UK be lower, and if so what should the age be?

- Select the main points of your argument and make a poster or leaflet to explain your views to others.
- Evaluate the posters and leaflets produced by your classmates. Which provide good summaries and make their arguments strongly?

→ *Floating and sinking*

The picture shows an experiment you could easily try at home. Two unopened cans of cola are placed in a bucket of water. One is a diet cola and the other is an ordinary cola. Will they float, will they sink or will one float and one sink? What do you think?

Key words
* downward
* upward
* upthrust

In fact the diet cola can floats – why do you think that is?

Enquiry ## Floating

Some things float in water and others sink. Can you predict which of these objects would float and which would sink?

apple	pound coin
lump of plasticine	brass door key
granite rock	pencil
oak log	bar of soap

What reasons would you use to justify the predictions you have made? If you think the brass door key would sink what is your reason for saying so?

Upthrust and Archimedes

When an object (such as a cork) floats, then there are no resultant forces acting on it. If there was a resultant force acting then the cork would move in the direction of the force. Any **downward** forces, such as gravity, must be balanced by an **upward** force. We call this upward force the **upthrust**. It is thought that the Greek scientist Archimedes was the first person to realise that if an object is weighed in a liquid there is an upward force or upthrust from the liquid, so that the object weighs less.

Archimedes lived between about 287 and 212 BC. He became an engineer and among the devices he invented was the Archimedes screw for lifting water. He was also the first person to make an accurate calculation of π.

1 What is upthrust?
2 What is the link between upthrust and Archimedes?
3 What job did the Archimedes screw do?
4 Archimedes is described as an engineer. Is this the same as a scientist? Explain your answer.

Enquiry ## Upthrust

The equipment shown in the diagram below can be used to demonstrate upthrust. A number of objects are hung from the forcemeter (spring balance or newtonmeter) and the reading is noted. The reading is also noted when they are suspended in the water. Some of the results are shown in the table below.

	Weight in air (N)	Weight in water (N)
aluminium block	5.4	3.4
steel bar	4.7	4.1
brass ornament	3.5	3.1
lead weight	5.7	5.2
oak log	12.1	

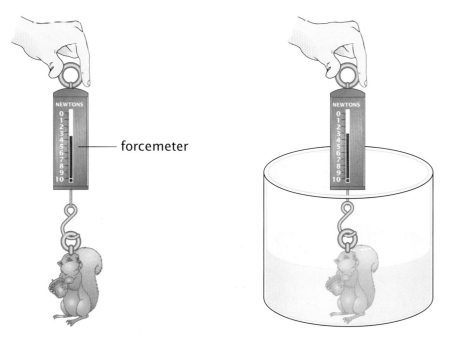

forcemeter

1 If an object floats in water how would this affect the results in the table?

2 What do you think the reading in the final column would be for the oak log?

It is said to be much easier to float in the Dead Sea, than in fresh water. This is because the upthrust is more. We could demonstrate this by repeating the experiment above using very salty water instead of fresh water.

➡ *Density*

Look at the pictures of the two lorries. One has a load of planks of wood and the other has a load of steel girders. The maximum load that each lorry can carry is 40 tonnes.

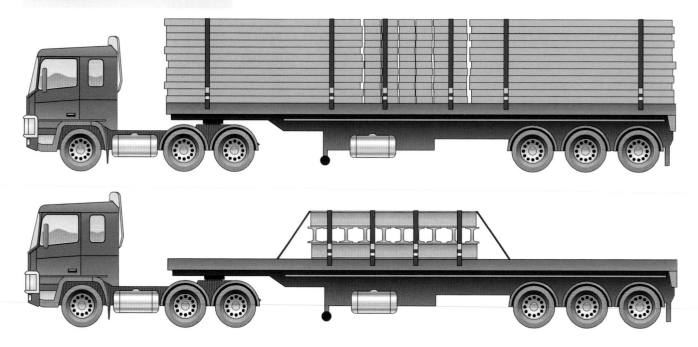

Both lorries are carrying the same **weight**. However there would be plenty of room on one lorry for some more steel girders. This would be illegal, as it would overload the lorry. Now look at the third picture.

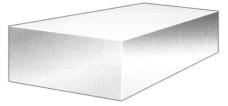

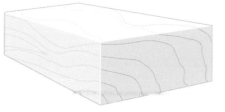

This shows two blocks, both the same size. One is made out of steel and one is made out of wood. If we weighed them we would find out that the steel one weighed the most.

So in the first pictures of the lorries, the wood and the steel weigh the same, but take up different amounts of space – they have different volumes. In the third picture the volumes are the same but the weights are different.

These objects all weigh the same but have different densities.

It would seem reasonable to say that a polystyrene cup is light and lead shot is heavy. But for this to be a fair comparison we must compare equal amounts of the materials. To do this we compare the **density** of each material. We need to compare the **mass** of 1 cubic centimetre (cm^3) of each material.

In everyday life we often use the word weight in a different way from the way it is used in science. In science, mass and weight are quite different.

For example when astronauts are in space, perhaps on a journey to the Moon in a spacecraft, we say that they are weightless. They are still made of the same amount of 'stuff'. They still have the same mass. The mass is the same whether they are on Earth, in space or on the Moon. However their weight changes because weight depends on the gravitational force acting on them. Mass is measured in kilograms and weight is a force measured in newtons.

$$\text{density} = \frac{\text{mass}}{\text{volume}}$$

If the mass is in kilograms and the volume is in cubic metres (m^3), then the density is in kilograms per cubic metre (kg/m^3).

If the mass is in grams and the volume is in cm^3, then the density is in g/cm^3.

The table shows the density of a few materials. The density depends only on what the object is made out of, not on its shape or size. If an object is made of something that is denser than water, then it will sink in water. If it is less dense it will float.

Material	Density (kg/m³)
oak	270
water	1000
ice	920
aluminium	2700
copper	8900
lead	11 400
steel	7800

6 Which materials from the table float in water?

7 Copy the table below. Fill in the gaps in the table.

Material	Density (g/cm³)	Mass (g)	Volume (cm³)
copper		890	100
oak	2.7		100
lead	11.4	228	

8 In this table which material has the smallest volume?

9 Which has the greatest mass?

10 Which has the highest density?

Word play

If we go to the greengrocers we would ask them to 'weigh out' a kilogram of potatoes. What we want is a 1 kg mass of potatoes. On the Moon the pull of gravity is about one-sixth as much as on the Earth. If an object on the Earth is placed on a newtonmeter and the reading is 18 N, what would the reading be on the Moon? Write a sentence to explain how the mass and weight of a 24 kg sack of potatoes would differ on the Earth and on the Moon.

Stretching

Key words
* extension
* load

Robert Hooke was born in 1635 and died in 1703. He worked at the Royal Society. He was interested in many areas of science. Here we look at some of the physics ideas he worked on. (Some of his biology work is discussed in chapter 7, page 132.) Robert Hooke investigated the way materials stretch. He used the word **extension** for the amount a spring stretches when a **load** is hung from it.

Information processing   *Stretching springs*

The picture shows an experiment to stretch a spring.

Some pupils did the experiment and plotted a graph of how the spring stretched as the load increased. They put their results in a table and then plotted a line graph.

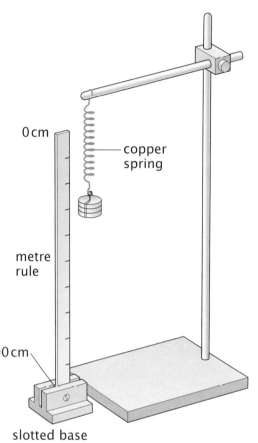

0 cm

copper spring

metre rule

100 cm

slotted base

Load (g)	Stretch (cm)
0	0
100	12
200	28
300	43
400	55
500	72
600	86

1 What is the input variable in this practical?

2 What is the outcome variable?

3 Which of the graphs (**A–D**) shown below is most likely to be correct? Remember 'what we change' (input variable) goes on the horizontal axis. 'What we measure' (outcome variable) goes along the vertical axis.

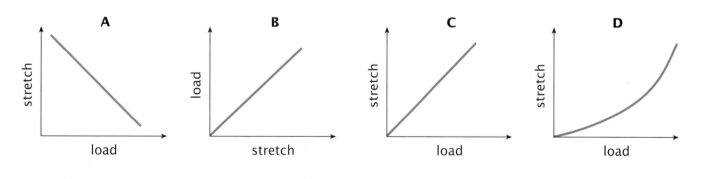

4 What was the relationship that Hooke found for springs? Start your sentence with: If you increase the size of the load . . . .

Reasoning *Stretching elastic bands*

A similar experiment is done using large elastic bands. In the first experiment one rubber band is used. The results are shown in the table below.

Load (g)	Length (cm)	Extension (cm)
0	10	0
100	16	6
200	22	12
300	28	
400	34	
500	37	
600	39	

The table shows the load and the length of the rubber band. The third column labelled extension is the amount that the rubber band stretches. This can be worked out by measuring the length without a load, measuring the length with a load and subtracting one from the other. The first three have been done for you.

1 Copy the table and complete the third column.

2 Sketch a graph to show extension against load. What will we put on the horizontal axis? (This is 'what we change' – the input variable.) What would go up the vertical axis? (This is 'what we measure' – the outcome variable.)

3 One pupil wrote a conclusion for this experiment like this: 'The bigger the load, the longer it got.' Her teacher underlined the word it. Can you write a better conclusion without this word?

4 If the experiment was repeated but this time two rubber bands were used side by side, how do you think the results would change?

5 If the rubber bands were joined together one below the other how would this change the results? Give a reason for your answer.

➡ # Friction, friend or foe?

Key words
* friction
* resists

Friction is a contact force. It acts when two objects move against one another. Friction is a force that **resists** or opposes motion. If you push a shopping trolley and then let go it will continue to move but will slow down and finally stop. This is because of the force of

pushing force

friction force

friction acting in the opposite direction to which it moves. To keep the trolley moving at a steady speed you need to keep pushing the trolley with a steady force. Now your pushing force and the friction force are balanced. This means that the pushing force is the same size as the friction force.

Friction is due to the roughness of the surfaces. It is the friction between the soles of our shoes and the ground that allows us to walk. If the friction is very low, such as when you walk on an icy surface, it is much harder to move.

Reasoning ## Friction

Some pupils performed an experiment to investigate friction and types of surface. They pulled a shoe along the floor at a steady speed. They repeated the experiment with the shoe on different types of surface. Their results are shown in the table.

Surface	Pulling force (N)
carpet	10
tiles	3
wood	6
concrete	7
tarmac	8
glass	4

1 How do we know what the size of the friction force is?

2 Either use a spreadsheet or graph paper to draw a bar chart of the results. Remember 'what we change' (the input variable) and 'what we measure' (outcome variable) form the headings on both the table and the graph.

3 Which surface had the greatest friction?

4 What is the order of the surfaces from the one with the least friction to the one with the most friction?

5 Can you make a prediction on what the friction force might be on a plastic tabletop?

6 What is your reasoning for this answer?

7 Suppose someone has spilt some cooking oil on a tiled kitchen floor. How do you think this would affect the friction?

8 Sometimes after a road accident, the road surface becomes covered in oil. What effect does this have? Why does the fire brigade often spread sand on the road?

9 Write a list of examples where friction is useful. Write another list of where it is a nuisance.

Bicycles

In the eighteenth century the first bicycle, the Hobby Horse, was built but it had a major disadvantage – it didn't have pedals! Pedals were introduced in 1839 by a Scottish blacksmith, Kirkpatrick Macmillan. Early bicycles were made out of wood and the first all-metal machines didn't appear until the 1870s. The pedals were still fixed to the front wheel. It was at this time that the penny-farthing bicycle was invented with its enormous front wheel and small rear wheel. For one rotation of the pedals the bicycle would move the circumference of the wheel. These bikes had solid rubber tyres to make the ride smoother but it was not very stable as the rider sat so high above the ground.

In the 1880s the safety bicycle was invented. This bicycle had a chain and sprocket drive on the rear wheel. It was the forerunner of the modern bicycle; although the idea of the chain and cog was said to have been suggested by Leonardo Da Vinci in the fifteenth century. By 1890 the pneumatic tyre had been invented by a veterinary surgeon called John Dunlop. Towards the end of the nineteenth century gears were introduced. The derailleur gear was invented in 1899.

Today there are several styles of bicycle, the main ones include the standard road bicycle, mountain bicycle, racing bicycle and recumbent bicycle. While the road bike looks similar in style to the bicycle of the 1950s there have been many technological advances. The classic Raleigh bicycle of the 1950s had a steel frame and weighed over 20 kg. Today modern bikes are made from a variety of materials including aluminium, titanium and carbon fibre. They are much lighter.

A pedal force is needed to start the bike moving and to change speed. Resistive forces have to be overcome; these include friction between the tyres and the road, and air resistance. Aerodynamics plays a major role in cycle races such as the Tour de France. This race covers 4000 km, and much of it is over mountainous terrain.

1 What was the origin of the name penny-farthing?
2 Why did the penny-farthing have a large front wheel?
3 Why is a ride on a modern bicycle smoother than it was in the nineteenth century?
4 Draw a timeline to show the development of the bicycle.
5 What factors led to changes in bicycle design?
6 List the factors you would consider when choosing a new bicycle.

Key words
* air resistance
* terminal velocity

➡ *Air resistance*

Galileo was an Italian astronomer and physicist. He made the first astronomical telescope and discovered the four moons of Jupiter. His work on the motion of the planets around the Sun questioned the work of Aristotle and the teaching of the church and he was forced by 'the inquisition' to give up his theory.

Today we can easily measure how two objects fall. At the time when Galileo lived it was much harder to make accurate measurements. But he was able to show that a heavy object and a light object both fall at the same rate. This is not quite true, however. There is one force that acts on a falling object to slow it down. That force is the friction force. This depends on the size and shape of the object and also what substance the object is falling through.

Sky divers falling from an aeroplane can reach a speed of 140 m.p.h. They do not keep on going faster and faster. They reach a steady speed when the air friction (or **air resistance**) balances the force of gravity. If they spread out their arms and legs, their maximum speed is less than if they point head down in a dive.

11 What country did Galileo come from and what was his profession?

12 How did Galileo add to the knowledge about astronomy at the time he lived?

13 Why was it more difficult for Galileo to do experiments on the way objects fall than it is now?

14 Can you explain what the purpose of a parachute is?

If an object falls through a liquid it will also reach a steady maximum speed. One factor is the material that the object falls through; an object will fall faster through water than through treacle. What factors do you think will affect this speed? The maximum speed that is reached is sometimes called the **terminal velocity**.

There are some useful CD-ROMs and websites for investigating terminal velocity.

Time to think   Now you have come to the end of this chapter, see if you can summarise the ideas by making your own concept map. To start you off, a few ideas are shown. You can use other words and ideas from what you have read in the chapter.

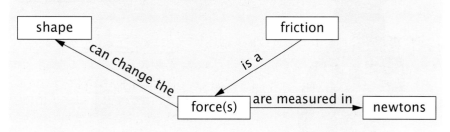

7 Cells

In this chapter you will learn:

- ➜ that all living things are either a single cell or made of many cells
- ➜ that cells are tiny and so you need a microscope to study them
- ➜ that a microscope uses lenses to magnify a specimen
- ➜ that cells respire and release energy for synthesis or movement
- ➜ about the structure of cells
- ➜ how some cells are specialised to do certain jobs
- ➜ that cells make up tissues which form organs and body systems
- ➜ that cells make new cells by dividing
- ➜ that cells make a copy of their DNA before they divide

You will also develop your skills in:

- ➜ sorting information and analysing evidence
- ➜ evaluating experiments
- ➜ using ratios to help you work out the size of small objects
- ➜ using models to help you learn about cell structure

➜ ➜ ➜ WHAT DO YOU KNOW?

All of these pictures show parts that are found in humans.

1 Do you know what any of them do?

2 Where are they found in the body?

3 Do any of them link together?

4 Have you any ideas about how big they are?

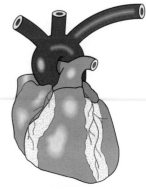
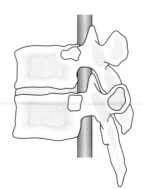
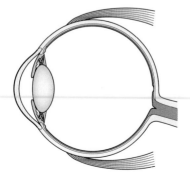

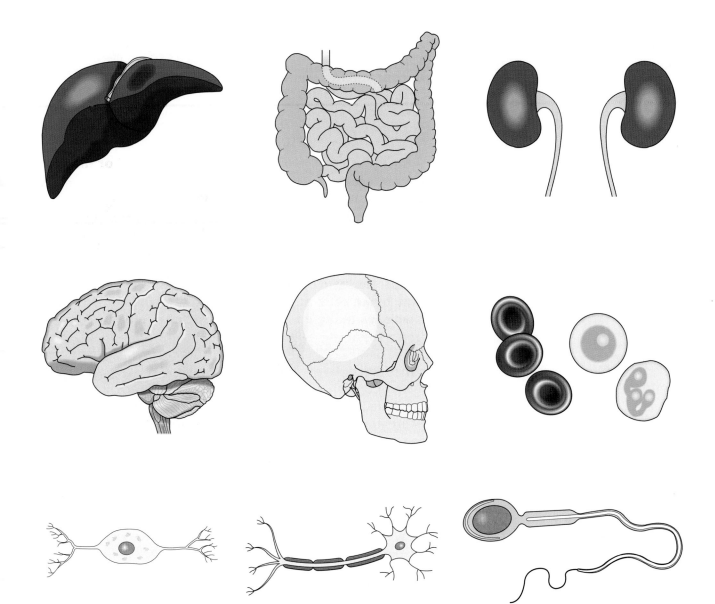

Plants have parts too. Most plants have a stem, roots and flowers.

5 What do the stem, roots and flowers do?

6 Draw a plant and label it. Make notes by each label to explain what each part does.

Key words
* microscope
* cell

Observing cells

Science and technology often work together. In the 1660s, the first **microscopes** were invented. Scientists, for the first time, were able to see things that were too small to see with their eyes alone. One of the first men to build and use a microscope was Robert Hooke (1635–1703), who worked at the Royal Society for Science. He was an astronomer, physicist and naturalist. He wrote a book that included the first illustrations of what various objects looked like under a microscope. One of the materials that Robert Hooke studied with his microscope was cork that is found under tree bark. Hooke noticed that the cork was made up of tiny boxes. These reminded him of the rows of monk's rooms in a monastery, and so he called each little box a **cell**.

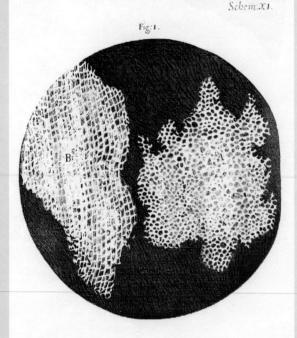

1 When was Robert Hooke born?
2 How old was Robert Hooke when he died?
3 Robert Hooke was an astronomer, physicist and naturalist. Explain what is studied in each of these areas of science.
4 What word would we use instead of naturalist today?
5 How did the fact that Hooke studied three areas of science help with the invention of the microscope?
6 What was special about the book that Hooke produced?
7 Why did Hooke choose the word cell for the small units he saw when he looked at plant material with his microscope?

➡ *What are cells?*

Key words
* multicellular
* respiration
* energy
* synthesis

The cell is often described as 'the basic unit of life'. This is because all living things are made of cells. Some living things are single cells.

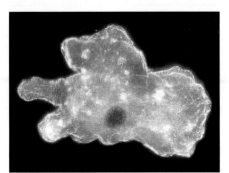

Here is an *Amoeba*, which oozes along the bottom of ponds.

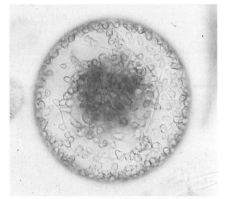

Here is an alga, which floats in the surface waters of ponds and lakes.

Here is a yeast cell, which we use to help us make bread and wine.

Most living things are made of a large number of cells. They are **multicellular**. The human body is made of around 100 million million cells. These cells are rather like tiny factories where many chemical reactions take place every second.

The most important reaction that happens in cells is **respiration**. This reaction releases **energy** from sugar. The energy can then help the cell move. Cells also need energy to make new materials. This process of making new materials is called **synthesis**.

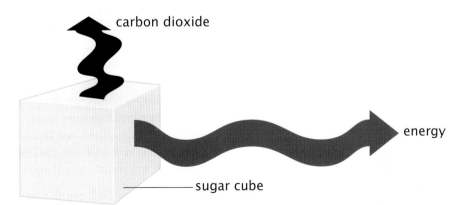

carbon dioxide

energy

sugar cube

Respiration happens in all cells. All cells need energy to keep alive and carry out their jobs in the body. It is difficult to observe single cells respiring but you can see the effect of all the cells respiring in the activity on the next page.

Enquiry Investigating yeast

The indicator changes from red to orange showing that the girl and the gerbil both release carbon dioxide.

Yes, plants do respire, but it's difficult to see this in an experiment because they use the carbon dioxide that they release in respiration, to make food in photosynthesis.

Now if I can stop photosynthesis, I might be able to show plants respire...

1 Can you draw the apparatus set-up that you would use to try to show that plants respire and release carbon dioxide? (Hint: remember that you have to stop photosynthesis taking place otherwise it will use the carbon dioxide as soon as it is released. Try using a similar set-up to the gerbil experiment above.)

Zainab wanted to find out if single cells respire in the same way as larger living things. She chose yeast as her single-celled organism. Yeast is a single-celled fungus used in making bread and wine. She wanted to see if single cells release carbon dioxide and whether she could detect any energy being released. She put some yeast and sugar solution into a flask, and placed a thermometer in the flask to

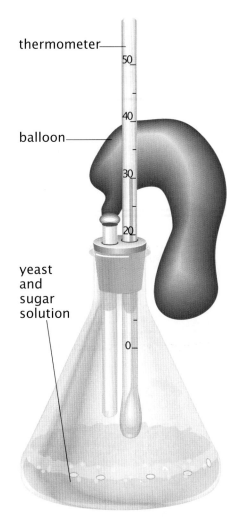

thermometer

balloon

yeast
and
sugar
solution

measure any temperature change. A balloon was attached to the flask to trap any gases released. Zainab also recorded the room temperature each hour, which stayed between 19 and 21 °C.

Time (h)	Temperature in the flask (°C)	Volume of balloon (cm³)
0	20	0
1	26	10
2	27	25
3	26	35
4	28	40
5	30	50

At the end of the experiment, Zainab tested the gas in the balloon with the carbon dioxide indicator and found that the yeast did release carbon dioxide.

2 What is the input variable in Zainab's experiment?

3 Zainab collected data on two outcome variables. What are these outcome variables?

4 What colour change would Zainab have seen when she tested the gas released by the yeast with the carbon dioxide indicator?

5 Why did Zainab take the room temperature as well as the temperature of the flask?

6 What happened to the temperature of the flask over the 5 hours of the experiment? What does this tell you about yeast respiration?

7 What happened to the volume of the balloon over the 5 hours of the experiment?

8 What does this tell you about yeast respiration?

9 What conclusion could Zainab give for this experiment? (Hint: use these words in your answer – carbon dioxide, energy, temperature change, respiration and yeast cells.)

10 If Zainab repeated the experiment using water instead of sugar solution, what would you expect the results to be? Why?

11 Zainab decided that yeast makes carbon dioxide when it respires. How is the carbon dioxide gas used in breadmaking?

12 What else do yeast cells make when they respire?

Word play

Many words are formed from other words. Microscope has the ending -scope which is from the Greek meaning 'to look at' or 'detect'. What do you think micro- means in Greek?

Copy the names of the instruments and match them to the job they do. The first one has been done for you.

stethoscope   to view stars and planets
oscilloscope   to look inside the gut and other body organs
endoscope   to examine waves, such as sound waves
telescope   to listen to heartbeat and lung movements

How big are cells?

We know that cells are small because we need a microscope to see them, but just how small are they? Some of the largest cells in humans are cheek cells. These are about 1 mm long. While we all know, from looking at the smallest division on our rulers, that 1 mm is small, it is hard to imagine how things that small work. The following examples give us some idea of what it means to be only 1 mm in size.

Imagine a jar of honey 1 m high. That's about the height of a school laboratory bench. Think about how you will remove the lid. How will you get the honey out?

Now imagine another jar of honey but this one is 10 times smaller than the last jar (only 10 cm high). This one will fit nicely on your outstretched palm. Think about how you will remove the lid. How will you get the honey out?

Next imagine a jar of honey that is 10 times smaller than the last jar (only 1 cm high). That's 100 times smaller that the first jar. You might need tweezers to pick it up. Think about how you will remove the lid. How will you get the honey out?

Finally imagine a jar of honey that is 10 times smaller than the last jar (only 1 mm high). That's 1000 times smaller than the 1 m jar that you first thought of. This jar is so small that it's just a tiny speck. Sneeze and you would lose it forever – so forget about trying to get the honey!

The last honey jar is the size of one of your cheek cells. A cheek cell is 1000 times smaller than a metre. Many cells are much smaller than this. A spot of blood will have around 5 million red cells in it and about 10 000 white cells. In fact red cells are around 0.001 mm, which makes them 1000 times smaller than cheek cells.

To see cells clearly, you need to use a microscope. You can then put the cells onto a glass slide and magnify them using the microscope lenses. Microscopes today are not that different to Robert Hooke's. They have an **eyepiece lens** that you look through. A second lens, called the **objective lens**, can be pushed into position above the slide. These two lenses **magnify** the specimen. Light is then directed up through the slide and the two lenses into the eye. In some microscopes, there are a range of objective lenses that vary in their magnifying power. Some things, like apple seeds or eyelashes, only need a low power of magnification in order to see them and you would use a ×4 or a ×10 objective lens for these. Others, like the tiny red blood cells, need a high power of magnification and you would need a ×40 objective lens to see these.

If you use a ×4 objective lens, then it magnifies things four times like this:

microscope

becomes

microscope

The eyepiece lens would then magnify things another ten times. This would make the m look about 6 centimetres high.

What you see, when you use these two lenses and look down the microscope, is forty times larger than the real thing. This is a **ratio** of 40 : 1.

1 How much bigger do you see things if you use a ×10 objective lens and the ×10 eyepiece lens? What is the ratio of real size : observed size with these two lenses?
2 How much bigger do you see things if you use a ×40 objective lens and the ×10 eyepiece lens? What is the ratio of real size : observed size with these two lenses?
3 If a cell is 0.5 mm wide, how big does it look using a microscope with a ×10 eyepiece and an objective lens that is:

    ×4
    ×10
    ×40

4 If a part of an apple flower looked 8 mm using a magnification of ×40 on a microscope, what is its real size?

Hooke's microscope

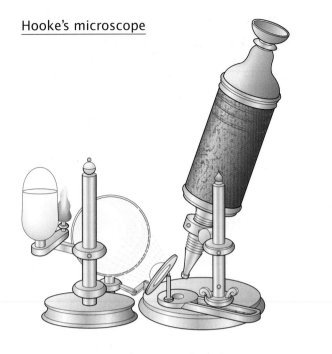

modern microscope

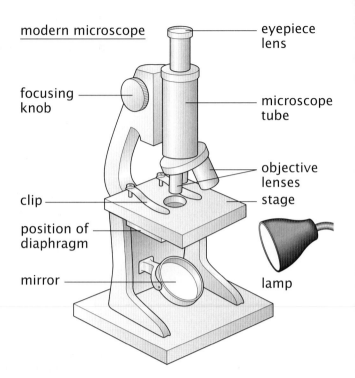

5 Find five ways in which Hooke's microscope is similar to a modern microscope.

6 Find two ways in which Hooke's microscope is different from a modern microscope.

7 Hooke used microscopes to look at cells and telescopes to look at stars and planets. Both microscopes and telescopes use lenses to help us see things better. Explain what microscopes and telescopes each do to the size of the things that they look at. How can we work out the real size of objects if the microscope and telescope change the size so that we can see it?

Information processing *What size is it?*

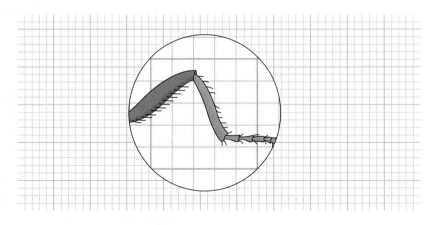

1 Look at the picture which shows what graph paper looks like under low magnification with a microscope. What you can see is called the **field of view**.

2 How much of the graph paper can you see in the field of view?

3 Measure the real size of the field of view in the diagram at the bottom of page 138 with a ruler. How many times has the microscope magnified the field of view? Now measure the length of the ant's leg. Work out the real size of the ant's leg.

4 If you looked down the microscope at pollen and estimated that you could fit about 20 pollen grains across one small square of the graph paper, what do you think the width of a pollen grain would be?

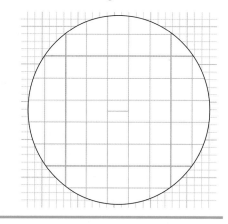

⇨ *What are cells made of?*

Key words
* cell surface membrane
* cytoplasm
* nucleus
* cellulose cell wall
* vacuole
* cell sap
* chloroplast

typical plant cell   typical animal cell

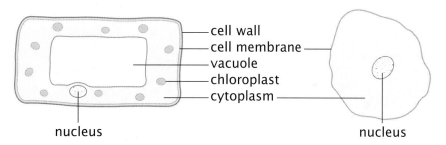

cell wall
cell membrane
vacuole
chloroplast
cytoplasm

nucleus   nucleus

A cell is a highly organised system. It has an outer boundary called a **cell surface membrane**. This surrounds a jelly-like material called **cytoplasm**. Some chemicals can pass through the cell surface membrane into the cytoplasm. The cytoplasm is the place where most of the reactions happen. It also helps the cell to keep its shape. The cytoplasm can also get rid of waste materials through the cell surface membrane.

All cells start life with a **nucleus**. This is the control centre of the cell. The nucleus carries all the information about what the living thing will look like and how it works, rather like a microscopic encyclopaedia.

Plant cells have a few extra structures compared to animal cells. They have a firm **cellulose cell wall** surrounding the cell surface membrane. They also have a tiny bag of fluid in the middle of the cytoplasm called the cell **vacuole**. The vacuole contains **cell sap**, which is a solution of sugar and salts. Many plant cells also contain little green sacs called **chloroplasts**. These help the plant cells trap light energy for food production.

Evaluation *Model cell*

Jake decided to make a model of an animal cell. He collected some runny jelly, a small ball and a plastic bag.

1 Which parts of the cell do you think each item in Jake's collection was for?

2 What other materials would be better for making a model of an animal cell? Why might these be better?

3 What other parts would he need to add to turn the model into a plant cell? What might he use for each of these parts?

Time to think

1 Produce a table that lists all the parts of a plant cell and the jobs that these parts do. Use a highlighter pen to highlight the parts of the cell that are also found in animal cells.

Look at the drawings below of the two cells, **A** and **B**. These show what they look like using a powerful magnifying glass.

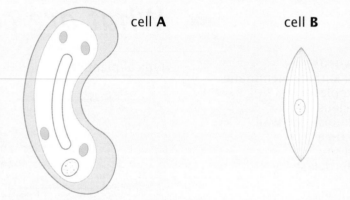

cell **A**   cell **B**

2 One of these is an animal cell and one is a plant cell. Which is which? How did you decide?
3 Both cells have been magnified using the same magnifying glass. Cell **A** on the left is 0.1 mm wide in real life. What is the width of cell **A** in the drawing?
4 How many times has the magnifying glass increased the size of cell **A**?
5 How long is cell **A** in real life? How did you work that out?
6 What is the real size of cell **B**? How did you work that out?

➡ *How are cells organised?*

Cells group together to form **tissues**. Often these cells are all the same type – like the cells that line the inside of your cheek. But sometimes a tissue is made of different types of cell – as in blood.

Key words
* tissue
* organ
* body system
* digestive
* circulatory

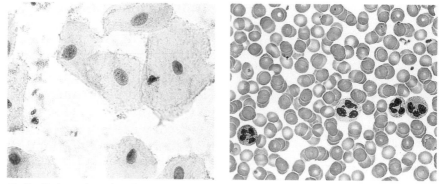

Cells lining the cheek.   Blood.

Organs are made of one or more tissues. The heart is an organ made of muscle tissue and tendon tissue. Several organs working together make up a **body system**. Each body system has one major role to play in the body. The liver, stomach and intestines form the **digestive** system. The role of the digestive system is to break down food to make it soluble so that the useful food can pass into the blood. Also the undigested food can be easily removed from the body.

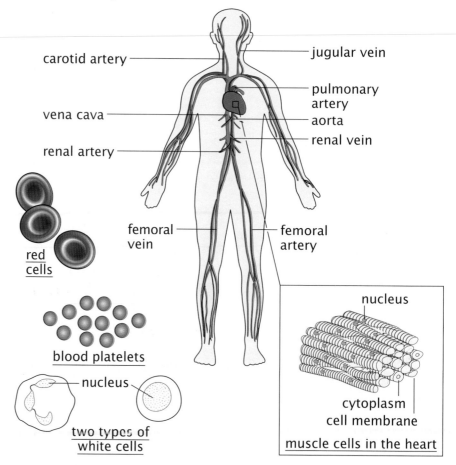

Blood cells make blood tissue. Muscle cells make the muscle tissue that forms the heart. Together these form the **circulatory** system. The circulatory system is the main transport system in the body.

It is sometimes difficult to think of our bodies being made up of cells. Some people imagine cells like being the bricks of a house. The organs would then be the different rooms in the house. Another way of thinking about it, is to start with a snowman. He is made from the tissue, snow. The snow comes from individual snowflakes, which would be the snowman's cells. It is easy to see the snowflakes when they are separate single items but when they join together to form snow and then a snowman, it becomes difficult to see the individual snowflakes. The same can be said of animals and plants that are all made of cells.

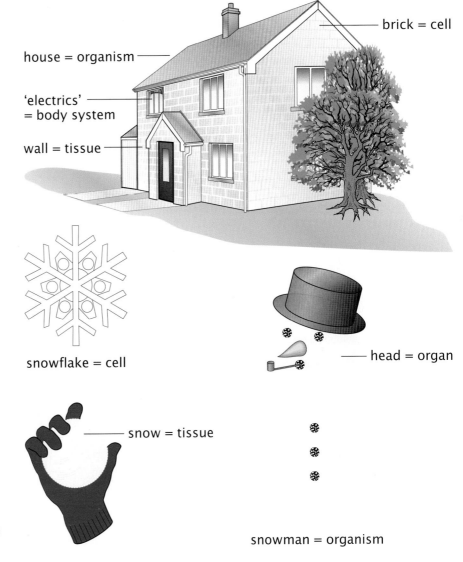

house = organism

'electrics' = body system

wall = tissue

brick = cell

snowflake = cell

head = organ

snow = tissue

snowman = organism

These are both models for explaining about cells, tissues, organs, organ systems and organisms. Which of the two models makes most sense to you?

Information processing *Body parts*

Look at the list below and sort them under the headings:

Cells, **Tissues**, **Organs**, **Body systems**.

lungs   white blood cells
nervous system   pancreas
brain   bladder
muscle   red blood cells
kidney   eye
circulatory system   excretory system
blood

Put these into a table, using the headings, and linking the correct bits together try to fill in the missing parts of the table.

➡ *Why are some cells specialised?*

Key words
* specialised
* axon
* capillary
* haemoglobin
* pigment
* antibody
* pollen

Some cells are **specialised** – they have a special job to do. Many are a special shape or contain extra things to do their job. Nerve cells have long, wire-like extensions called **axons**. Some of the nerve cells in our legs are over 1 metre in length. The axons of nerve cells are insulated by a special fat layer so that they can carry messages better.

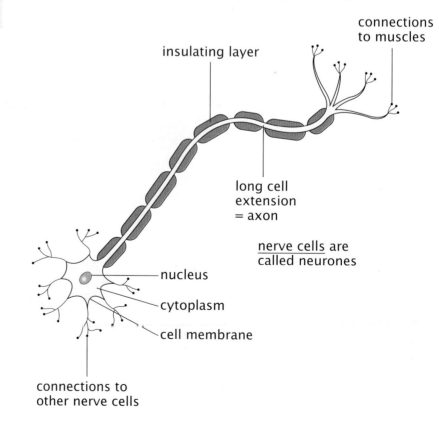

connections to muscles
insulating layer
long cell extension = axon
nerve cells are called neurones
nucleus
cytoplasm
cell membrane
connections to other nerve cells

Cheek cells fit together like paving stones and are very thin. They make an excellent lining for the inside of our mouth. The cells that line our intestines have a frilly surface. This increases the outside surface of the cells which helps them absorb digested food better.

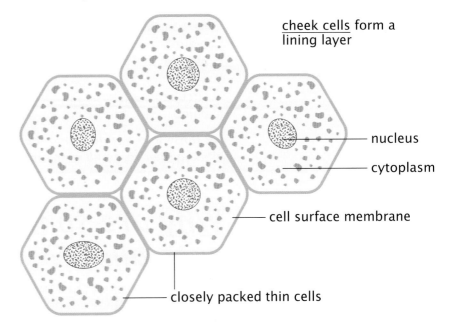

cheek cells form a lining layer

nucleus

cytoplasm

cell surface membrane

closely packed thin cells

Red blood cells are small enough to travel through tiny **capillaries**. They also have a shape that has a large surface area for absorbing oxygen. However, the most specialised bit in red cells is **haemoglobin**. This is a red **pigment** that attracts oxygen. So red blood cells are specialised to carry oxygen around our bodies.

cytoplasm soaked in haemoglobin

Red blood cells do not have a nucleus. How does this help them do their job? What problems might this cause for them?

White blood cells are the soldier cells in our bodies. If bacteria get through a break in our skin or sneak past the traps in the nose or stomach, then the white blood cells can detect them. The white blood cells move to the infected area and kill the bacteria that are starting to attack our body cells. They can do this by flowing round a bacterium and swallowing it up. Other types of white blood cell produce chemicals called **antibodies** which destroy the bacteria.

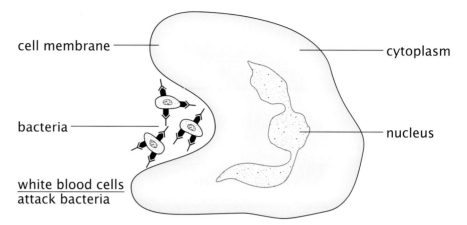

cell membrane

cytoplasm

bacteria

nucleus

<u>white blood cells</u>
attack bacteria

Plants have specialised cells too. Plant roots have root hair cells that increase the surface area of the root. With more space this means that they can take in more water. These cells make sure that the plant takes in as much water as they can. This replaces water lost by evaporation through the leaves. Water, which is also the main component of cell sap, is very important to plants as it pushes on the cell wall keeping each cell full and hard. These rigid plant cells help keep the plant stem firm and upright so that the leaves and flowers are held above the soil.

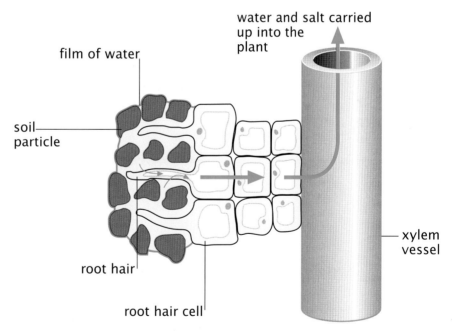

water and salt carried up into the plant

film of water

soil particle

root hair

root hair cell

xylem vessel

Plants also have specialised cells called **pollen** for reproduction. Pollen are the male sex cells and they need to reach the female parts in another flower. Some flowers have pollen that is very light and can float on the wind. Some flowers have pollen that can stick to bees or other insects and be carried from flower to flower. Pollen cells also have ridges or sticky surfaces to help the pollen anchor when it lands on the female part of the flower. A pollen cell carries DNA from one plant to another in its nucleus. This is the special chemical code that is needed to make new plants.

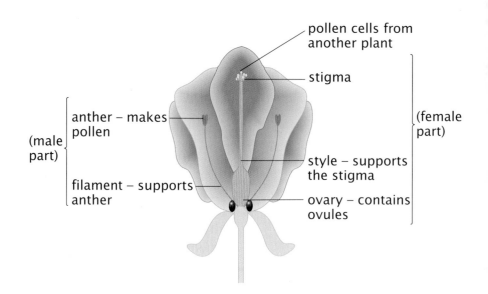

pollen cells from another plant

stigma

anther – makes pollen

(male part)

filament – supports anther

(female part)

style – supports the stigma

ovary – contains ovules

Pollen cells are specialised to help them reach and stick onto the female parts in another flower.

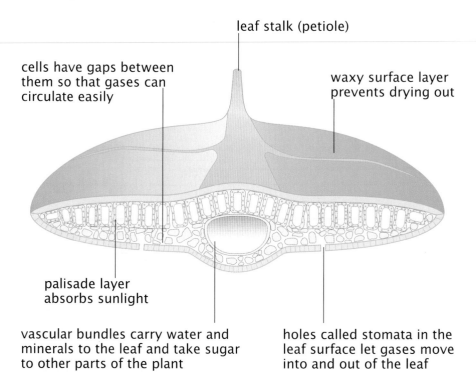

leaf stalk (petiole)

cells have gaps between them so that gases can circulate easily

waxy surface layer prevents drying out

palisade layer absorbs sunlight

vascular bundles carry water and minerals to the leaf and take sugar to other parts of the plant

holes called stomata in the leaf surface let gases move into and out of the leaf

Cells in a leaf are specialised to absorb as much sunlight as possible and to exchange gases with the air outside the plant.

8 Which cells look like they are specialised for absorbing sunlight? Why?

9 Which cells look like they are good at taking in or getting rid of gases? Why?

Then and now – our knowledge of cells

COLOURLESS CORPUSCLES. 115

there; the colouring matter being broken up and forming the bile pigment, and probably the colour of the urine.

The red corpuscles are more than half water (68 per cent.). The rest is composed of hæmoglobin, hæmatin and globulin, salts of phosphate of potassium, sodium and calcium, fatty matters (including cholesterin) and gas, principally O.   Chemical Composition.

The colourless or white corpuscles (discovered by Hewsen, 1773) are larger than the red ($\frac{1}{2800}$ in. diam.), but are only spherical in death; during life their shape constantly varies. Their numbers are about 1 to 500 of the red, or about 10,000 in a cubic mm. Like the red corpuscles, they have no   Colourless Corpuscles.

Fig. 48.—Amœboid movement of a White Blood Corpuscle of Man; various phases of movement.

cell walls, but unlike them they have one or more distinct nuclei. They have a finely granular appearance, which on examination under a high power is seen to be due to a meshwork that pervades them, the corners of the meshes being formed into knobs. Part of the granules may be food material. The colourless corpuscles or leucocytes of the blood are identical with the smaller description of lymph cells that are found all over the body, and particularly in the spleen and lymphatic glands.

The function of these cells has long been obscure, and is only now beginning to be understood. The last utterance of a leading physiologist (Landois) is that they do "an important work in the blood of an uncertain character." Austin Flint says "their   Their functions.

I 2

116   *ELEMENTARY PHYSIOLOGY FOR STUDENTS.*

use is doubtful." We have seen that they are believed to be the parents or forerunners of the red corpuscle. They have very active habits during life. Having the power of traversing the walls of the blood-vessels with the greatest ease into the lymph space around, or the body tissues, they are found in enormous numbers wherever any active inflammation is going on, and they form the principal part of pus or "matter."

Metschnikoff regards them as our defenders against germs of all sorts, and has lately shown how active they are in eating and destroying bacteria and germs, and also refuse of all sorts; while the curious fact has been discovered that in Peyer's patches in the intestines, where they abound, they migrate into the tube, seize on all the bacteria they can find, carry them down into the deeper tissues, where they and their spoil both become the prey of the larger description of lymph corpuscle which we have already alluded to in the spleen as feeding on the used-up red corpuscles.

Enough has been said to show what a life of varied interest and usefulness they lead, and to encourage us to hope for still further discoveries respecting it.

They increase rapidly by fission, and appear in amazing quantities in a very short time wherever they are wanted.

One great source of them is the spleen, as seen in the splenic vein, where they number 1 to 80 of the red. Another is the thoracic duct, for it is found that they vary from 1 to 800 red corpuscles when fasting, down to 1 to 300 after a meal; the increase being due to the large numbers poured into the blood by the chyle through the thoracic duct.   Their Qualities.

Their numbers in certain diseases are enormously increased.

The most remarkable feature about these corpuscles is their constant change of shape (which is always very irregular) by so-called "*amœboid*" movement, from its similarity to that of the "amœbæ" of stagnant waters. This movement is best seen by drawing a cell under the

This book, which was written in 1894, shows that scientists did not know about the job that white blood cells do in the body.

Write a paragraph about white blood cells comparing what we know about them today with what was written in the book.

Research Sir Alexander Fleming discovered antibiotics. These work in a similar way to antibodies because they can destroy bacteria. Find out more about Fleming's discovery and write a paragraph for a modern science encyclopaedia or website.

➡ *How are new cells made?*

Key words
* cell division
* DNA
* grow

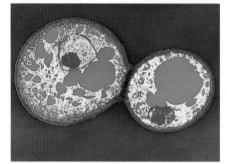

Budding yeast cells.

Copied algal cells.

Most cells are able to make copies of themselves just like the yeast and algal cells in the photographs above. Making new cells is called **cell division**. Each new cell needs the same cell parts as the original cell. The code for making these new parts is found in a special chemical called **DNA** in the nucleus of the cell. The cell makes copies of the DNA and then divides the DNA into two batches – one batch for the new cell and the other for the original cell. It is a little bit like making a copy and then peeling it away from the original page.

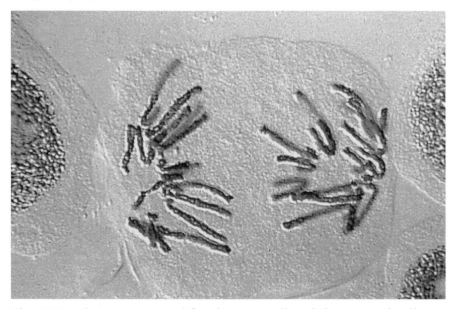

The DNA is being separated for the new cell and the original cell.

The cell then has to make more cell surface membrane, more cytoplasm and other cell parts for the new cell. Often the new cell looks a little smaller than the original cell because its new parts are still being made.

Making new cell parts requires quite a lot of energy. Cell division usually happens when there is lots of food around to provide the energy that is needed. Making more cells causes the animal or plant to **grow**.

Reasoning ## Bacteria

A bacterium is a single cell, but not for long. A bacterium can divide about every 20 minutes in warm conditions. In a very short time, there can be lots of bacteria. Look at the table below that shows the number of bacteria produced in 2 hours.

Time (mins)	0	20	40	60	80	100	120
Number of bacteria	1	2	4	8	16	32	64

1 Which type of graph, from **A**, **B**, **C** and **D** below, do you think these data will look like? Why?

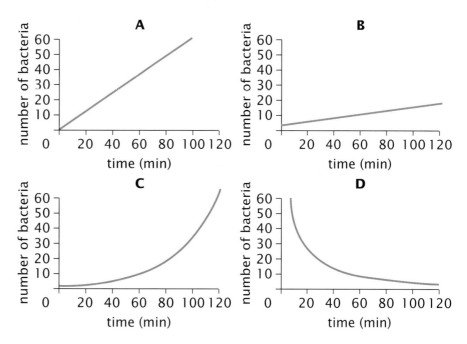

Draw a line graph of the data in the table to check which graph shape it gives.

Look at the four graphs above to help you get your axes the right way round.

Use a scale that goes up in 20 s for the 'Time' axis.

Decide if you want to use a scale that goes up in steps of 5 s and 10 s for the 'Number of bacteria' axis.

2 There are 64 bacteria after 2 hours (120 minutes). Estimate how many of these bacteria are produced in 3 hours, and in 4 hours. Now work out how many are produced. If your estimate differs from the number that you have worked out, try and explain why this is.

Evaluation **Investigating liquid soap**

Bacteria can be grown on a jelly-like material, called agar, in dishes. Bacteria are very small organisms. In order to identify them, hospitals sometimes need to grow colonies of bacteria. A colony of bacteria can have thousands of individual cells.

Jerome and Clare wanted to test whether a new liquid soap called Bactfree killed all the bacteria on their hands as claimed in the advert. They did the following experiment to put Bactfree to the test.

Jerome put one hand in a large beaker of water and the other in a large beaker which had a mixture of Bactfree soap and water. Clare took a cotton bud from a new pack and wiped it once across each of Jerome's hands. Each time she quickly lifted the lid on an agar dish and wiped the cotton bud across the agar. The lids were replaced on the agar dishes and loosely stuck down with two small pieces of tape. A third agar dish was wiped with a cotton bud dipped in clean water and its lid also loosely stuck down. Jerome and Clare labelled the agar dishes and put them in a warm place for 3 days. They put the cotton buds in disinfectant and then into a sealed plastic bag before putting them in the bin.

After 3 days the agar in the dishes looked like this.

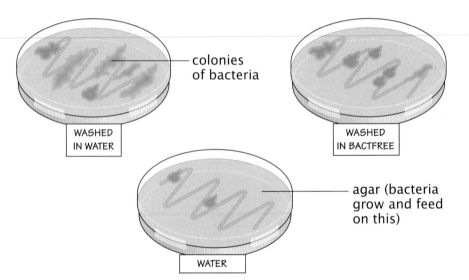

colonies of bacteria

WASHED IN WATER

WASHED IN BACTFREE

agar (bacteria grow and feed on this)

WATER

Jerome and Clare had to look at their results through the dish lids because it was not safe to remove the lid. After they had recorded their results, the technician took the agar plates away to dispose of them in a special pressure cooker called an autoclave. Jerome and Clare wiped down their table with hot soapy water and then washed their hands after handling the agar dishes.

1 What question were Jerome and Clare trying to investigate in this experiment?

2 What title would you suggest for Jerome and Clare's experiment?

3 What was the input variable?

4 What was the outcome variable?

5 Why did Jerome and Clare set up the third agar dish which had only clean water wiped across it?

6 Why did they put lids on the dishes?

7 Why did they put the three dishes in a warm place?

8 How long did Jerome and Clare wait to get their results? Why did they need to wait so long?

9 List three safety precautions in this investigation. Explain why each was necessary.

10 Look at the results of Jerome and Clare's investigation and decide on the best way to record the results. Check on the way that others in your group have decided to record the results and discuss the advantages and disadvantages of each way.

11 Jerome and Clare's teacher wrote the following comment on their investigation write-up 'Good, but how certain are you of these results? It could have been just chance that the bacteria grew at different rates in each of the three dishes'. What would you do to try and improve the reliability of your results if you had to plan this investigation?

Time to think   What do you know now?

- Look back at the start of this chapter and see if you can add more to your ideas about the body parts that you can see in the pictures.
- Try to explain how small our cheek cells and red blood cells are.
- Explain why cells look bigger when you use a microscope.
- List all the things that cells have in common.
- Note down the three main differences between animal and plant cells.
- List the special things about some cells and the jobs they do.
- Describe how cells make new cells.
- Check how many of the key words you have used in your ideas above.
- Find out how your ideas compare with others in your group.

8 *Reproduction*

In this chapter you will learn:

→ **about human reproduction, pregnancy and the menstrual cycle**
→ **how offspring are protected and nurtured**
→ **about the changes that occur in adolescence**
→ **how birds, fish and frogs reproduce and their life cycles**
→ **the importance of sample size in biological investigations**

You will also develop your skills in:

→ **collecting, presenting and interpreting data in bar charts and graphs**
→ **reading and sorting data to look for relationships between variables**
→ **calculating proportions, scales and ratios to help you work out the real size of objects**
→ **drawing and using models of life cycles**

→ → → WHAT DO YOU KNOW?

Key words
* reproduction
* sexual intercourse

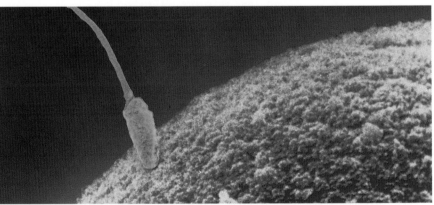

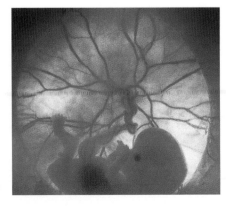

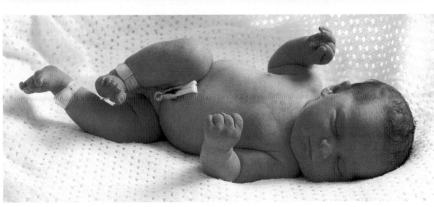

All living things produce young. This is called **reproduction**. In animals it usually involves two individuals of the same species, a male and a female, mating together. This is sexual reproduction. In humans it is sometimes called **sexual intercourse**. In your groups decide what you think each of these words mean and write a group sentence to explain them:

A life cycle is . . . . One life cycle we know about is . . . .
Reproduction is . . . .
An adolescent is a person who is . . . .
When things grow they . . . .

What do you know about how a human baby is made? Tell each other. Make a few notes to show your teacher.

Human reproductive organs

Key words
* reproductive organs

Males and females of the same species are different to each other. Men and women look different on the outside and have different **reproductive organs** on the inside.

1 Make a list of all the differences you know about between men and women. You can include any differences you think there are in the way men and women behave.

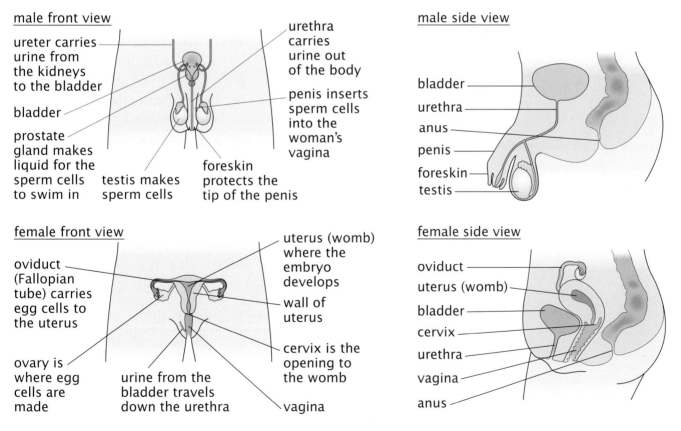

male front view

ureter carries urine from the kidneys to the bladder

bladder

prostate gland makes liquid for the sperm cells to swim in

testis makes sperm cells

foreskin protects the tip of the penis

urethra carries urine out of the body

penis inserts sperm cells into the woman's vagina

male side view

bladder
urethra
anus
penis
foreskin
testis

female front view

oviduct (Fallopian tube) carries egg cells to the uterus

ovary is where egg cells are made

urine from the bladder travels down the urethra

uterus (womb) where the embryo develops

wall of uterus

cervix is the opening to the womb

vagina

female side view

oviduct
uterus (womb)
bladder
cervix
urethra
vagina
anus

2 Look at the diagrams of the reproductive organs in a man and a woman. List the labels and by each label write down its function. The information above and on page 154 should help you.

Fertilisation

All sperm cells have to swim to egg cells. This is a problem for animals that live on land. The sperm cells cannot move across land, so most land animals have a way of putting the sperm cells inside the female where it is moist. Humans are land animals.

Fertilisation happens when a **sperm cell** from a man fuses with an **egg cell** (**ovum**) inside the woman. Sperm cells are made in a man's **testes**. Another word for testes is testicles. The testes make a liquid to feed the sperm and help them swim. The sperm and this liquid make up the **semen**. The woman makes her egg cells in her **ovaries**.

Thousands of sperm cells are released inside the woman's **vagina** when the man inserts his penis and ejaculates. This is called sexual intercourse. The sperm cells swim very rapidly up into the **uterus** (womb), and into the **oviducts**. If the sperm cells are making this journey when a woman has released an egg cell (an **ovum**) from one of her ovaries, fertilisation could take place. Usually only one sperm cell can enter the egg to fertilise it. As the first sperm pierces the egg's surface a chemical change happens to make the egg cell too tough for other sperm to enter.

Although it is only a short distance from the vagina to the top of the oviduct, the sperm are very small so the journey is long. Many never reach the egg and die on the way.

3 How does a man ensure that his sperm cells have a moist environment to swim towards a woman's egg cell?

The nucleus of the sperm cell moves inside the egg to fuse with the nucleus of the egg cell. This is the first cell of the new baby and is called a **zygote**. After about 3 days inside a woman's body, all the sperm cells that have not managed to fertilise an egg cell die.

The zygote is a single cell that very quickly starts to divide. Cell division occurs many, many times to produce a new human. Each time the cell divides, it makes a new copy of the DNA that is inside its nucleus. In this way every cell in a new human has the same DNA, which came originally from its parents' sex sperm and egg cell.

There are about 500 million sperm in a teaspoonful of semen.

Information processing   *Comparing male and female sex cells*

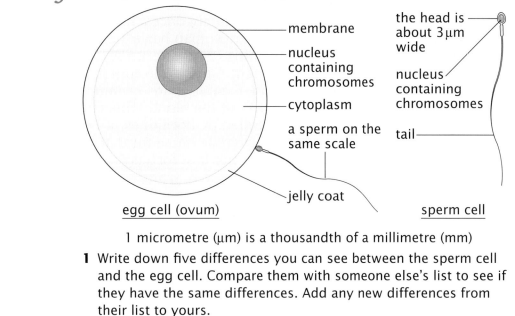

1 micrometre (μm) is a thousandth of a millimetre (mm)

1 Write down five differences you can see between the sperm cell and the egg cell. Compare them with someone else's list to see if they have the same differences. Add any new differences from their list to yours.

2 The picture above left of an egg being fertilised by a sperm has been drawn 500 times bigger than real sperm and egg cells. Measure the width of the egg cell and the length of the sperm cell in the picture. Write the measurements down. What must this measured size be divided by to calculate the real sizes of eggs and sperm cells?

3 Work out the real life-sized diameter of an egg cell and the length of a sperm cell. (Hint: you can use a calculator to help you with the maths.)

4 What is the ratio of the drawing to a life-sized egg cell?
(Hint: it helps to think 'how many times would the width of one life-sized egg cell fit inside the drawing of the egg cell? Look back at chapter 7 to help you do this.)

5 Why have we drawn the cells much bigger than they really are?

Time to think

Check back to what you have done in this chapter so far and see if you have the knowledge to answer these questions:

- Where inside the woman's body does fertilisation take place?
- Why can only one sperm cell fertilise one egg cell?
- What happens to the millions of sperm cells that do not fertilise the egg?
- Where does a woman make her egg cells?
- Where does a man make his sperm cells?
- Why do you think that semen contains such a large number of sperm cells?
- What are the cells called that join together to make the first cell of a new baby?

Compare your answers with at least two other pupils. Add any improvements that you find to your answers.

The menstrual cycle

Key words
* puberty
* fertility
* menstrual
* menstruation
* menopause

Approximately once a month from **puberty** to about the age of fifty, a woman has a 'period'. This is when she gets rid of the lining of her uterus because she has not become pregnant. During the course of 4–5 days blood leaves her womb. Sanitary pads or tampons are worn to collect and dispose of the blood. This is part of her **fertility** cycle and is controlled by hormones. It is known as the **menstrual** cycle. The scientific name for a period is **menstruation**.

From her late forties (although the precise age can vary from woman to woman) she becomes less fertile as her hormones change. She will not develop an egg cell each month. This is called the **menopause**.

Menstrual bleeding is the main sign a woman has each month that she is not pregnant. If she is pregnant she will not bleed because the fertilised egg will have begun to develop in the thick lining of her uterus.

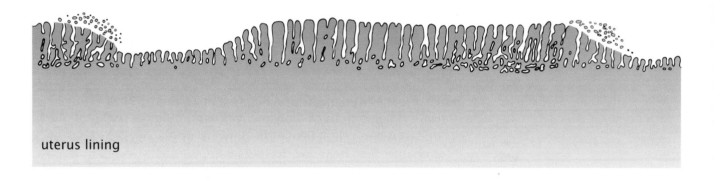

	ovulation	uterus	
lining thickens	(egg released by ovary)	ready to receive embryo	lining breaks down if no egg implantation takes place

uterus lining

1 2 3 4 5 6 7 8 9 10 11 12 13 14 15 16 17 18 19 20 21 22 23 24 25 26 27 28 1 2 3 4 5

days

intercourse
could result
in fertilisation

4 On which days does menstrual bleeding start in the menstrual cycle picture shown above?

5 When is it most likely that an egg can be fertilised by a sperm cell?

6 What happens to the lining of the uterus between days 28 and 5 if the egg is not fertilised?

7 Why does the lining of the womb get thicker from day 5 to day 13?

Infertility

⇒

Key words
* infertility
* *in vitro* fertilisation
* hysterectomy
* miscarriage

Some women easily become pregnant. They are described as fertile. But, sometimes a couple finds it very difficult to make a baby. One or both of the people may be infertile. There are many reasons for **infertility**. Some of the most usual reasons are that:

* The man may not produce many sperm cells; he has what is called a 'low sperm count'.
* The woman may have a blockage in her oviducts or an under-developed uterus.
* The woman may not have any egg cells to develop in her ovaries.
* The woman may have problems with her menstrual cycle.

Hormone treatment or surgery may solve many of these problems. But sometimes infertility has no obvious cause so cannot be treated.

A woman's egg cell can be artificially fertilised outside her body. This is called '***in vitro* fertilisation**' which literally means 'inside glass'. This is because the sperm cells are mixed with the egg cell in a glass container. Some people refer to this as making 'test-tube' babies. Later, the zygote that is formed '*in vitro*' can be put into the woman. The zygote can then grow inside the uterus.

Some women may have problems with their reproductive organs and may have to have a **hysterectomy**. This is when the uterus is removed by surgery. The oviducts may be removed too.

8 What is meant by infertility?
9 Why might a man be infertile?
10 How might surgery help an infertile woman?
11 How might hormone treatment help an infertile woman?
12 Why are children, born as a result of *in vitro* fertilisation, sometimes called test-tube babies?
13 Can a woman become pregnant after a hysterectomy? Explain your answer.

DID YOU KNOW?

A sperm cell swimming up inside a woman's reproductive system to reach the egg is like a man trying to swim across the Atlantic Ocean full of treacle.

Some women cannot manage to carry the developing baby for the whole 9 months of pregnancy. If they lose the foetus in the first few months this is called a **miscarriage**.

Growth

All living things grow. Growth is the increase in size as an organism develops. The cells divide into two which increases the number of cells. The more cells that there are, the bigger the organism. Cell division is the basis of all growth.

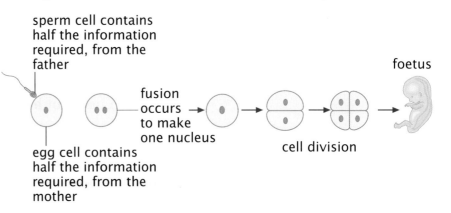

sperm cell contains half the information required, from the father

fusion occurs to make one nucleus

egg cell contains half the information required, from the mother

cell division

foetus

The nucleus of a sperm cell fuses with the nucleus of an egg cell to form the first new cell, the zygote. This one cell divides into two, two into four, four into eight and so on to grow into a ball of cells called an **embryo**. The zygote grows into an embryo by cell division. Once the embryo becomes more developed it is called a **foetus** and later, after birth, it is called a baby.

14 Put these stages in the correct order for the human life cycle: foetus, zygote, embryo, baby.

How twins are made

Occasionally the ovaries produce two, three or even four eggs at the same time. Each egg can be fertilised by different sperm. This results in **twins**, **triplets** or **quadruplets**. These multiple births are more likely to happen if a woman has been given fertility drugs to help her ovulate (release eggs). As you can imagine, if there are more than two foetuses in the womb it gets harder and harder for the mother's uterus to hold them, so she is more likely to give birth early, often around 7 months. There is also an increased chance that not all of the babies will survive.

Sometimes identical twins are created when a single fertilised egg (a zygote) splits in two at a very early stage, so that two foetuses develop from the one egg. Siamese twins occur if the egg only partly splits in two, so that the two foetuses develop joined together at some point. The babies can be separated by an operation after birth but if the babies have shared organs it is very hard for both to survive.

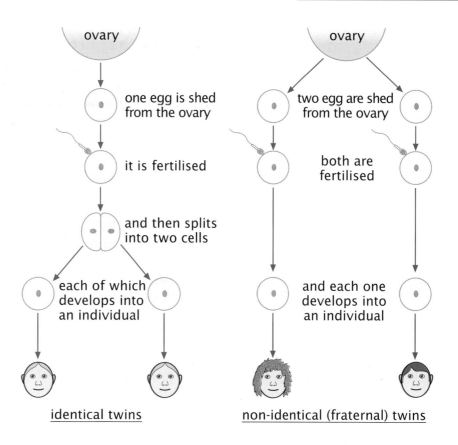

15 Draw a series of pictures to show how you think triplets are made. (Hint: decide if the triplets are formed in a similar way to either identical or non-identical twins.)

➡ *What do you think? Science and society*

Jodie and Mary were Siamese twins that shared one set of working lungs and heart. The doctors believed that Jodie could survive if she were separated from Mary, although it was highly likely that Mary would not survive. They believed that if the twins were not separated, both would die. Their parents did not want them separated after birth by an operation, because they believed that only God could decide if one or other twin should survive. This is a very difficult situation. In the end, judges decided that the doctors should perform an operation to separate the twins.

16 What do you think about this decision?
17 What arguments would you make to support the parents' view?
18 What arguments would you make to support the doctors' views?
19 If you were the judge, what decision would you reach and how would you come to that decision?

Fertilisation in other animals

Birds and humans have internal fertilisation. The sperm cells fuse with the egg cells inside the female's body. The male bird does not have a penis to insert the sperm cells into the female's body; he only has an opening like a female bird. He mounts the female and presses his opening against hers so that sperm is transferred into her body. Some birds manage to do this while they are in flight!

20 What do you think is the advantage, for a bird, of fertilisation taking place inside a female's body?
21 Where does the zygote of a bird grow? (Hint: what do birds use nests for?)
22 What time of year do you think is the most popular time for birds to mate?
23 How do you think male birds attract mates? (Hint: think of a peacock, and think how you sometimes can detect a bird when you can't see it.)

Frogs and fish have external fertilisation. The male sprays the sperm cells over the female egg cells outside the female's body, as she lays them. Fish live in water but frogs only go back to the water to mate.

24 What would happen if frogs tried to mate on land?
25 Why do you think female frogs and fish lay over a thousand eggs at a time, whereas birds only lay a few eggs and humans usually give birth to one baby at a time?
26 How do you think frogs and fish protect their eggs from being eaten? You may need to look and touch some eggs to find out. Perhaps you have already looked at frogspawn.

➡ *Development and birth in humans*

After a human egg has been fertilised it becomes implanted in the wall of the uterus. It stays in the uterus for 9 months as it grows and develops.

27 Look back at the diagrams of the menstrual cycle on page 156. If a woman becomes pregnant what do you think happens to her menstrual cycle?

Information processing ## Human embryo development

Look at the drawings of the human embryo at different stages of its development.

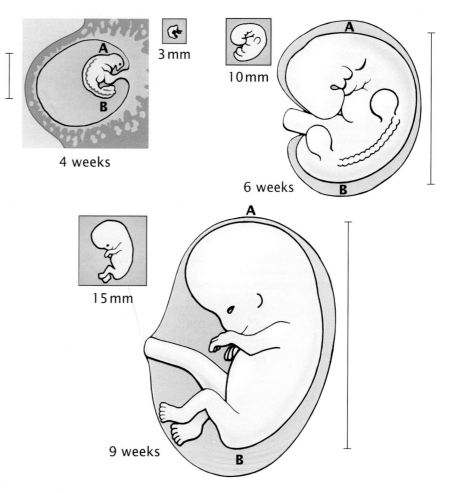

3 mm

4 weeks

10 mm

6 weeks

15 mm

9 weeks

1 Describe to a partner what you can see in each diagram.

2 Measure the length of each embryo from **A** to **B** in each diagram. How many times larger is each drawing than the real embryo?

3 What is the ratio of the drawing to the real embryo?

4 Are these pictures 'scaled up' or 'scaled down'?

5 Why have the pictures been 'drawn to scale'?

This is a photograph of a foetus inside the uterus when it is 20 weeks old.

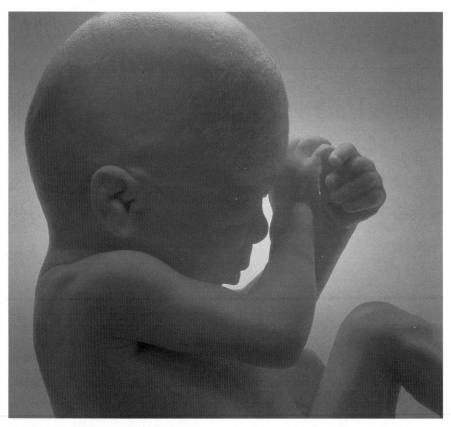

6 How many months of pregnancy is shown in the photograph above?

7 What proportion of the pregnancy still remains before the baby is born?

If the baby was born after 7 months, it could live. It would weigh about 1 kg and be about 37 cm long.

DID YOU KNOW?

A 3-week-old embryo is no larger than a sesame seed. At a month old it weighs the same as a piece of paper inside an envelope and is the size of a teardrop.

Key words
* amnion
* umbilical cord
* placenta

By the time the foetus is 10 weeks old all the organs have been formed. As it develops, the sac of fluid it is in (the **amnion**) expands like a balloon so that the foetus floats in a warm, safe environment. The foetus is a bit like a deep-sea diver, it is cut off from the outside world but must keep a 'lifeline' to supply it with what it needs to live and to get rid of the waste materials its growing body produces. This lifeline is the **umbilical cord**. Where the cord joins the wall of the uterus, it becomes the **placenta**. The placenta provides the growing foetus with digested food and oxygen. It also removes any waste that the foetus has produced. The mother's blood and the foetal blood do not mix. Instead the food, oxygen and waste materials pass between the thin walls of the blood vessels.

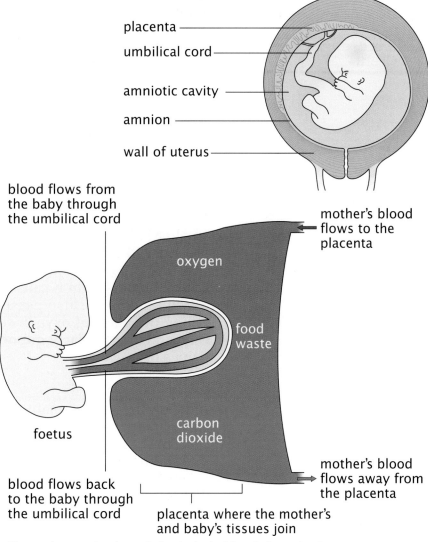

placenta

umbilical cord

amniotic cavity

amnion

wall of uterus

blood flows from
the baby through
the umbilical cord

mother's blood
flows to the
placenta

oxygen

food
waste

foetus

carbon
dioxide

mother's blood
flows away from
the placenta

blood flows back
to the baby through
the umbilical cord

placenta where the mother's
and baby's tissues join

Note: the mother's and the baby's blood do not mix

28 Where is the cord attached to the foetus? Think about
this area on the outside of your own body. What have
you got there?

29 Remember the seven characteristics of living things.
Talk in your groups and discuss:
- How does the foetus get its energy?
- Does it excrete waste in the same way as a baby after
birth?
- Does it have the other characteristics of living things?
How do you know?
- What protects the foetus in the womb?

30 Look carefully at the drawing above. Work with a
partner to write a short paragraph that describes what
the foetus gets from its mother to help it live, and what
it gets rid of to stop it being poisoned.

31 Notice that the mother's blood does not mix with the
foetus' blood. Discuss why you think the two blood
supplies should not mix.

Harming the unborn baby

Rubella

This is the name for the disease sometimes called German measles. It is generally not very harmful to people if they get it, just very itchy. However, if a pregnant woman catches rubella it can seriously harm her unborn baby. The rubella virus can pass from the mother's blood through the placenta and into the unborn baby's blood. For this reason most young girls are **inoculated** against it.

Smoking

Mothers that smoke throughout pregnancy tend to have smaller babies than those from non-smoking mothers and are more likely to have a miscarriage or stillborn baby. Nicotine is a poisonous drug and if it gets into the unborn baby's bloodstream it causes the heart to beat too fast. Carbon monoxide also passes into the baby's bloodstream taking the place of oxygen so that the baby receives less. Oxygen is particularly important for healthy growth of the baby's brain cells.

Other drugs

Alcohol, heroin and many prescribed pills and medicines can all be absorbed into the baby's bloodstream across the placenta. As a result, babies may be deformed or can be born addicted to the drug because of their mother's habit.

Food

It is very important that a pregnant woman eats healthily, both for her own health and for that of the unborn baby. If she does not eat a balanced diet, both her health and that of her unborn baby can suffer.

32 Design an eye-catching poster that could be put up in a health centre as part of a campaign to help women who want to conceive to be healthier. You might want to concentrate on warning against one of the dangerous substances described above, or you might want to be more informative about healthy lifestyles for pregnant women.

Research | Find out what inoculations are.
What have you been inoculated against? You may need to ask your parents or the school nurse.

Information processing ## Lifespans and pregnancy times

Animals have different lifespans and different pregnancy times.

Mammal	Approximate lifespan (years)	Gestation (time taken for pregnancy)
beaver	15	about 90 days
chimpanzee	25	231 days
dog	12	about 60 days
killer whale	20	64 weeks
elephant	70	84 weeks
shrew	1	15 days
skunk	10	54 days
tiger	20	110 days
lion	25	109 days
human	85	40 weeks

1 What are the variables in this table? What are the values for each variable?

2 Is there a relationship between the lifespan of an animal and the time taken for it to develop inside the uterus of the mother before it is born? You may find it helpful to rearrange the data in rank order. That is, from the largest to the smallest value for one of the variables.

3 Can you think of a better way to show the data in this table so that it shows timescales more visually? Work in a group to produce a visual representation of the data. Make sure that you use the same unit for time in each case.

You could think about designing a bar or pie chart. Which would be better here? You could use a computer to help you. You could use a very large piece of paper and draw a scale along one side.

Experiment, make sketches, draft and redraft – see what your group thinks works best to make the data interesting and easier to look at.

DID YOU KNOW?

A baby giraffe is 2 m tall when it is born. A baby whale is 7.5 m long when it is born.

Time to think

Write down all the key words in the chapter so far on pieces of card. Arrange the cards on a large piece of paper to form a concept map for reproduction. Write in the links between the key words. Compare and discuss your concept map with others in the class.

The birth of a baby

Here is a short story that will give you some idea about what it is like for a woman to give birth.

'My name is Mina and my husband is John. We have wanted a baby for ages. We've been married 3 years and I am 23. John's the same age as me, we have our birthdays in the same week! When I missed a period I thought I might be pregnant but I wasn't sure. I have missed periods before. When I was a teenager my periods were not very regular. I was twenty before I seemed to get a regular pattern. Anyway, when my period was three weeks late I couldn't wait anymore. I bought one of those 'do-it-yourself' kits from the supermarket and the little stick went blue when I tested my urine. I was overjoyed and immediately told John. He said we needed to make sure, so we went to the clinic and had a proper test done by a doctor. The results were positive.

In the beginning I was quite sick because my hormones, the chemicals in my body, were changing as the baby developed. It's called 'morning sickness', although I felt sick at any time of the day! For the next 8 months we were busy buying baby things, decorating the baby's room and telling all our friends and family.

When I got to 40 weeks' pregnancy I started getting cramping feelings in my tummy. They went on for a day or so but were not very regular or painful. I thought I was beginning to go into **labour**. This bit can be very different for each woman and I found it hard to know if birth had begun as this was my first baby! By 10 o'clock that night I could really feel my uterus contracting and it was quite painful, so John took me to hospital where they said I had started labour. Then my waters broke (I think this is the amniotic sac breaking open). I had to control my breathing and push the baby out – making sure the head was coming out first. I finally gave birth to a lovely little girl after about 8 hours. I did not have a very long labour. The midwife was great. After she cleaned up the baby and cut the umbilical cord she handed her to me and John and I just cried with happiness. The baby is called Mary.'

33 Do you know how long your mother was in labour with you? Was it 8 hours like Mina?

Some babies are delivered by **Caesarean** if the vagina is too narrow for the baby to pass through or if there are difficulties and the mother or the baby's health is at risk. This involves surgery. The mother's outer wall and uterus are cut open to remove the baby. Surgeons are skilled at doing this operation and only a tiny scar remains on the woman's skin afterwards.

Human development

Months after birth	Development
1	feeds on milk, sleeps and cries
2	responds to sounds
3	begins to make noises when spoken to, cries are more varied
4	turns head to noise
5	reaches out to grip objects, often puts them in mouth to suck
6	lower front teeth develop
7	chews everything
8	upper front teeth appear
9 to 12	sits up, crawls
15 to 17	starts to stand, may walk, starts saying words
18	walks well, talks to be understood

In a growing child, cell division takes place all over the body so that the child gets steadily larger. Different parts of the body grow at different rates because cells divide at different rates depending on which part of the body they are forming. For example, the head grows very quickly at first and then slows down.

When a baby is born its head is a third of its total length. By the time he or she is 15 years old it is only an eighth of the total length. Legs and arms grow slowly to start with and then speed up later. A newborn baby should show six special **reflexes**:

- The swallowing and sucking reflex. If you put your (clean!) finger in a baby's mouth it will suck it and try to swallow.
- The rooting reflex. If you gently stroke a baby's cheek it will turn its head and open its mouth.
- The grasping reflex. The baby will grip a finger very strongly.
- The startle reflex. When a baby is startled it will spread its hands wide then bring them in across its chest and clench its fist.
- The walking reflex. If the baby is held as if to stand, one leg straightens and the other foot moves slightly as if to walk.
- The falling ('moro') reflex. If the baby has a feeling that it will be dropped, it will fling back its arms and open its hands, the arms will then be brought together as if to catch something.

34 Discuss with each other why you think each of these six reflexes might be important for the survival and protection of a very young baby.

Research

Imagine you have been asked to produce a leaflet for new parents explaining to them how a baby is made, and how they must look after a newborn baby as it grows in its first 2 years of life. You will need to do some research. Perhaps you could interview some parents of 2 year olds, or your own parents, and find out what advice they would give to parents so that their children grow up to be healthy and loved.

Information processing ## Growth patterns

Look at this diagram of growth pattern in humans.

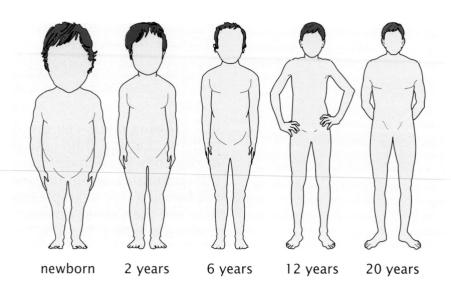

| newborn | 2 years | 6 years | 12 years | 20 years |

1 Measure the head in each picture and measure the length of the whole body. This picture is scaled down from real life. What proportion of the body is the head at birth, 2, 6, 12 and 20 years?

2 Organise your answers into a table of data that shows the ratio of the head to whole body measurement. This means dividing the whole body measurement by the head measurement. At what age is the head relatively large compared with the whole body, and when is the head small compared with the whole body?

3 A sample of people will have been measured to get these data. Discuss how many people you think should be in this kind of sample. How do you think they should be selected?

Growth is one of the characteristics of life. Your DNA codes for how tall you might grow, but your final height will also depend on your health and diet.

Humans are taller today than they were 500 years ago. Do you think this is likely to be the effect of genetics or the environment? Why?

Puberty in humans

The reproductive organs of a human do not work during childhood. They begin to work when we reach our early teens. Hormones (for example, chemicals like **testosterone**, **progesterone** and **oestrogen**) are released and these cause changes in our bodies. Boys' and girls' bodies begin to develop differently so that by the time they are men and women they look very different. This stage of development is **puberty** and it can last from 2 to 4 years. The start of puberty can be quite young in girls; some girls start changing at about 10 years old. Other girls may be 13 or 14 before any noticeable changes begin. Boys tend to start puberty a little bit later, at about 13 years old. There is great variation in the age these changes start between different people.

A boy's voice breaks in puberty because his vocal cords get longer. Up until puberty boys and girls have similar length vocal cords.

When a baby girl is born, her ovaries already contain the beginnings of all the egg cells she will release from puberty to menopause. One of the biggest changes for a girl during puberty is that she will start to menstruate. Look back to 'The menstrual cycle' (see page 156) to explain why, about once a month, a woman passes blood out of her body from her uterus.

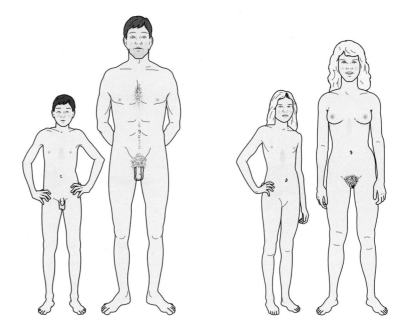

35 Write down the changes you think happen when a girl develops into a woman and a boy develops into a man.

36 Do you know any other words for 'menstruation'? Some women refer to menstruation as 'their time of the month'. Can you explain what they mean by this?

Frog development

Only mammals give birth to small versions of adults, and feed their babies with milk from the female's mammary glands (breasts). Amphibians, reptiles, fish and birds do not give birth to offspring, they all lay eggs.

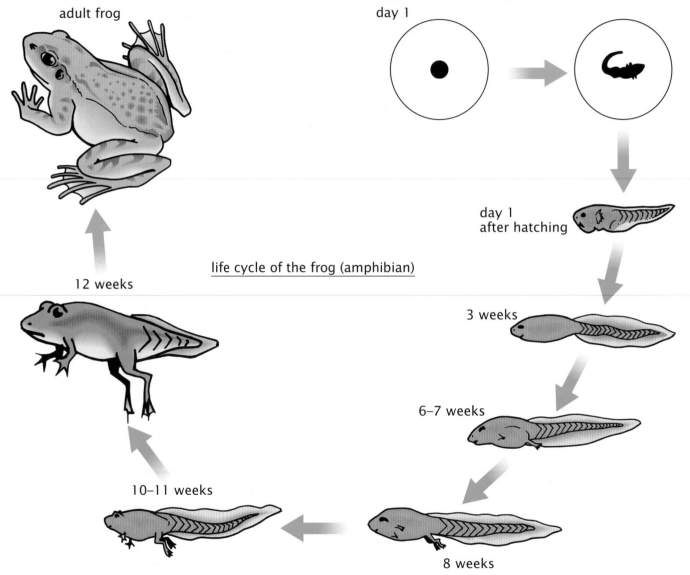

adult frog

day 1

day 1 after hatching

life cycle of the frog (amphibian)

12 weeks

3 weeks

6–7 weeks

10–11 weeks

8 weeks

37 Look back at the table (see page 167) and the picture showing the development of a human baby into an adult (see page 168). Use the information to produce a life cycle, with some notes that explain each stage. You can model it on the frog life cycle shown above.

38 Why do you think it takes a human so long to develop compared with a frog?

39 Which do you think will stand more chance of growing up to become an adult – the young of a frog or a human? Why?

40 What do you think is the right age for a woman to start a family? Why?

Time to think

Go back to the notes you made in your groups when you began this chapter.

- Do you know more about reproduction in humans and other animals now that you have read this chapter? If so, what new things have you learnt? List them.
- Show other people in your group your list and look at theirs. Have they learnt the same new things as you have?
- What were the most and least interesting things in this chapter for you? Do the rest of the group agree with you?
- When you are revising for a test, which bits do you think you will find it hard to remember? Why?
- Work in your groups to find at least one way of helping each other to remember something each of you finds difficult.

9 Solutions

In this chapter you will learn:

→ **how to explain dissolving**
→ **about solvents and how to measure their dissolving power**
→ **how to separate salt from rock salt and water from sea water**
→ **how scientific detectives track down criminals**

You will also develop your skills in:

→ **using ratios and proportionality in solubility calculations**
→ **controlling variables for fair testing**
→ **planning an experiment to produce accurate results and reliable evidence**
→ **interpreting graphs**
→ **using models to explain observations**

→ → → WHAT DO YOU KNOW?

Key words
* boiling
* condensing
* dissolving
* filtering
* freezing
* melting

You will need to refer to the picture and the key words above to answer the following questions.

1 Read through this passage and decide what missing key words **A–F** are.

You can make coffee using instant coffee powder or coffee grains. Some coffee was made by heating water until it was _____ **A** _____ and then pouring it onto the coffee grains. The resulting brown liquid was separated from the grains by _____ **B** _____ it. The drink was then sweetened by _____ **C** _____ sugar in it.

The ice cubes in the orange drink were made by _____ **D** _____ water. After a while, the cubes became smaller because they were _____ **E** _____.

It was difficult to see through parts of the window because water vapour was _____ **F** _____ on the cold glass.

2 After the waitress had swept up the sugar and broken glass from the accident shown in the picture opposite, a discussion broke out about how the sugar could be separated from the bowl without getting cut fingers. They thought of two methods but only one would work perfectly.

Can you think of the two methods? Give details of each step using flow diagrams.

➡ # *Is there a solution?*

Key words
* solution
* soluble
* dissolve
* solute
* solvent
* insoluble

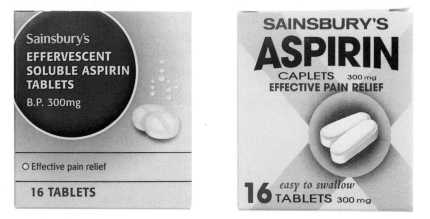

Solutions are liquids. When a **soluble** aspirin is added to water and stirred, it **dissolves** to form a solution. This aspirin is soluble in water. The substance that dissolves is called the **solute** (aspirin) and the liquid it dissolves in is called the **solvent** (water).

If an ordinary aspirin is stirred in water, it does not dissolve. It is **insoluble** in water.

DID YOU KNOW?

Aspirin was the first manufactured drug. It was discovered by a German scientist called Hoffmann in 1899. He tested out a range of chemicals, similar to aspirin, on his father and found that aspirin was the most successful. Many of the other chemicals had unpleasant side effects. Soluble aspirin was produced much later.

Evaluation ## Where has the solute gone?

... and now I will make this salt disappear.

When salt dissolves in water, it seems to 'disappear'. A group of pupils produced three different methods to prove that the salt was still present in the solution:

- Tom's plan – About $50\,cm^3$ of water was poured into a $100\,cm^3$ beaker and weighed. $10\,g$ of salt was weighed out, added to the water and stirred with a glass rod until the salt dissolved. The solution in the beaker was weighed.
- Nisha's plan – Some water was poured into a $100\,cm^3$ beaker and then some salt was added. This was stirred until the salt dissolved and then heated gently on a tripod and gauze with a Bunsen burner until the water evaporated.
- Zoe's plan – Some water was poured into a $100\,cm^3$ beaker and then some salt was added. This was stirred until the salt dissolved and then the solution was tasted.

1 Which plan was too dangerous to do in a science laboratory? Give a reason.

2 What did Nisha expect to happen that would prove that the salt was still in the solution?

3 What did Tom expect to happen that would prove that the salt was still in the solution?

4 What would your plan be to prove that salt is present in a salt solution? Try to use the words soluble, solute, solvent and solution in your explanation.

Time to think

1 Some people describe solutions as a 'mixture'. Think about what is mixed together and how easy or difficult it is to split up this mixture.

2 Think back to chapter 4. Use your understanding of the particle theory to make a drawing of:

- the solute
- the solvent
- the solution.

Compare your ideas with at least two other people.

Get cleaning

Sometimes we need to dissolve away substances that are insoluble in water. In this case we use a different solvent that the solute will dissolve in. This is often needed in cleaning jobs.

How would you clean these two paint brushes?

How would you remove the nail varnish?

Dry-cleaning

Some clothes need to be dry-cleaned because they are damaged by washing with water and detergent. Dry-cleaning uses a solvent called 'trichlor'. This dissolves away the grease that sticks the dirt onto the clothes. The solvent is then drained away and the clothes are dried. Sometimes a small amount of solvent remains on the clothes for a few hours before it fully evaporates away.

Danger – solvents!

If you use any solvents other than water, you must be very careful because they can be hazardous.

highly flammable

harmful or irritant

toxic

1 When clothes are picked up from some dry-cleaners, there is a label saying: 'Driving home by car? If so, please leave a window open on the journey.' Explain why this label is necessary.

2 Look at the following extract from a magazine and answer the questions.

How to remove those nasty stains from clothes and carpets

Stain	Cleaning fluid			
	dry-cleaning fluid	amyl acetate	methylated spirit	white spirit
adhesive tape	✓		✓	
chewing gum	✓			
grass			✓	
creosote	✓			✓
ballpoint pen			✓	
nail varnish		✓		
tar	✓			✓

Note: before using any of these fluids, test them out on a small, hidden part of the fabric.

a) Which two stains can be removed with white spirit?
b) Name a cleaning fluid that will remove both chewing gum and tar.
c) Cleaning fluids are all examples of which key word?
d) Why do you think that it recommends testing out a fluid on a small, hidden part of the fabric before use?

➡ Concentration

Key words
* dilute
* concentrated
* ratio
* concentration
* proportional

Orange squash is placed in three glasses as shown below.

A   B   C

The glasses are then topped up with water and the drinks are tasted. The drink in **A** is the most **dilute** and has the least taste of orange. The drink in **C** is the most **concentrated** and has the strongest taste of orange. The drink in **B** is twice as concentrated as the drink in **A**.

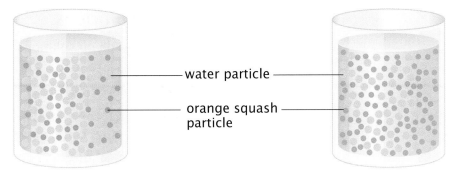

water particle

orange squash particle

3 Which of these glasses is **A**? How do you know?
4 Glass **C** is twice as concentrated as **B**. Can you draw the particle picture that shows this?

Concentration calculations

10 g of sugar in 100 cm^3 of water   30 g of sugar in 100 cm^3 of water

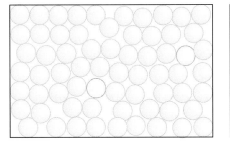   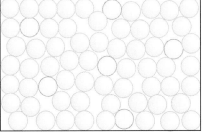

There are three times as many sugar particles in this solution compared with the other one.

A sugar solution was made by dissolving 5 g of sugar in 20 cm^3 of water. The **ratio** of sugar to water is 5:20 which is the same as 1:4. To make up a different volume of sugar solution of the same **concentration**, the ratio must remain the same, that is 1:4. So we could have:

2 g of sugar dissolved in 8 cm^3 of water
25 g of sugar dissolved in 100 cm^3 of water
250 g of sugar dissolved in 1000 cm^3 of water.

The concentration of a solution is usually calculated as the mass of solute dissolved in 100 cm^3 of water.

When the ratio of one variable to another is always the same, we say that one variable is **proportional** to the other.

5 If we wanted the same concentration as above, how much sugar would we need in
a) 40 cm^3 of water
b) 200 cm^3 of water
c) 2000 cm^3 of water
d) 500 cm^3 of water?
For each of these, discuss with a partner how you worked out the answer.
Did you always use the same method? Were any of the calculations easier than the others?

Different solutions

1 Two pupils made up solutions of sugar.

Rajit dissolved 12 g of sugar in 25 cm³ of water.
Anna dissolved 20 g of sugar in 40 cm³ of water.

a) Calculate the concentrations in g per 100 cm³ of water.
b) Whose solution is the more concentrated?

2 Vinegar is mainly ethanoic acid dissolved in water.

BigSave vinegar contains 24 g of ethanoic acid in 400 cm³ of water.
LowPrice vinegar contains 14 g of ethanoic acid in 250 cm³ of water.

a) Calculate the concentrations in g per 100 cm³ of water.
b) Which vinegar is the more dilute?
c) For BigSave vinegar, what mass of ethanoic acid would be dissolved in 50 cm³ of water?

Solubility

Key words
* saturated
* solubility

If you keep adding salt to water and stirring, you reach a point when no more salt will dissolve. Undissolved salt remains at the bottom of the solution. The solution is said to be **saturated**. In everyday language, we say something is saturated when it is soaked in water. In science, a solution is saturated when it is full of the dissolving solid (solute).

The **solubility** of a substance in water is calculated as the mass of solute needed to make a saturated solution in 100 cm³ of water.

Different solutes have very different solubilities. The following planning exercise compares the solubility of sugar and salt.

Enquiry   ## Which is more soluble in water: salt or sugar?

Julie's teacher gave the following instructions to solve this problem.

One method is to weigh out 10g of salt in a beaker. Pour 10 cm³ of water into a test tube and add a 'spatula end' of salt from the beaker. Keep adding salt and shaking until no more dissolves. Any extra salt added will just sink to the bottom of the test tube. The solution is now saturated. The remaining salt in the beaker is weighed. By subtraction, the amount of dissolved salt can be worked out.

The experiment is then repeated for sugar.

1 A variables table can help you to plan a fair test. Here is Julie's variable table.

Variable (what can change)	Values	Type of variable (input, outcome, fixed)
type of solute	sugar and salt	input
mass of dissolved solute	number of 'spatula ends'	outcome
type of solvent	water	fixed

  a) Julie's teacher wrote 'You can use a more accurate value for your outcome variable'. What did her teacher mean by this?
  b) Give three other important fixed variables for this experiment. What value would you use for each of them?
  c) Explain why the investigation would be fair.

2 What would you do to make the results more reliable?

Word play   Some words have very different meanings when used in science and everyday language. Other words have quite similar meanings in both science and everyday language.

  1 Write down a sentence containing the word 'solution' using
    a) scientific language
    b) everyday language.
  2 Review your two sentences above. Does the word solution have a very different meaning in science, or is it similar to its meaning in everyday language? Explain your answer.

Increasing the solubility

Key word
∗ accuracy

I like *lots* of sugar in my tea!

For most chemicals, the higher the temperature – the greater the solubility. This can be investigated and the results plotted on a graph.

Methods of measuring solubility at different temperatures

Method 1

This method is similar to that used to measure the solubility of salt earlier:

- Measure out a volume of water and heat it to a particular temperature.
- Add a 'spatula end' of salt, one at a time, and stir until dissolved. Keep adding until no more salt dissolves.
- Find out what mass of salt has been added.

Method 2

An alternative method is:

- Weigh 40 g of salt and dissolve it in 100 cm^3 of water in a water bath at about 90 °C.
- Carefully put about 10 cm^3 of the hot solution into a test tube and place in a rack.
- Stir the hot solution and let it cool down.
- Note the temperature when the first few crystals of salt appear. This happens around 42 °C for 40 g of salt dissolved in 100 g of water.

In method 2, the solubility of salt at 42 °C would be 40 g in 100 cm^3 of water.

In both methods, scientists would repeat the experiment using different temperatures in method 1, and different amounts of salt in method 2. This would give them sets of results that they could turn into a line graph.

Enquiry ## To investigate the effect of temperature on the solubility of salt using method 2

The **accuracy** of an investigation depends on:

- the accuracy of the apparatus used for measuring
- a method that allows the apparatus to be used to its full accuracy.

There is no point in using very accurate apparatus if it is not needed.

Apparatus list

All pieces of apparatus are made in different sizes or have different ranges.

- Thermometers range:
  0–50 °C
  0–100 °C
  0–200 °C
- Sizes of containers:
  test tube: 15 cm^3
  boiling tube: 40 cm^3
  beakers: 50 cm^3
       100 cm^3
       250 cm^3

- Balances accurate to:
  1 g
  0.1 g
  0.01 g
  0.001 g
- Measuring cylinders size:
  50 cm^3
  100 cm^3
  250 cm^3

1 Which piece of apparatus would you choose from the list for:
    a) measuring the temperature
    b) measuring out the water to make up the solution
    c) weighing the potassium chloride
    d) making up the solution
    e) placing the sample of hot solution in, for the cooling step?

2 Why is method 2 more accurate than method 1, even if the same equipment is used?

Information processing   *Solubility data*

1 The following table gives the solubility of potassium chloride at different temperatures.

Temperature (°C)	0	10	20	40	60	80	100
Solubility (g in 100 cm³ of water)	28	31	34	40	46	51	56

    a) What is the relationship between temperature and solubility for potassium chloride? Start your sentence with 'As the temperature increases...'
    b) What is the largest mass of potassium chloride that can be dissolved in 100 cm³ of water at 60 °C?
    c) To what temperature would you need to heat 51 g of potassium chloride in 100 cm³ of water to make sure that it dissolves?
    d) Estimate the largest mass of potassium chloride that can be dissolved in 100 cm³ of water at 50 °C.
    e) What is the largest mass of potassium chloride that can be dissolved in 20 cm³ of water at 40 °C?

2 The following graph shows how the solubility of copper sulphate varies with temperature.

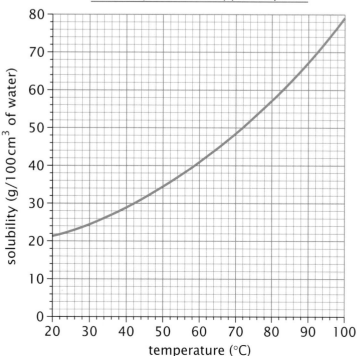

solubility curve of copper sulphate

a) What is the relationship between the solubility of copper sulphate and temperature?

b) What is the solubility of copper sulphate at 30 °C?

c) What is the solubility of copper sulphate at 85 °C?

d) What is the minimum temperature that is needed to dissolve 40 g of copper sulphate in 100 cm³ of water?

3 The following table gives the results of an experiment cooling different concentrations of benzoic acid solution and recording the temperature when crystals first appeared.

Temperature (°C)	20	33	51	63	65	74	81
Concentration (g of benzoic acid in 100 cm³ of water)	0.25	0.5	1.0	1.5	2.0	2.5	3.0

These results were plotted in the graph shown below.

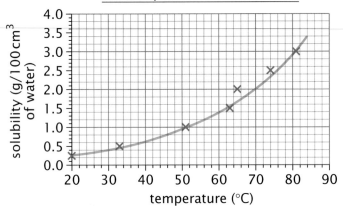

solubility curve of benzoic acid

a) Which concentration gave an 'odd' (anomalous) result?

b) How do we spot an anomalous result on a line graph?

c) Suggest a possible reason why this result could have gone wrong.

d) What is the relationship between the solubility of benzoic acid and temperature?

e) What do you predict the temperature would be when the first crystals appeared for:

i) 0.75 g of benzoic acid in 100 cm³ of water?

ii) 3.25 g of benzoic acid in 100 cm³ of water?

The salt industry

Key word
* brine

The salt in the above pictures should really be called common salt or table salt because there are many other types of salt such as bath salt, washing salt and Epsom salts (see chapter 5).

The scientific name for common salt is sodium chloride. Sodium chloride is found underground in thick layers called rock salt. It is also found in sea water. The underground layers of rock salt were formed millions of years ago. Ancient seas evaporated, leaving beds of salt that were covered by other sediments and turned into rock. Rock salt is obtained by digging out wide tunnels in the layer of rock. It contains bits of rock in addition to the salt. Salt mines are found in many parts of the world. In the UK, they are found in Cheshire. Some of the rock salt is crushed into a powder and used for gritting the roads in winter. The remainder is used to obtain pure common salt.

An alternative method of extracting salt from rock salt is to drill bore holes down into the salt layers and pump water down. This dissolves the salt to form **brine** (salt solution) which is then pumped up to the surface.

Sea salt is obtained from sea water in hot countries. It contains common salt and other salts that are dissolved in the sea.

DID YOU KNOW?

An adult human contains about 250 g of salt. You cannot live without it. It helps your muscles and nerves work properly and it is vital for the digestion of food. However, too much salt is harmful.

Time to think

Split into groups and discuss:

- How you would extract salt from sea water in a hot country.
- How you would extract salt from brine in the UK.
- How you would extract salt from large lumps of rock salt.

Try to use some of the key words you have learnt in your answers.

Research

1 Why is rock salt put on roads in winter?
2 **a)** Find two direct uses of salt other than table salt and road salt.
   b) Find two substances that are made from salt.
3 Supermarkets sell 'low sodium' salt.

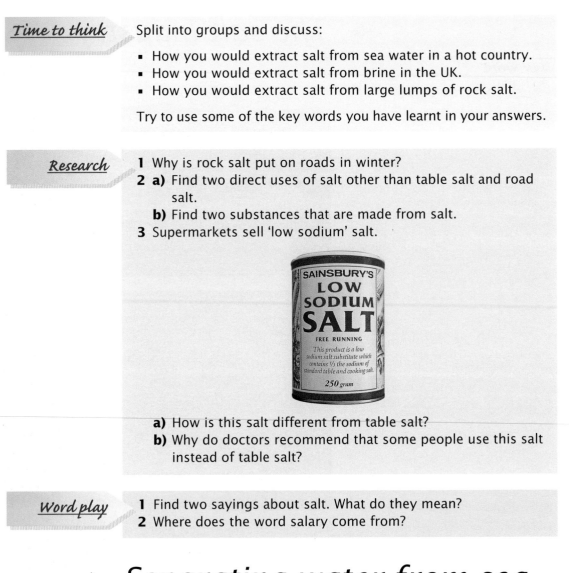

a) How is this salt different from table salt?
b) Why do doctors recommend that some people use this salt instead of table salt?

Word play

1 Find two sayings about salt. What do they mean?
2 Where does the word salary come from?

➡ *Separating water from sea water*

Key words
* dehydration
* extract
* desalination
* distillation

Fresh water is vital for humans. They need it for drinking, washing, growing food and for industry. Humans need roughly 2.5 litres of water per day. It takes 430 litres of water to grow enough wheat to make a loaf of bread. About 140 000 litres of water are required to make a tonne of steel or a tonne of paper.

Millions of homes in Africa, Asia and South America have no running water. The people must carry it from the village well, or from pools and rivers far from home. Many people spend 5 hours or more per day on collecting water. The tragedy is that, having **spent** so much time and effort, the water is sometimes polluted and a health hazard. It causes illnesses such as diarrhoea and dysentery. In developing countries one in ten children die of diarrhoea and **dehydration**. It is estimated that over 1 billion people do not have access to safe water.

Only 3% of the water on Earth is fresh water, and two-thirds of this is water locked up in ice caps and glaciers. Rivers and lakes contain only about 0.02% of the Earth's water.

Water, water everywhere but not a drop to drink . . . .

Some countries that are short of water **extract** it from sea water. To do this, you must remove all of the dissolved solids, such as common salt. This is called **desalination** and it uses a process that involves **distillation**.

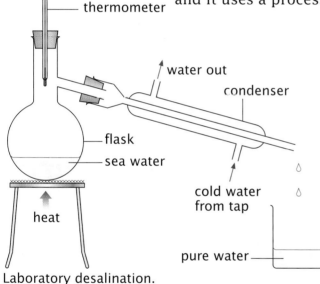

thermometer

water out

condenser

flask

sea water

cold water from tap

heat

pure water

Laboratory desalination.

Desalination plant.

6 Look at the diagram of the laboratory desalination.
   a) Copy out the flow diagram shown below and complete it to say how the water travels from the heated flask to the beaker.

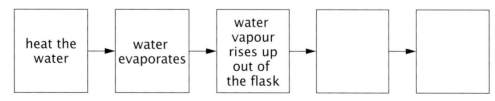

| heat the water | water evaporates | water vapour rises up out of the flask | | |

   b) Why is the salt left behind in the flask? (Try to use some of the key words in your explanation.)
   c) What temperature will be recorded on the thermometer during the distillation?
   d) What would the inside of the flask look like at the end of this practical? Why?

Time to think

1 Some countries have to extract drinking water from sea water on a very large scale. Distillation is sometimes used but it is very expensive – why is distillation expensive?
2 Imagine that you are a particle of water in some sea water. Write a story called 'The long journey' that describes what you see and feel on your journey through the laboratory distillation apparatus shown on page 185.
3 Design some emergency equipment for distilling drinking water from sea water that can be carried in a life-raft. It must take up little storage space and use the Sun's energy.

Chromatography

Key words
* chromatography
* chromatogram

Chromatography is a process that is used to separate a mixture of soluble substances. For example, some plants contain useful chemicals and chromatography can be used to separate them. Chromatography is often used by scientific detectives.

Forger's ink

Many inks contain a mixture of different dyes to make one colour that always looks the same on paper.
Chromatography can be used to separate out these different dyes to identify a particular ink. A forged cheque can be linked to the forger by comparing the ink on the cheque with the ink in the forger's pen.

A small spot of each ink is placed separately near the bottom of the filter paper. When it is placed in the beaker, the paper soaks up the solvent and carries the different colours at different speeds. The most soluble dye is carried the fastest and travels furthest up the paper. The final result is called a **chromatogram**.

➡ *Analysing foods*

Some processed foods contain additives that have been put in by the manufacturer to improve things like the colour or the flavour. Each additive is given an E-number. Some additives can cause allergies in certain people; they may develop spots or a rash. They must carefully check everything that they eat to make sure that it does not contain an additive that they are allergic to.

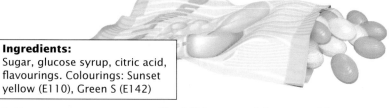

Ingredients:
Sugar, glucose syrup, citric acid, flavourings. Colourings: Sunset yellow (E110), Green S (E142)

7 Some new sweets called 'Lime and Lemons' have appeared in the shops. A food inspector decides to test the sweets to see if the list of colourings on the food label is correct. The resulting chromatogram is shown below.

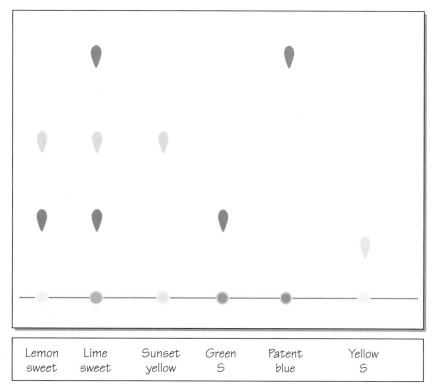

| Lemon sweet | Lime sweet | Sunset yellow | Green S | Patent blue | Yellow S |

a) Which sweet contains three colourings?

b) Does the lime sweet contain colourings not mentioned in the ingredients list? Does the lemon sweet contain colourings not mentioned in the ingredients list?

c) Mary is allergic to the colouring Patent blue. Which sweets are safe for her to eat?

d) Rashid is allergic to the colouring Yellow S. Which sweets are safe for him to eat?

Forensic science

Forensic scientists are called on by the police to help solve cases. Chromatography is an important tool in their fight against crime. Some of the uses are to:

- detect small traces of explosives on a suspect's hand
- detect small traces of drugs in a person's body
- identify traces of substances on clothing that may have been picked up at the scene of the crime
- detect the type of ink used for a letter or a signature on a cheque.

If a person is suspected of a crime, the police often take away the clothes that they have been wearing. These are then given to a forensic scientist to check for evidence to link the person to the crime scene.

If the substances to be separated and identified are not coloured, there are other ways of detecting them. Some substances glow (fluoresce) in ultraviolet light.

8 Can you name any TV programmes or books where chromatography played an important role in solving a crime or problem?

9 Draw a cartoon strip that shows chromatography providing vital clues in a crime story.

DID YOU KNOW?

DNA fingerprinting was invented by a British scientist Alec Jeffreys in 1984. A sample of DNA is obtained from the suspect (for example, from hair or blood). It is partly broken down and the mixture of DNA fragments is separated by chromatography to give a unique pattern that belongs to only that person.

Word play

The word chromatography is derived from two Greek words: 'chroma' and 'graphe'.

1 Chroma means 'colour'.
   a) Where are *chrom*osomes found in living things?
   b) Find out why the word chromosome contains the prefix 'chrom'.
   c) Find out why the name of the metal chromium contains the prefix 'chrom'.

2 Graphe means 'writing'. What is a seismograph?

Time to think

- Make a card game where you have a key word on one side of the card and a definition or piece of information about it on the other side. Place all the cards with the key word facing downwards and see if you can work out what the key word is from the definition or information given.

  Now turn the cards with the key word showing. Can you give a definition or information on each?

  Try again with sets of cards from two other people in your class.

- In the chapter, you have investigated:
  - dissolving a solute in a solvent
  - separating a mixture of solids by dissolving, filtering and evaporating
  - separating a solvent from a solution by evaporating and condensing
  - separating a mixture of solvents by chromatography.

Get into a group of four and each select one of the above to prepare a presentation. Try to explain how your selected process works by using the particle theory.

Take it in turns to give your presentation.

After each one, the rest of the group 'traffic light' the performance.

Green means a clear explanation has been given with all of the correct scientific terms.

Amber means a reasonable explanation but some terms have been missed or used incorrectly.

Red means the explanation was not clear.

Make sure that the reasons for red or amber scores are explained. If you score amber or red, then use the advice given to you to write an improved draft of your presentation. If you score green, then select a second presentation to write about.

10 The Solar System

In this chapter you will learn:

➜ about the relative sizes and positions of the planets
➜ how our ideas about astronomy have changed over time
➜ about the place of our Solar System within the Milky Way galaxy
➜ about the reasons for day and night, year length and day length
➜ the differences between stars, planets and satellites
➜ how to describe the motions of the Earth, Moon and planets
➜ the reason for a solar eclipse
➜ how a lunar eclipse occurs
➜ why the height of the Sun in the sky changes with the seasons
➜ about comets and meteors

You will also develop your skills in:

➜ plotting and interpreting graphs
➜ using ratio
➜ using models
➜ presenting data in tables

➜ ➜ ➜ WHAT DO YOU KNOW?

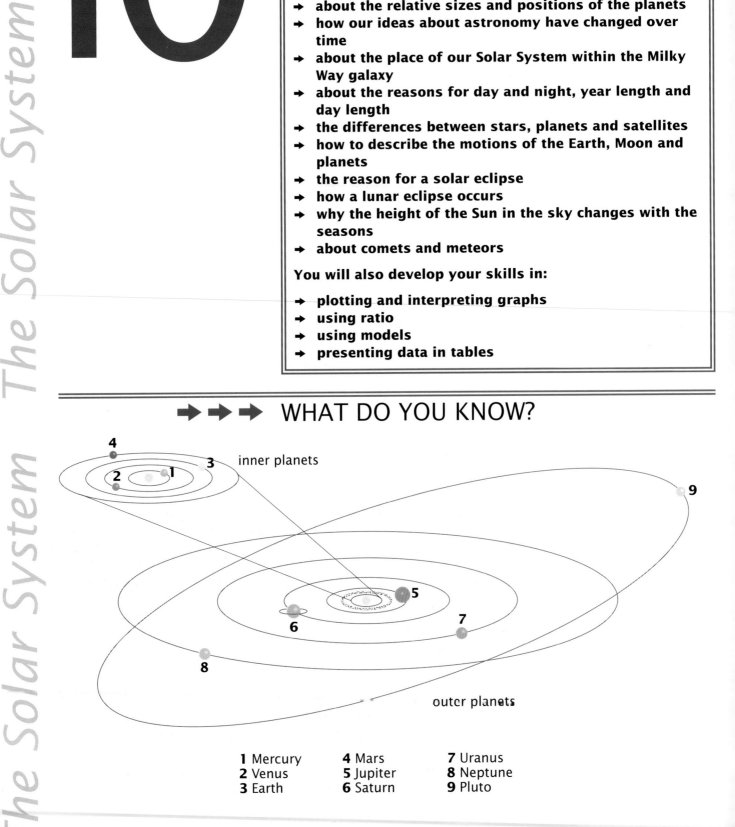

inner planets
outer planets

1 Mercury	**4** Mars	**7** Uranus
2 Venus	**5** Jupiter	**8** Neptune
3 Earth	**6** Saturn	**9** Pluto

1 Look at the diagram of the Solar System opposite. Can you explain what it is all about? With a partner, write down all you know about the diagram. You could do this by brainstorming or making a concept map. To help you complete your own concept map, here are some more objects and link words. See if you can complete your own concept map.

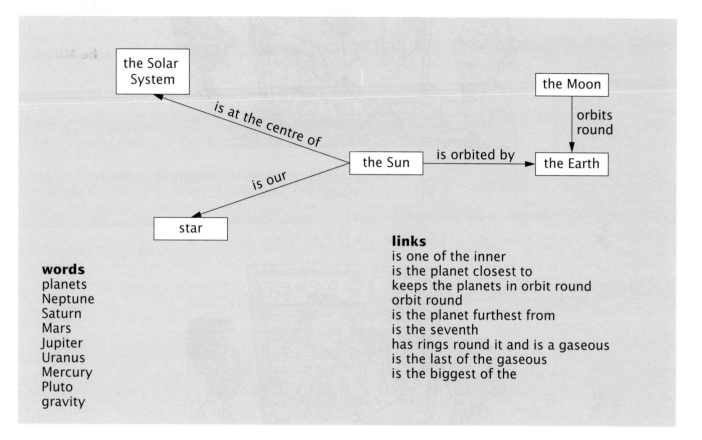

the Solar System

is at the centre of

is our

star

the Moon

orbits round

the Sun — is orbited by → the Earth

words
planets
Neptune
Saturn
Mars
Jupiter
Uranus
Mercury
Pluto
gravity

links
is one of the inner
is the planet closest to
keeps the planets in orbit round
orbit round
is the planet furthest from
is the seventh
has rings round it and is a gaseous
is the last of the gaseous
is the biggest of the

You may have seen a computer simulation of the movement of the Earth and Moon in space, or you may have seen or done a demonstration using a globe and a lamp.

These may help you to answer these questions. Working in groups, discuss possible explanations for the following problems. One member of the group should write down the group's answers. Another member of the group will be the reporter who will feed back your answers to the class.

2 Three pupils are discussing the position of the Sun in the sky at different times of day. Look at the cartoon and word bubbles.

I think this means that the Sun goes round the Earth

I think it is because the Earth goes round the Sun

I think it is because the Earth spins on its axis

a) Which statements are correct? How do you know?
b) Which statement explains the position of the Sun in the sky? Why?

3 Consider the next cartoon.

We get day and night because the Earth goes round the Sun once every day

The Earth turns round once a day to give us day and night

The Sun goes round the Earth once a day to give day and night

a) Which statements do you agree with and why?
b) Why is a day 24 hours long?

4 Referring to the light source and globe, explain:
a) why the Sun appears to rise in the east, climb higher in the sky and then set in the west.
b) whether the Earth spins clockwise or anticlockwise when viewed from the North Pole.

Key words
* astronomy
* civilisation
* eclipse
* equator
* hieroglyphics
* codex (plural: codices)
* comet
* satellite

DID YOU KNOW?

The Sun makes up 99.86% of the Solar System whereas the Earth is about 0.0003%.

The origins of astronomy

Many different civilisations have been interested in the sky. The Egyptian astronomer, Ptolemy (2nd century AD), revived the study of **astronomy** and produced a book called the *Great System*. It was originally written in Greek.

The ancient Mayan **civilisation** in Central America showed a good understanding of both mathematics and astronomy. They developed their own number system. The Mayan number system was based on 20 not 10 and was written like this:

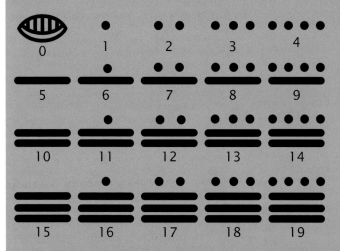

The Maya used a system of bars and dots – a dot stood for one and a bar stood for five.

Because the base of the number system was 20, larger numbers were written down in powers of 20, for example 32 is (1 × 20) + 12 which is shown as:

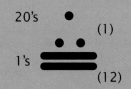

Numbers were written from bottom to top.

They also calculated information on the planets and on **eclipses** many years before Europeans discovered America. Most of the Mayan cities were located in a region near the **equator** where the Sun could be observed directly overhead at midday twice a year. The Maya could easily determine these dates, because at midday a stick

would not cast any shadow. The Maya had a complicated system of writing using pictures, symbols and bars. We call this **hieroglyphics**. Folding tree books made from fig tree bark were placed in royal tombs. They also made books from bark paper coated with lime and leather bound. Only four remain today. These books are called **codices** and contain information on the motion of the planets. The Maya were able to predict eclipses and other astronomical events. Unfortunately the Spanish destroyed much of the original material, as they regarded the hieroglyphics as the work of the devil. Even today, much of the hieroglyphics have not been deciphered.

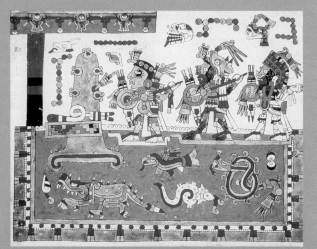

Other civilisations made many discoveries in astronomy. For example, the Ancient Chinese recorded solar eclipses over 2500 years ago. They compiled star maps around 300 BC. Halley's **comet** was first recorded by the Chinese in 240 BC, and in 365 BC the Chinese observed Jupiter's **satellites**.

1 What did Ptolemy contribute to scientific understanding nearly 2000 years ago?
2 Where did the Mayan civilisation live?
3 How did living near the equator help Mayan astronomers work out when the Sun would be directly overhead?
4 Where and how did Mayan astronomers record their data and predictions?
5 Why are so few codices found today?
6 Who first recorded evidence of Halley's comet, and how long ago was this recorded?

→ *Models in science*

We use models to represent an idea, to help our understanding of a topic. An example is when we use objects of different sizes to represent the **planets** in our **Solar System**. We could use a hazelnut to represent Mercury, big marbles for Venus and Earth, a small marble for Mars, a large beach ball for Jupiter, a football for Saturn, a grapefruit for Uranus, a large orange for Neptune and a pea for Pluto.

A particular feature of the model is used to represent a particular feature of the Solar System. In this example it is the relative sizes of the objects that represent the relative sizes of the planets of the Solar System.

Another way of modelling the Solar System is to represent the relative distances of the planets from the Sun (see page 190).

Mercury Venus Earth Mars Jupiter Saturn Uranus Neptune Pluto

→ *The Earth, Sun and Moon*

There are millions and millions of stars in the sky. Stars give out light. This is why we can see them. The Sun is our star. It seems much bigger than all the other stars because it is much closer to the Earth. The stars, including the Sun, give out light because they are very hot. It is an important source of heat and light for us on Earth. Without the Sun there would not be any life on Earth. We see the Moon and the planets because they reflect the light from the Sun.

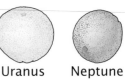

The Earth spins **anticlockwise** (as you look down on the North Pole). The time for one complete **revolution** is just under 24 hours. You will see that the **axis** along which the Earth spins is an imaginary line that passes through the North and South **Poles** and the centre of the Earth. Note that this axis is **tilted** at an angle of about 24°.

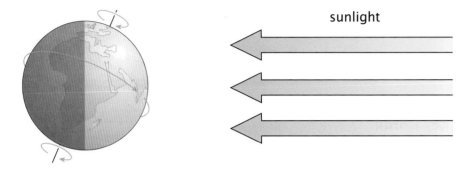

We have already referred to a model of the Earth and Sun where the Earth is shown as a globe and the Sun is a bright light source. Choose any point on the surface of the Earth. As the Earth rotates on its axis, sometimes that point is facing the Sun, sometimes it is facing away from the Sun. This explains why we have day and night. Because of the direction of spin, the Sun always appears to rise towards the east and set towards the west. As well as spinning on its axis, the Earth is moving round the Sun and it takes $365\frac{1}{4}$ days to go round once.

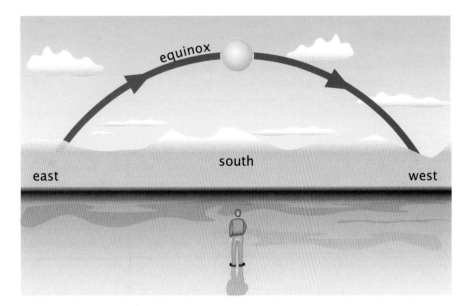

1 What is a day in terms of the movement of the Earth?
2 Suppose the Earth were spinning much more slowly. What difference would we notice?
3 Which is the nearest star to Earth?
4 Can you explain why we sometimes have 29 days in February?

The stars in the sky give out light. Do the following words or expressions use this idea and, if so, how?

1 film star
2 starfish
3 star turn
4 superstar

→ *The height of the Sun in the sky*

Key words
* altitude
* clinometer
* autumnal equinox

We cannot measure the height in kilometres, but we can measure how far the Sun is above the horizon as an angle. We measure the **altitude** of the Sun. To do this we use a **clinometer**.

SAFETY! **Never look directly at the Sun.**

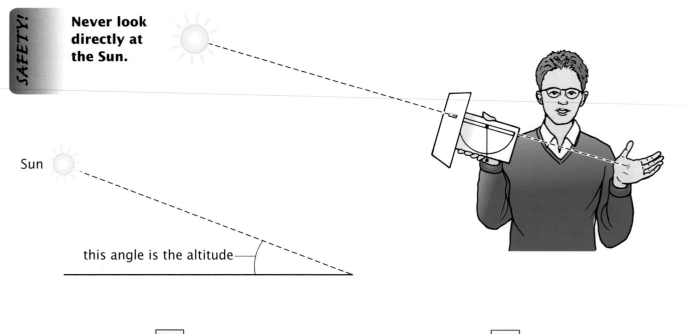

Sun

this angle is the altitude

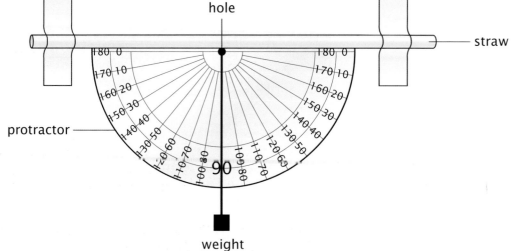

hole

straw

protractor

90

weight

Reasoning *Sunrise to sunset*

Some pupils used a homemade clinometer to measure the altitude of the Sun. Their results are shown in the table.

Time of day (h:min)	Altitude of Sun (degrees)
9:00	17
10:00	24
11:00	29.5
12:00	33
13:00	34
14:15	32
16:00	24
17:00	17
17:45	11

The experiment was done towards the end of September, at the **autumnal equinox**, when day and night are equal length. The results are shown in the graph.

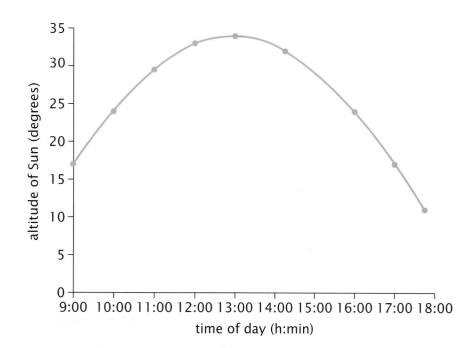

You could plot your own graph using the results. You could plot it on graph paper or use a spreadsheet such as Excel. Although the pupils were not able to be at school for sunrise, you could estimate when the Sun rose by working out where the graph line would cross the time axis if it was extended.

1 Can you predict the time of sunrise and sunset from the graph? For how long is the Sun visible?

The graph in winter is a similar shape, but the Sun rises later and sets earlier. The second graph shows the shape in the middle of winter.

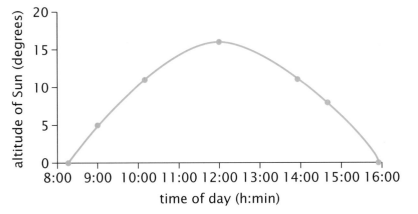

2 How does the graph differ from one drawn in July? There is one other factor we should really take into account (Hint: the times shown are for Greenwich Mean Time (GMT).) What is this other factor?

3 For how long is the Sun visible in winter?

4 What is the maximum altitude that the Sun reaches?

5 From which direction does the Sun rise?

6 From which direction would the Sun rise if you lived in Australia?

7 In which direction is the Sun at midday in Australia?

→ *Sundials*

Sundials come in many shapes and sizes.

5 What time do the sundials in pictures **b**–**d** show?

You may have made a sundial or followed the path of the Sun with a shadow stick.

6 In the picture when would you expect the length of the shadow to be shortest, and when would it be longest?
7 What would be the difference between the shadows formed by the stick on a summer's day and those on a winter's day?
8 Can you explain why a sundial that is set up to give the correct time in Greenwich in London, does not give exactly the correct time in Penzance in Cornwall?

In **Antarctica**, during the summer months, November, December and January, the Sun never sets, so the Sun casts a shadow all the time. The composite picture below is taken over a period of 24 hours and shows how the height of the Sun varies throughout the day.

9 To take a similar photo at the **Arctic Circle**, when would you need to take it?

The seasons

We have already seen that the position of the Sun in the sky is different in winter and in summer. The diagram below shows how the Earth moves around the Sun during a year. Look at it again. You will see that the tilt of the Earth's axis is always the same. This means that when the North Pole is tilted away from the Sun, less sunlight reaches the northern **hemisphere**. It is winter in Europe and North America. In the summer the North Pole is tilted towards the Sun. It receives more light and heat and therefore it is summer in the northern hemisphere.

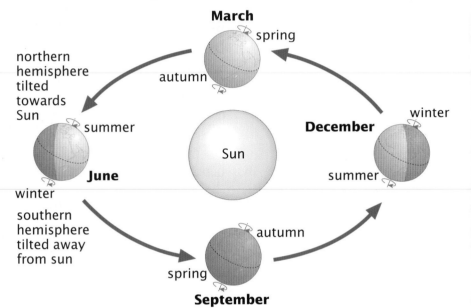

The picture shows an experiment to demonstrate these **seasonal** changes. It uses a globe and a lamp. In winter the low angle of the Sun means that the energy is spread over a big area. Also the sunlight has to pass through more of the Earth's **atmosphere** before it reaches the ground. Both of these facts mean that it is colder in winter. In summer the energy from the Sun falls more directly on the Earth and so it is more concentrated on a smaller area. So summer should be warmer than wintertime.

The Moon

You may already have observed and recorded the shape of the Moon in the sky. You may have made a 'flicker card' booklet to show the shape of the Moon over the period of a month. These changing shapes are known as the **phases** of the Moon. When the Moon is directly opposite the Sun, half the Moon is lit and this is a full Moon. When the Moon is between the Earth and the Sun, the dark half is facing us and so we cannot see it at all. This is called a new Moon. As the Moon orbits the Earth the amount of the lit half that we can see changes. It increases (or **waxes**) until we have a full Moon and then it decreases (**wanes**). Just after a new Moon the amount we can see appears as a **crescent**.

Sun

Moon Earth

The picture left shows an experiment to model the phases of the Moon. The overhead projector represents the Sun, the ball on the stick represents the Moon and the person's head is the Earth. The Moon goes around the Earth. In the model you represent this by turning anticlockwise on the spot while holding the Moon out at arm's length in front of you and slightly above your head. The light shines on the ball (the Moon) to show how the Moon is lit by the Sun.

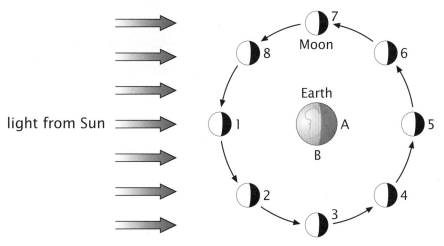

light from Sun

If you were standing on the Earth at A and you were looking at the Moon when it was in position 5, you would see a full Moon.

10 If you were standing at position B and the Moon was at position 3, what would you see?

11 What would you see if the Moon was at position 4?

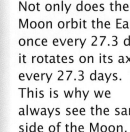

DID YOU KNOW?

Not only does the Moon orbit the Earth once every 27.3 days, it rotates on its axis every 27.3 days. This is why we always see the same side of the Moon.

Eclipses

Key words
* solar
* annular
* elliptical
* annulus
* lunar
* scattered

The last total eclipse of the Sun (or **solar** eclipse) in England took place on Wednesday 11 August 1999. It was also visible in many other countries from France across to India. Before that, the last solar eclipse in Britain had been in 1927, and we will have to wait until 2090 for the next one. There will be total eclipses visible in other countries. What is an eclipse? In France the newspapers described the appearance of 'le soleil noir', the 'black Sun', and as the pictures show it is a good description. The black is in fact the Moon passing between the Earth and the Sun. The Moon covers the Sun, and the sky goes dark.

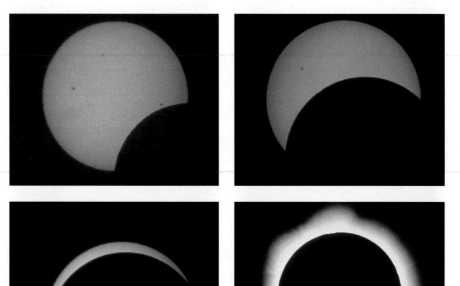

The diagram below shows the eclipse as though you were looking from space.

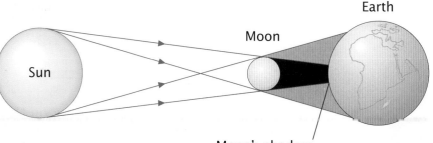

The longest possible time for a total eclipse to last is about 7½ minutes.

12 Where would you have to stand on the Earth to see a total eclipse?

It is pure coincidence that we are able to see an eclipse. The Sun is about 400 times bigger than the Moon, but it is also 400 times further away. They both seem to be the same size in the sky. However, the Moon is getting further away from the Earth and in a few million years it will be too far away for a total eclipse to take place.

As the Moon passes between the Earth and Sun every month, you might expect that we should see an eclipse of the Sun every month. This does not happen because the orbit of the Moon is at a slight angle relative to the Earth's orbit.

Sometimes we see an **annular** eclipse. This happens because the orbit of the Moon is not circular but **elliptical**, and sometimes the Moon is just too far away to appear to cover the Sun. The result is that the edges of the Sun can still be seen as a bright ring or **annulus**. The diagram shows how an annular eclipse can happen. A person at B would see an annular eclipse. A person at A would see a partial eclipse.

A solar eclipse.

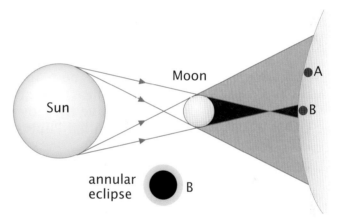

As well as eclipses of the Sun there are also eclipses of the Moon. An eclipse of the Moon is called a **lunar** eclipse. These happen when the Earth comes between the Moon and the Sun, and the Moon is passing through the Earth's shadow. Usually in a lunar eclipse there is sufficient light **scattered** by the Earth's atmosphere for the Moon to be seen as a red–orange colour. The diagrams below show the lunar eclipse on Tuesday 9 January 2001.

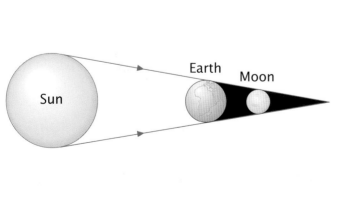

A lunar eclipse.

Find out about the solar eclipse on 11 August 1999. Here are some things you may wish to discover:

- Where was the eclipse visible?
- What time was it visible?
- How long did the eclipse last?
- Did the eclipse have any effect on plants or animals?
- Were there any noticeable changes in temperature, light level or humidity?
- How fast does the shadow of the Moon race across the Earth's surface?

The Solar System

Key words
* orbit
* asteroid

The planets travel in **orbits** around the Sun. The Sun is at the centre of the Solar System. The planets are kept in their orbits by the pull of the Sun's gravity. Without the Sun the planets would fly off into space. We can divide the planets into two main groups. These are the four inner planets closest to the Sun and the five outer planets. Between the two groups there is a large space, which is called the **asteroid** belt.

Many of the planets also have satellites which orbit them. Our satellite is the Moon. We do not think that Mercury and Venus have their own moons. We know that Mars has two moons called Phobos and Deimos. The four giant planets have many moons. Jupiter is known to have 17, Saturn has 18, Uranus has 15 and Neptune has eight.

The planet closest to the Sun is Mercury. It is still a very long way from the Sun – 58 million kilometres. The next planet, moving out from the Sun, is Venus, then the Earth and beyond that Mars. They are all made mostly of rock.

The five planets furthest away are the four giant gas planets: Jupiter, Saturn, Uranus and Neptune, and the small distant cold planet, Pluto. Jupiter is the biggest of all the planets and is made up mostly of hydrogen. Saturn is the second largest planet in our Solar System and is well known for its ring system. Uranus is the seventh planet from the Sun. It is a cold gas planet. It appears a blue–green colour because of methane in its atmosphere. It was discovered by William Herschel in 1781. Neptune is the last of the gas giants. It is a similar size to Uranus. The outermost planet Pluto was not discovered until 1930.

William Herschel.

Because Pluto has an elliptical orbit it sometimes moves inside the orbit of Neptune. It is only since 1999 that it has, again, moved away to become the furthermost planet from the Sun.

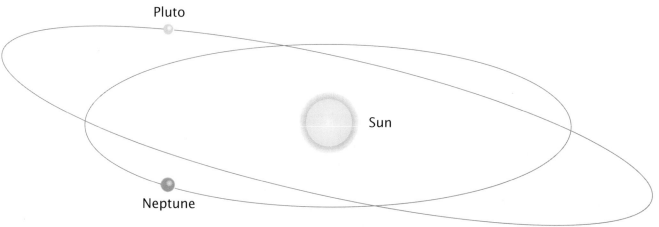

Orbits of Neptune and Pluto.

Information processing   ## The Solar System

To get a better idea of the relative sizes of the planets in the Solar System, use either the internet, books or CD-ROMs to collect information so that you can produce your own data. Some possible headings are suggested in the table below.

Planet name	Diameter in 1000 km	Distance from the Sun in million km	Relative mass compared to Earth	Time to orbit the Sun in Earth days

A spreadsheet would be a useful way of presenting the information.
Other facts you could find out include the surface temperature, how many Moons each planet has, the length of their day, and when they were discovered.

Information processing   ## Scale models

Suppose you are asked to produce a scale model of the planets' distances from the Sun on the walls of your school corridor. You would need to choose a suitable scale. A possible scale could be 1 cm = 1 000 000 km (1 million km). The Earth is 150 000 000 km (150 million km) from the Sun. To draw this to scale we would need to place it 150 cm away from the Sun.

1 How far away would we place Mercury?

2 Saturn is 1 430 000 000 km (1 430 million km) away from the Sun. On our scale model how far away would Saturn need to be from the Sun?

→ *Comets and meteors*

When a **comet** appears it can be a spectacular sight. In 1997 Hale-Bopp comet was visible for several weeks in our sky. Although it looked impressive, comets are not all they seem. Their actual core is quite small and made of ice, gas and dust. Their tails are mainly vapour. When Halley's comet visited in 1986 rockets were sent up and it was found to have a core about 15 km long. Halley's comet can be seen from Earth every 76 years. It will next appear in 2062. How old will you be then?

Halley's comet.

Halley's comet is shown on the Bayeux Tapestry, which was completed in 1080.

It is estimated by some scientists that 25 tonnes of meteor dust falls on the Earth every day. That's about a lorryload a day!

Other objects that can sometimes be seen in the sky on a clear night are **meteors**. (They are sometimes, incorrectly, called shooting stars.) A meteor is a chunk of rock. As it enters the Earth's atmosphere it burns up. You see a streak of light across the sky. If they are big enough they occasionally crash into the Earth. They are then called **meteorites**. Sometimes they form a crater where they hit the Earth. If you look at the Moon through binoculars you can clearly see examples of craters.

Many scientists think that a huge meteorite crashing into the Earth wiped out the dinosaurs. In recent years very few meteorites of any size have crashed into the Earth. It is thought that a meteorite crashed into Western Siberia, a remote part of Russia in 1908. Luckily this is not a populated area. Recently however, a well-known German scientist has claimed that it was a 'volcanic blowout' of millions of tonnes of natural gas. The picture below shows a crater formed in the USA tens of thousands of years ago.

View of a meteor crater in Arizona, USA.

Suppose a meteorite crashed into Britain. It could kill millions of people. Some scientists predict that a large meteorite is on a collision course with Earth around the year 2030.

13 Do you think we should take this seriously? What could we do? What should we do?

Time to think

Check that you can answer these questions.

1 Which planet is closest to the Sun?
2 What is the order of the planets starting from the Sun?
3 Which planet is furthest from the Sun?
4 Which planet has a ring system around it?
5 Why is it difficult to see other planets from Earth?
6 What is a year in terms of the movement of the Earth?
7 Do we see different stars in the summer and winter skies? If so, why?
8 What in our Solar System is the source of light and heat?
9 Why can we see the Moon?
10 What is the Milky Way?
11 Where is the asteroid belt found?

Use this information to prepare an explanation of one astronomy topic for a friend.

→ Constellations and galaxies

Key words
* constellation
* Milky Way
* galaxy
* Andromeda

From the Earth the stars appear still. In fact they are a huge distance away from the Earth and moving very fast.

Many years ago groups of stars were given special names. The most famous group of stars is the Plough. Another is Orion. These groups of stars only appear to exist in this pattern from the Earth. They are billions of kilometres apart. These imaginary groupings were invented to help us to map the sky. There are 88 of these **constellations**.

Research

Find out the answer to one of the following.

- How can you use the Plough to locate where the Pole Star is? (The Pole Star is sometimes called Polaris.)
- Twelve of the constellations are the zodiac constellations. What are they called?
- In which direction do the constellations move across the sky?

DID YOU KNOW?

The brightest star in the sky is Sirius. It is 8.7 light years away.

Our Sun is just one of 100 000 million stars that make up the **Milky Way** galaxy. If it was possible to look at the Milky Way from above, you would see that our Sun is located on an arm of this spiral **galaxy**.

There are at least 20 galaxies relatively closely grouped with the Milky Way, the nearest of which is the **Andromeda** galaxy. Even so it is still an enormous distance away – over 2 million light years! Beyond this group of galaxies there are billions more, each containing millions more stars.

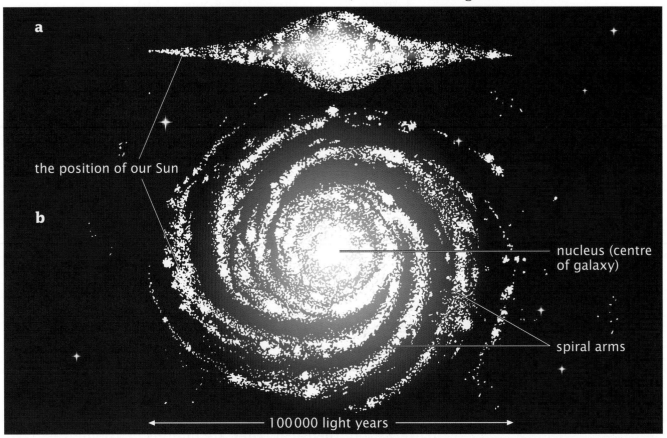

a

b

the position of our Sun

nucleus (centre of galaxy)

spiral arms

◄────────────── 100 000 light years ──────────────►

The position of our Sun in the Milky Way galaxy, **a** is the side view and **b** the view from above.

The Milky Way galaxy.

Andromeda galaxy.

Enquiry ## Craters

You can investigate the impact of craters by modelling the effect. You will need a tray or box, suitable 'soil' and 'meteorites'. You could use different 'soil' such as play sand, flour or plaster. Your 'meteorite' could be a marble, ball or ball-bearing. What do you think will happen?

Think about what measurements you will take: what you will vary (input variable); what you will keep the same (fixed variables); what you will measure or observe (outcome variable); what you will use to take the measurements; how many measurements you will take; how you will present your findings; what key words you will use in your conclusion.

Time to think

Using the information you have learnt and the number grid below, try to answer the following questions. If you have to decide the units, check that you get them correct.

365	27	8.7	240
24	9	400	150
76	58	1781	

- How many planets are there?
- How far away is the brightest star, Sirius, in light years?
- How many days does it take approximately for the Moon to go round the Earth?
- How many days does it take approximately for the Earth to go round the Sun?
- In what year BC did the Chinese first record seeing Halley's comet?
- What is the approximate angle of tilt of the Earth's axis?
- How many hours of daylight does the Arctic have during the summer?
- How many times bigger is the diameter of the Sun compared to the Moon?
- How many million kilometres is the Earth from the Sun?
- In which year was Uranus discovered?
- In millions of kilometres, how far is Mercury from the Sun?
- How long is it between appearances of Halley's comet?

Can you think of any more questions or numbers for the grid?

11 Simple chemical reactions

In this chapter you will learn:

→ **how to recognise a chemical reaction**
→ **how acids react with metals and carbonates**
→ **what new substances are made when materials burn in air or oxygen**
→ **the chemical test for hydrogen, carbon dioxide and oxygen**
→ **about the fire triangle and fire safety**
→ **to investigate what is needed for materials to burn**

You will also develop your skills in:

→ **looking for patterns in data**
→ **identifying variables**
→ **constructing and analysing graphs**
→ **evaluating experiments**
→ **predicting results**

→ → → WHAT DO YOU KNOW?

Key words
* reversible
* temporary
* irreversible
* permanent

Most science teachers can find their way to the chemistry laboratory blindfolded. They use their sense of smell to tell them the way. Chemistry lessons can get very smelly. But chemical reactions don't just happen in school. They happen all around us especially at home in the kitchen. Most of the things around you are manufactured. That means they have been specially made. Many of them are made during some sort of chemical reaction.

1 Look carefully at the photographs on these two pages. Which of the changes can be described as **reversible (temporary)** changes? Which of the changes can be described as **irreversible (permanent)** changes?

2 Which photograph shows both a temporary and permanent change? Explain your answer.

➡ *What is a chemical reaction?*

Key words
* chemical
* physical

Chemical reactions are irreversible; that means you can't change them back. You always end up with one or more new chemicals. If you burn sugar, you cannot get the sugar back even if you cool it down in the freezer. **Physical** changes do not result in new chemicals being produced and are reversible. You can melt ice but if you put the water back in the freezer it changes back to a solid again.

How do you decide that what you are observing is a chemical change? Good scientists are good observers. Here's what to look out for:

- colour changes
- bubbles appearing
- temperature changes
- chemicals appearing or disappearing.

1 Look carefully at all the changes in the pictures on pages 210 and 211 and decide which are physical changes and which are chemical changes. Put the changes into a table using the headings physical and chemical.

2 Split into groups and look at the list below. You need to decide which column each change should be added to.

- making toast
- boiling an egg
- a light bulb getting hot
- burning charcoal in a barbecue
- adding sugar to a cup of tea
- making ice cubes in the freezer
- setting off a firework
- food going mouldy

- Alka Seltzer fizzing in water
- brewing beer
- making a cup of tea
- using Rennies to cure acid indigestion
- treating wasp and bee stings
- diluting orange juice with water
- plaster of Paris and water mixed together and going hard

3 Pupils were testing what happened when they put two different solids, salt and chalk, in clear, colourless vinegar. Here are their results.

Salt in vinegar	Chalk in vinegar
We noticed that most of it just sank to the bottom but a little dissolved when we stirred it.	We observed lots of bubbles and the powder quickly disappeared. The container felt warm.

a) Which chemical seems to change reversibly in vinegar? Is this a physical or chemical change?
b) Which chemical seems to change irreversibly in vinegar? Is this a physical or chemical change?

Acids and metals

Key words
∗ metal
∗ hydrogen

Have you ever tried cleaning your old dirty coins? Put a dirty penny into some cola and leave it overnight. Next morning it will be gleaming!

Acids are corrosive. They attack some (but not all) **metals**, eating them away, just like the coins left in cola. **Hydrogen** gas is produced when acids attack metals.

For those concentrated and strong acids that can damage metals or skin, a hazard sign marked 'corrosive' is placed on the container.

corrosive

Information processing   *Reaction between magnesium and hydrochloric acid*

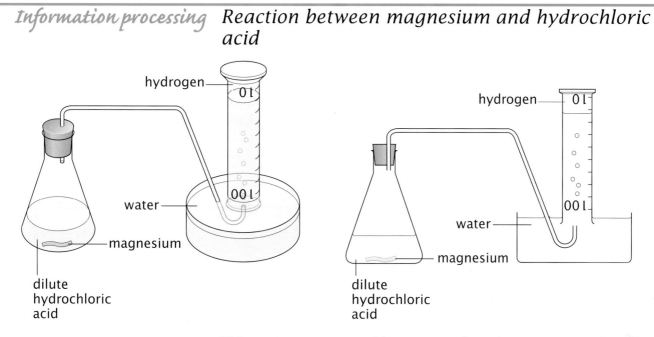

This apparatus was used by a group of pupils to investigate how the volume of hydrogen would change when different amounts of magnesium were added to a large excess of hydrochloric acid.
Here are their results:

Length of magnesium (cm)	1	2	3	4	5	6
Volume of hydrogen (cm³)	10	21	25	40	50	

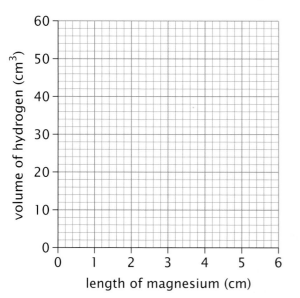

On graph paper, copy the axes shown on the left and plot the results.

1 Which is the input variable?

2 Which is the outcome variable?

3 Which other variables would they have to control (keep the same)? What type of variable do we call these?

4 What relationship is there between the input and outcome variables?

5 Which result would you want to check again? Why?

6 From your graph estimate what the result would be for:
   a) 6 cm of magnesium
   b) 1.5 cm of magnesium
   c) 3.5 cm of magnesium.

7 How much magnesium would they need for:
   a) 50 cm³ of hydrogen
   b) 45 cm³ of hydrogen
   c) 15 cm³ of hydrogen.

8 List two things that might affect the accuracy of these results. How could you improve the accuracy of the results?

Testing for hydrogen

Hydrogen is the lightest gas. The proper way to say this is to use the term **low density**. It will float upward out of open test-tubes and containers.

Once you have trapped some hydrogen you can test it by bringing a burning splint near to the open end of the test-tube. You will hear a 'pop' if the gas is hydrogen. This is called the **'pop' test** because when hydrogen burns it is like a small explosion.

Evaluation *Preparing hydrogen*

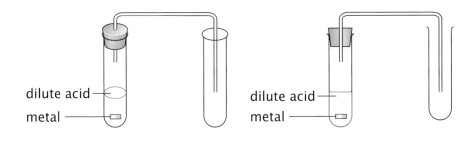

dilute acid
metal

dilute acid
metal

1 A group of pupils set up their experiment to collect and test some hydrogen using the apparatus in the diagram but they did not get a positive test. What changes would you make to their apparatus? Explain why their set-up would not work.

In 1933 a German airship, the Hindenberg (shown left), exploded as it arrived in New York on its maiden voyage. It was full of hydrogen that somehow caught fire. There was a massive explosion and in less than a minute the airship was totally destroyed. Airships and weather balloons are now filled with helium instead.

2 Can you suggest two reasons why helium is now used to fill weather balloons and airships?

3 Your science teacher has brought in a display of solids, liquids and gases. The balloon full of carbon dioxide is still fully inflated, but the balloon full of hydrogen has shrunk. What do you think has happened to the hydrogen particles?

→ *Acids and carbonates*

Key words
* calcium carbonate
* neutralise
* limescale

The antacids shown above are taken to relieve acid indigestion. You can see from the label the chemical contents in this antacid cure. The main ingredient is the chemical **calcium carbonate** that **neutralises** the extra acid in the tummy. Carbon dioxide is produced when the acid reacts with the carbonate.

We also make use of this reaction in the kitchen. Have a look at the picture of the kettle. It is covered in calcium carbonate but you might know it better as **limescale**. This limescale is a real nuisance but can be removed with the correct acid.

4 We can use a weak acid to remove the limescale. How many can you name?
5 Why should a strong acid not be used? What would it do to your metal kettle?
6 Many kettles are now made of plastic. How could you find out if strong acids attack plastic?

Rocks at risk

Limestone, **chalk** and **marble** all contain calcium carbonate. Rainwater has a pH of 6 and is sometimes called **acid rain**. Chemical **weathering** is the result of acid rain attacking certain rocks. The photograph shows how damaging this effect can be.

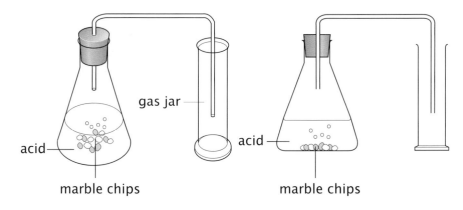

This apparatus shows the reaction of a strong acid on some pieces of marble rock.

7 Why is rainwater sometimes called acid rain?
8 Is carbon dioxide a low or high density gas? Look carefully at the apparatus for the answer.

Testing for carbon dioxide

When carbon dioxide is bubbled through **limewater** the solution turns milky. Solid particles of calcium carbonate are formed in the liquid. The full chemical name for limewater is **calcium hydroxide** solution.

Time to think Try these four questions as a check on your learning so far.

1 Name one of the chemicals produced when an acid reacts with iron.
2 Vinegar can be used to remove limescale (calcium carbonate) from your kettle. Which gas will be produced?
3 Read 'Testing for carbon dioxide' on the opposite page. Has a chemical reaction taken place? Give as many reasons as you can to support your answer.
4 Look carefully at the diagrams opposite that show acid attacking marble chips. What evidence is there that a chemical reaction is taking place?

Now compare your answers with at least two other pupils. Improve your answers to each question and highlight any key words that you use.

Word equations

Key words
* word equation
* reactant
* product

Word equations are a type of shorthand. We can summarise a chemical reaction using word equations which all take this form:

reactants → chemical reaction → products

Reactants are the chemicals that react together. **Products** are the new chemicals produced.

In chapter 5 you learnt that acids and alkalis are chemical opposites. They neutralise each other to form salts.

The word equation for acids reacting with alkalis is:

acid + alkali → salt + water

We can write a word equation for the reaction between acids and metals like this:

metal + acid → salt + hydrogen

We can write a word equation for the reaction between acids and carbonates like this:

carbonate + acid → salt + water + carbon dioxide

The chip shop mystery

There is a huge queue at the local chip shop. You ask the person in front of you what the problem is.

'Somebody asked for sodium chloride and ethanoic acid on their fish and chips' came the reply. 'They've been searching the store cupboard for nearly half an hour.'

Can you sort this problem out? Explain what you would tell the chip shop owner.

➡ *The burning question*

Key words
* fuel
* combustion

This picture shows early humans keeping warm in their cave. In the Stone Age, fire kept you warm, cooked your food and frightened off wild animals.

Fire has been important throughout history. All through the ages we have burnt **fuels** to keep us warm and cook our food. It is probably one of the most important chemical reactions we have ever discovered. However burning can be dangerous and very destructive.

About 6000 years ago an important discovery was made about rocks and minerals. Some could be roasted in a fire to produce metals. The first metal discovered in this way was copper.

9 What sorts of materials burn? Name as many as you can.
10 Is getting copper from roasting rock a chemical or physical change? Explain your answer.

Burning is a very obvious example of a chemical change. Burning is also called **combustion**.

11 Will we be able to get the wax back? Is this a reversible change?
12 What types of energy does the burning candle produce?
13 Where has this energy come from? Where is it stored?
14 Name one of the reactants when a candle burns.

What is needed for things to burn?

Things need air to burn. Providing extra air will help things to burn better. You will see people blowing on a small fire to help it burn better. Air is used up so quickly during a fire that firefighters need to have a cylinder of oxygen on their back so they can breathe inside a building that is on fire.

Fire-fighting often involves smothering the fire to remove the supply of air. Look around the laboratory. You will see a fire blanket, a sand bucket and a fire extinguisher containing carbon dioxide. Each of these can be used to smother a fire so that it is starved of air and cannot carry on burning.

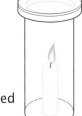

candle extinguished after 12 s

candle extinguished after 8 s

candle extinguished after 4 s

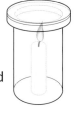

15 How does the amount of air inside the jar affect how long the candle burns?

Have you seen this warning sign when you have been to a petrol station?

Some fuels burn very easily – they are **flammable**. Petrol catches fire very easily. Below is the hazard sign for substances that catch fire easily. A careless person lighting or smoking a cigarette could cause a serious explosion.

Petroleum spirit Highly flammable

No smoking or naked lights

Word play

Flammable means to catch fire easily. **Inflammable** sounds like the opposite but it means exactly the same thing! **Non-flammable** describes a material that will not burn.

Imagine that you are a Scout leader advising a Scout pack on how and where to light a fire safely.

Try to use the words flammable, inflammable and non-flammable at least once in your explanation.

➡ *Fire fighting: the fire triangle*

Every year many lives are lost through house fires and large areas of forests are burnt to the ground. We need to understand how things burn so that fire can be controlled and used safely. In summer 2000 some of the worst forest fires ever broke out across the eastern states of the USA, destroying millions of acres of forest. The photo shows a forest fire that happened at Meru National

Park in Kenya. One technique used to control them was to carefully burn down or cut down parts of the forest to remove the fuel. This helps to prevent the fire spreading to new areas of the forest.

In the UK in 1999 house fires killed over 400 people and injured about 14 600 people. They can be so easy to start but so difficult to extinguish (put out).

Fighting fires involves one of the following:

* Removing the fuel – a fuel is anything that will burn.
* Removing the heat – throwing water onto a fire cools it down.
* Smothering the fire to cut the supply of air.

These three things make up the fire triangle. You can put out a fire by taking away any one of the three.

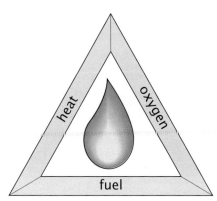

16 Look at the following fire-fighting methods and decide how they work.

Fire-fighting		How it is used	How it works
carbon dioxide extinguisher		pointed and sprayed onto the fire forming an invisible blanket	
fire blanket		a non-flammable blanket is placed over the fire	
water		water is hosed onto the fire	
sand		sand is thrown onto the fire	

Research

One of the first people to use the fire triangle was Sir Humphrey Davy (1778–1829). Methane gas (the gas that comes out of our Bunsen burners) caused many explosions in coalmines. Because the mines were very dark, miners used candles to see deep underground. Very often the methane caught fire and caused massive explosions and many miners died. Davy realised that it was the heat of the flame that was the problem so he designed a lamp that stopped this happening.

Find out about the life of Sir Humphrey Davy and about his important invention, the Davy Lamp. How does it manage to reduce the heat of the flame?

Which part of air is needed for burning?

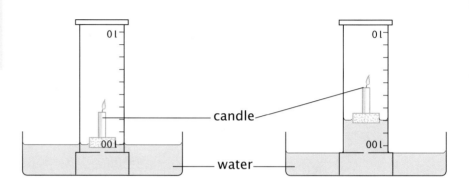

candle

water

When the candle burns the water level in the jar rises. The water only rises part of the way up the jar. This tells us that only part of the air is used up during burning. The part that is being used is the gas **oxygen**. Once the oxygen in the jar has been used up the candle can no longer burn and the flame goes out.

Air is a **mixture** of gases that can be separated into more useful pure gases. Air is about one-fifth oxygen, four-fifths **nitrogen** and the rest is mainly argon. There is a tiny amount of carbon dioxide (0.03%) and the amount of water vapour changes depending on the weather and where in the world you live!

17 What is the water level reading in the first diagram?
18 What is the water level after the candle has finished burning?
19 What percentage of the air is made up of oxygen?

Oxygen has many uses such as in hospitals, treating polluted rivers, steel making and in space rockets. Rockets need fuel and they have to take their own oxygen so that the fuel can burn.

Every cell in our body needs oxygen for the chemical reaction that we call respiration (see chapter 7). This is also true for cells in plants and in other animals. Oxygen is an important gas for life on Earth.

→ *What about the products?*

Key words
* element
* atom
* oxide

So far we have learned that burning is a chemical change (chemical reaction) that uses up oxygen, one of the gases found in the air.

The next question is: What new substances are formed? What are the products?

To begin this section we must pick simple chemicals to burn so we can start with simple word equations before we tackle chemicals like wax and other fuels.

The simplest group of chemicals we can choose are called **elements**. Remember Sherlock Holmes and his famous phrase: 'It's *elementary* my dear Watson'. Meaning it's *simple*. Elements contain one type of particle or **atom** so we can work out the products of burning more easily.

When elements burn they react with oxygen. The product is called an **oxide**. All substances form oxides when burned.

Enquiry ## *What will happen?*

Imagine you have a gas jar full of air (21% oxygen) and another of pure oxygen (100%).

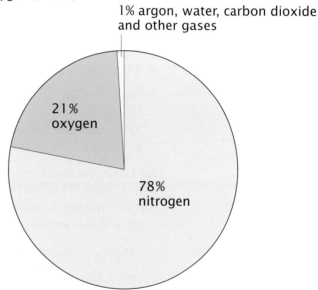

1% argon, water, carbon dioxide and other gases

21% oxygen

78% nitrogen

1 What difference do you expect between burning substances in air and in pure oxygen? Use the information in the pie chart to help to explain your answer.

2 Can you predict what the new substances (products) will be when you burn carbon in air or pure oxygen?

3 What test will you carry out to prove your prediction was correct? What result will you get if you are right?

Information processing Metal and non-metal oxides

Each of the elements in the table below was burned in pure oxygen to form oxides. The product was tested with litmus (see chapter 5).

Element	Metal/non-metal	How the element burns	Appearance of product (oxide)	Colour of litmus
magnesium	metal	bright white light	white solid	blue
carbon	non-metal	glows red	colourless gas	red
calcium	metal	red flame	white solid	blue
sulphur	non-metal	blue flame	dense fumes	red
phosphorus	non-metal	bright white flame	white fumes, some solid	red
sodium	metal	yellow flame	yellow/white solid	blue

1 What colour was the litmus with the metal oxides?

2 What does this tell you about these metal oxides?

3 What colour was the litmus with the non-metal oxides?

4 What does this tell you about these non-metal oxides?

5 Predict what colour the litmus would change to when these elements burn:
   a) potassium (metal)
   b) silicon (non-metal).

We can write word equations for all of these reactions. Let's start with carbon. The reactants were carbon and oxygen and the product turned limewater milky. The product was carbon dioxide.
   Here is the word equation:

carbon + oxygen → carbon dioxide

To write the word equation for the burning of magnesium start off with the reactants:

magnesium + oxygen

The product is an oxide; in this case it is called magnesium oxide.

6 Copy the start of the equation for burning magnesium. Add the arrow and write in the product on the right-hand side of the arrow. Then you have the finished word equation.

7 Try to write word equations for burning the elements calcium and sulphur.

Sparklers contain tiny pieces of iron that burn really well. They are much hotter than you think.

8 Write the word equation for the chemical reaction taking place in the sparklers.

Enquiry ## Acid drops investigation

Many of the chemicals in fossil fuels form acidic oxides when they burn. The most harmful are carbon dioxide, sulphur dioxide and nitrogen oxide. These gases dissolve in rain to make an acidic solution that falls to the ground as acid rain. This acid rain is a mixture of mainly sulphuric and nitric acid.

In many cities and towns, buildings have been gradually destroyed by acid rain. Steel railway lines in parts of Eastern Europe can be seen fizzing as the acid rain attacks the metal. The photograph on page 216 shows the effect of acid rain on buildings, which is also known as chemical weathering.

1 Make a list of all the different materials that are used in building. Which ones do you think are most at risk from acid rain? Which ones might be 'acid proof'?

2 Plan an investigation to test your ideas.

Think about the variables: input, outcome and fixed.
What values will you choose? Use a variables table to help you.
Check you have thought about all the safety issues.
Choose sensible equipment.

3 Check out your plan with your teacher before you get started.

4 A local builder wants your advice on which materials are acid resistant. Write a report showing your evidence and clearly explain your conclusions.

The lakes that died

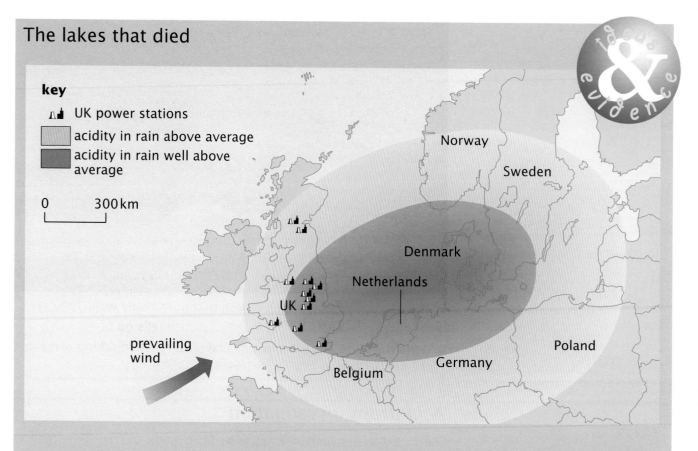

key

🏭 UK power stations

acidity in rain above average

acidity in rain well above average

0   300km

Norway
Sweden
Denmark
Netherlands
UK
Belgium
Germany
Poland

prevailing wind

Most of Sweden is covered with lakes and pine forests. Acid rain has made these lakes a hundred times more acidic than normal. Scientists have noticed that the amount of damage to the trees is increasing. The Swedes are spending more and more money on adding lime to the lakes. Many blame the power station fumes from the UK. The prevailing winds blow the fumes across the sea to Scandinavia.

Lapland is in the northern part of Scandinavia. Factory fumes 200 miles away in Russia are responsible for damage to the trees and are making the lakes very acidic.

1 How would adding lime ('liming') help remove the acid from the lakes?
2 Should the Swedes blame other countries for the pollution?
3 Why do some people say that the lakes have died?
4 Should other countries be helping Sweden pay for liming the lakes?

DID YOU KNOW?

The Earth's crust consists of over 45% oxygen. Most of this is combined with the element silicon to form minerals, such as quartz. You will know this better as sand. The oxygen also occurs in the form of oxides and as carbonates, which make up limestones.

Testing for oxygen

Things burn better in pure oxygen than they do in air. This gives us a way of testing for oxygen. A splint is lit and the flame blown out so the splint is just glowing. When placed in pure oxygen the splint relights. This is the test for oxygen. We say it relights a glowing splint.

Time to think

All elements are pure because they contain just one type of particle called an atom. Remember all the atoms in an element are identical (exactly the same). When elements burn in oxygen (another element) these atoms join together in a chemical reaction to form oxides. All the oxides you have made are called compounds because they have two different elements joined together.

It's a lot easier if you can picture this, so let's go back to using models. You'll remember we used these to explain the differences between solids, liquids and gases in chapter 4.

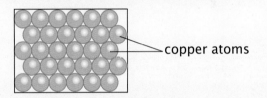

copper atoms

We can do the same for oxygen. Remember, oxygen atoms will be different from those of copper. In fact, oxygen is diatomic. This means that it is made up of two oxygen atoms. Oxygen is also a gas, and not a solid like copper. Think about how you will draw them in a box. Try out your idea.

When copper and oxygen react together the atoms become joined. Copper oxide would look like this:

copper atom

oxygen atom

1 Draw particle diagrams for the following word equations.

magnesium + oxygen → magnesium oxide
sulphur + oxygen → sulphur dioxide
('di' in front of the word oxide means TWO oxygen atoms)
carbon + oxygen → carbon dioxide

Using symbols

It's a bit awkward writing copper atom or oxygen all the time so scientists have agreed a sort of shorthand language. They gave each element its own symbol. These are used all over the world and are the same in every language. So you could pick up a French science book and still understand some of it.

COMMENT FONCTIONNENT LES FORMULAE

Cela permet aussi de montrer d'une façon plus détaillée, comment les atomes des éléments se combinent. Par exemple, la réaction entre le calcium et le chlore s'exprime ainsi:

$$\text{calcium} + \text{chlore} \rightarrow \text{chlorure de calcium}$$
$$Ca + Cl_2 \rightarrow CaCl_2$$

En remplaçant lesmots par les formulae, il faut faire bien attention parce que le nombre d'atomes de chaque élément d'une côté de l'équation doit égaler le nombre de l'autre côté. Il est possible que, pour faire équilibrer les nombres, il faut ajouter d'autres nombres devant l'une ou l'autre des formulae pour les réactifs et les produits. Par exemple:

$$\text{calcium} + \text{oxygène} \rightarrow \text{oxyde de calcium}$$
$$Ca + O_2 \rightarrow CaO$$

Dans cette forme il y a deux atomes d'oxygène à gauche, mais il n'y en a qu'une à droite. On équilibre l'équation en ajoutant le 2 devant le CaO pour équilibrer les atomes d'oxygène, et en ajoutant le 2 devant le Ca pour équilibrer les atomes de calcium. L'équation équilibrée est le suivant:

$$2Ca + O_2 \rightarrow 2CaO$$

En équilibrant les équations, il ne faut pas changer les formulae ni des réactifs ni des produits. Par exemple:

$$\text{sodium} + \text{chlore} \rightarrow \text{chlorure de sodium}$$
$$Na + Cl_2 \rightarrow NaCl$$

Cette équation n'est pas équilibrée. Quoiqu'on pourrait l'équilibrer en écrivant $NaCl_2$, ce composé ne se produit pas, donc l'équation ne serait pas correcte.

On ne peut équilibrer cette équation qu'en le changeant en:

$$2Na + Cl_2 \rightarrow 2NaCl$$

4 Vérifiez ces équations et équilibrez-les si nécessaire.
a) $H_2 + I_2 \rightarrow HI$,
b) $2C + O_2 \rightarrow 2CO$,
c) $K + H_2O \rightarrow KOH + H_2$,
d) $Mg + O_2 \rightarrow 2MgO$,
e) $KI \rightarrow 2K + I_2$,
f) $CuO + H_2SO_4 \rightarrow CuSO_4 + H_2O$,
g) $H_2O_2 \rightarrow H_2O + O_2$.

Figure 14.2 En étudiant les réactions avec attention, on peut découvrir la structure de grosses molécules.

177

How much of this do you understand?

The chemical symbol for gold is Au. Next time you watch the James Bond film *Goldfinger* look carefully at the number plate of the car owned by the villain Goldfinger: Au 1.

Burning fuels

Key words
* Bunsen burner
* methane (natural gas)
* air hole
* fossil fuels
* hydrocarbons

Earlier in this section the word fuels was mentioned. Fuels are chemicals that we burn in order to produce heat and light energy. They contain more than one element and so produce more than one oxide.

20 How many fuels can you name?

Most **Bunsen burners** use a fuel called **methane (natural gas)**. In your school laboratory, methane is supplied through the gas taps. The Bunsen burner is connected to the tap using a rubber hose. The size of the flame can be adjusted by turning this tap. The type of flame is controlled by opening and closing the **air hole** as shown below.

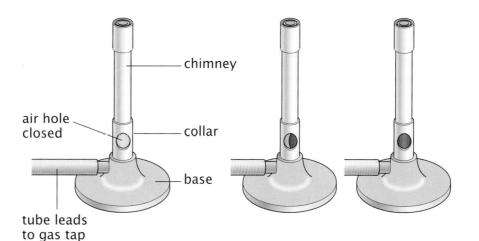

Air hole closed: yellow flame. (This is the flame you need when the Bunsen is not in use.)

Air hole half open: heating flame.

Air hole fully open: roaring blue flame.

We burn fuels because they provide lots of heat and light. Just like our ancestors we use fuels to keep us warm, cook food and much more. The most important ones are coal, oil and gas. These are the **fossil fuels**.

21 Coal is mainly made of carbon. What is the main product when coal burns?
22 Look at the table on page 224. What type of solution will you get when carbon dioxide dissolves in rainwater?

Oil and gas are fossil fuels that are known as **hydrocarbons** because they contain two elements joined together.

23 Can you name the two elements in oil and gas?

The bad news about fossil fuels

When fossil fuels such as coal and natural gas are burnt in power stations they produce large amounts of carbon dioxide. The Mauna Loa Observatory in Hawaii has been measuring the levels of carbon dioxide in the atmosphere since the mid 1950s. In the past, trees and other plants were able to control the level of carbon dioxide by using the gas during photosynthesis. This reaction releases oxygen into the atmosphere. However, we are now burning so much of our fossil fuel supplies that levels of carbon dioxide are building up. In other parts of the world, rain forests are being cut down to make way for farming. This has an effect on the build up of carbon dioxide in the atmosphere.

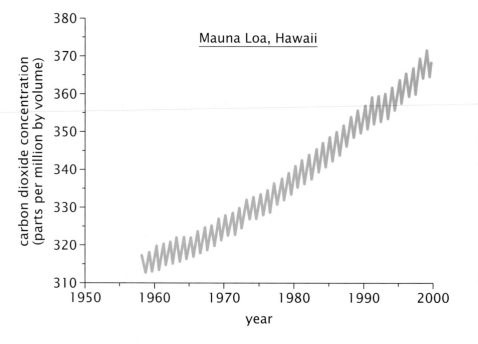

24 When did the observatory first begin measuring carbon dioxide levels?

25 Estimate the increase in levels between
   a) 1970 and 1980
   b) 1985 and 1995.

26 Trees and other green plants are often called the 'lungs of the Earth'. What do we mean by this?

27 Increase in carbon dioxide levels has been blamed for causing global warming. Imagine you were Prime Minister, what would you do about:
   a) getting people to save energy at home
   b) destruction of the rain forests
   c) using other energy sources instead of fossil fuels
   d) getting people to use buses and trains instead of cars?

What are the products of burning gas?

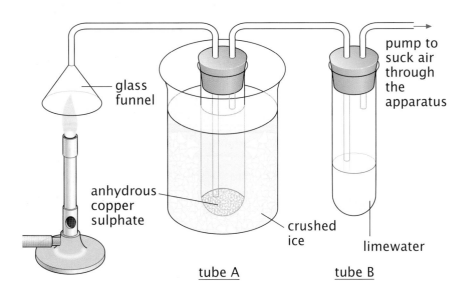

glass funnel

anhydrous copper sulphate

crushed ice

pump to suck air through the apparatus

limewater

tube A   tube B

This apparatus identifies the products of burning methane (natural gas).

There are two simple tests for water. Cobalt chloride test paper turns from blue (dry) to pink (wet/damp), and dry copper sulphate turns from grey/white to blue when water is added. The chemical name for water is hydrogen oxide.

In the experiment shown above small drops of a clear liquid are seen in tube A and some of the white powder has turned blue. The limewater has turned cloudy.

I'm very thirsty. I need a glass of hydrogen oxide!

28 Copy these sentences into your books and complete:

The hydrogen from the _____ has reacted with the _____ from the air to produce water (_____ oxide).

The carbon from the burning gas has joined up with _____ from the air to form _____ dioxide. This gas turns limewater _____.

➡ *Incomplete burning*

Key words
* combustion
* carbon monoxide

Sometimes fuels don't get all the oxygen they need. This is called incomplete burning or incomplete **combustion**. This happens inside a car engine where the petrol burns. It can happen in the home when rooms are not properly ventilated and even when cigarettes burn. In each case, **carbon monoxide** is produced. This is a dangerous, poisonous gas.

29 Write a word equation for this reaction.
30 Explain why a car mechanic should always work with the garage doors open.

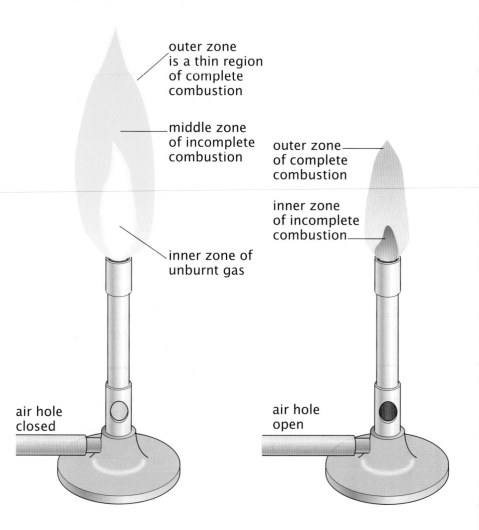

outer zone
is a thin region
of complete
combustion

middle zone
of incomplete
combustion

outer zone
of complete
combustion

inner zone
of incomplete
combustion

inner zone of
unburnt gas

air hole
closed

air hole
open

31 Can you explain why the yellow flame has a very small region of complete combustion?

Time to think

In this chapter you have investigated the difference between physical and chemical changes. You have studied a number of important chemical reactions.

Acids and metals
Acids and carbonates
Combustion of elements
Combustion of fuels

You have begun to use your ideas of particles to help you write word equations for the reactions you have studied.
You have also learnt how to identify these gases:

hydrogen
carbon dioxide
oxygen.

Check that you can explain each of the above parts of this chapter.
Now try to answer these questions.

- Explain why the exhaust of a petrol-driven car may give out carbon monoxide, carbon dioxide and water vapour.
- Explain the difference between complete and incomplete combustion.
- The labels have fallen off three gas cylinders. They are known to contain hydrogen, carbon dioxide and oxygen. Describe the tests that could be used to find out which cylinder contains which gas.
- You are given a 100 cm³ measuring cylinder, a candle and a bung. How could you measure the percentage of oxygen in air?
- Explain the differences between a physical change and a chemical change. Give three examples of each.

Check your answers with at least two other people. If any of your answers are different from theirs check in this book, or your exercise book, to see if you can find out who is correct.
If you cannot work it out between you, ask your teacher to give you a clue.

12 *Energy resources*

In this chapter you will learn:

→ that burning fuels release energy in the form of heat
→ to identify a variety of energy resources including oil, gas and coal
→ the names of renewable energy sources
→ the names of non-renewable energy sources
→ to identify the Sun as the ultimate source of most of the Earth's energy resources
→ to explain how oil, coal and gas are formed
→ to describe in simple terms how electricity can be generated using a range of energy resources
→ to describe how wind and waves can be used as an energy source
→ to consider the advantages and disadvantages of using different energy sources

You will also develop your skills in:

→ finding information from the internet
→ producing bar charts from data in tables
→ planning investigations
→ looking for patterns in data

→ → → WHAT DO YOU KNOW?

Water is being stored behind this dam, and used to generate electrical power. Can you think of any other sources of energy?

You often hear the word energy used in everyday life. Perhaps someone has said to you 'I don't know where you get the energy from'. You may have heard someone else say 'I'm worn out, I haven't got any energy today'.

Often, words we use in different ways in everyday speech, have a very specific meaning when they are used in a scientific context. Energy is one of these words. It has an exact meaning in science. While the idea of energy is very important it is not something that can be easily imagined.

1 In pairs discuss what we mean by energy and write down three sentences that contain the word energy. Share your ideas with another pair. If any of your sentences are unclear try to rewrite them or discuss how you could make them clearer.

➡ *Fuel*

Key words
* fuel
* generate
* primary fuel

We can think of a **fuel** as a concentrated source of energy. So oil, gas, wood and coal are fuels. They are burnt in air to give out heat. We often burn these fuels in power stations to **generate** electricity. We call coal, oil and gas **primary fuels**. Electricity is not a primary fuel because it has to be generated by burning another fuel in the power station.

1 Produce a list of the fuels you use in your home. What do you use each fuel for? Which are primary fuels?

Information processing ## Energy sources

The table below shows the four main energy sources in our homes for the years 1949 and 1999. In recent years the amount of fuel which each of us uses has increased greatly. Today the amount of fuel used by an average family in the UK is much more than was used 100 years ago.

Fuel	Amount of fuel used in 1949 (%)	Amount of fuel used in 1999 (%)
coal	52	13
oil	5	10
gas	28	55
electricity	14	22

1 Use a spreadsheet to produce the data for 1949 as a pie chart. Also produce a bar chart for both 1949 and 1999.

2 What was the main fuel used in 1949?

3 Which energy source has shown the greatest increase from 1949 to 1999?

4 Which energy source has shown the greatest decrease from 1949 to 1999?

Key words
* fossil
* decay
* compressing
* non-renewable
* consumption

Fossil fuels

Coal, oil and natural gas are **fossil** fuels. They were formed millions of years ago from the remains of plants and animals between the layers of rock deep in the Earth's crust.

Coal comes from the fossilised remains of plants. The plants **decayed** and over the years were covered by water, sand and mud. Over millions of years new layers of rock built up **compressing** the decayed plants. Oil comes from the remains of plants, animals and bacteria from ancient seas. They too decayed and over millions of years were covered by water, sand and mud. Once again layers of rock built up above them compressing these remains.

Research | Find out more about how coal, oil and gas were formed.

DID YOU KNOW?

The first town in the UK to have natural gas supplied to it was Burton upon Trent in Staffordshire.

Unfortunately we do not have a never-ending source of these fuels. We have a limited supply. They are **non-renewable**. When they are used up there will be no more available. Some people predict that in less than 50 years we will have no oil or gas left if we carry on using them at the same rate as now. Many people are very concerned about our use of fossil fuels. They think we should try to reduce the amount of fuels we use.

Fuel	Reserves (years)
coal	300
oil	30
gas	50

The chart above shows our fossil fuel reserves. This is based on data from 1997.

2 If we keep using fossil fuels at the same rate when would we be most likely to run out of the fuels shown?
3 Our demand keeps on increasing. From 1987–1997 demand increased by 16%. Can you predict how this may affect how long the resources last?
4 Look at the map below which shows fuel use by different countries of the world. Which countries use the most fuel? Which countries use the least? (See 'Measuring energy' on page 238 for an explanation of the units used on this map.)

Fuel consumption each year measured in tonnes of oil equivalent per person

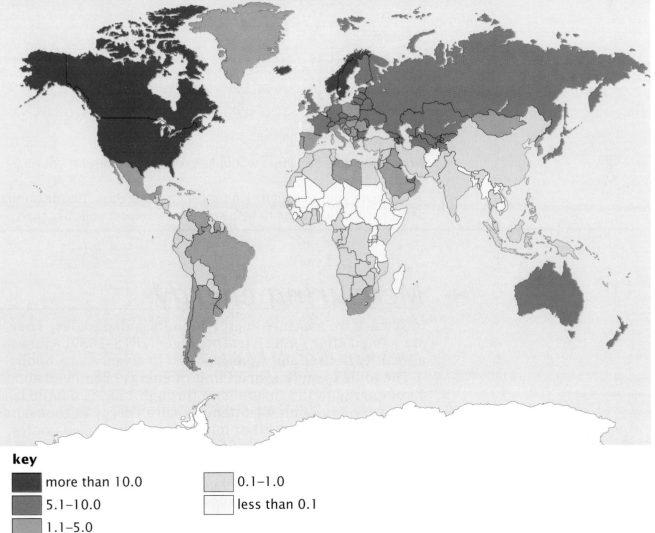

key

- more than 10.0
- 5.1–10.0
- 1.1–5.0
- 0.1–1.0
- less than 0.1

Using fuels

The amount of fuel used depends on various factors. A very useful way of looking at fuel use is to compare how much fuel each person uses in a year.

The table below shows the primary fuel **consumption** (use) per person for different countries of the world. Use a spreadsheet or graph paper to produce a bar chart of fuel consumption. Do the most populated regions have the highest consumption?

Country	Consumption per person per year in MWh	Population in millions
Australia	43	20
Brazil	5	172
Canada	75	31
France	31	59
Germany	40	82
India	1	1033
Japan	26	127
Mexico	10	100
Nigeria	2	127
Sweden	48	9
UK	44	60
USA	88	284
Zambia	3	10

Write three questions that would help someone interpret your bar chart.

Compare your questions with others in your class. Decide on the best possible questions to help someone interpret your bar chart.

→ *Measuring energy*

In science we measure energy in units called joules. They are named after James Prescott Joule (1818–1889) who was a wealthy brewer and experimented in science as a hobby.

The joule is quite a small unit of energy. You need about 1 J of energy to lift an apple up through 1 m. As a joule is not a very large unit we often measure energy in thousands of joules (kilojoules, kJ) or millions of joules (megajoules, MJ). However in everyday life we will come across lots of other units. Common measurements used are kilograms or tonnes of oil equivalent. This means that whatever type of fuel is actually used, it has been converted to the same amount of oil that would be used.

5 Why do you think this is done? Why couldn't some of the information be in tonnes of coal burnt, or cubic metres of gas burnt?
6 We use fossil fuels in a number of ways. For example, oil is used to produce petrol. With a partner, write down a list of all the uses you can think of for the fossil fuels.

When fuels burn, energy is transferred to do various jobs or make things work. For example, petrol or diesel fuel is burnt in a car engine. Different fuels provide different amounts of energy. When fuels are burnt it is useful to compare the amount of energy provided by 1 kg of each fuel. This information is shown in the table below for a range of fuels.

Fuel	Energy (MJ/kg)
coal	36
petrol	46
methane	56
methyl alcohol	22
diesel	45
wood	15

7 What type of graph would you draw to present this information? You may wish to use a spreadsheet.

Enquiry *Energy from fuels*

Plan an investigation to find out which solid fuel gives out the most heat when it burns. You can do this by burning the fuel to heat up some water. You could test some of the following:

- fuel tablets for a model steam engine
- different brands of firelighter
- barbecue fuel beads
- solid fuel for cooking a fondue.

How can you measure the amount of energy transferred to the water? What equipment will you use? How will you set it up?
  What safety measures will you take?
  Decide which factors should be changed and which should be kept the same. What are the input, outcome and fixed variables?
  Design a table for your results. How will you present your results? Will you plot a graph?
Ask your teacher to check your plan before you carry it out.

➡ *Renewable energy resources*

Key words
* renewable
* hydroelectric
* solar power
* wind turbine
* wave generator
* tidal barrage
* biomass energy
* geothermal energy
* heat exchanger

Because fossil fuels took millions of years to make, they cannot be renewed. Other sources are **renewable**. Examples of these are electricity produced at **hydroelectric** power stations (power from water pressure); energy directly from the Sun (**solar power**); **wind turbines**; **wave generators**; **tidal barrages**; firewood (**biomass energy**) and **geothermal energy**.

The pictures show examples of each of these 'renewable energy resources'.

Research Find out more about renewable energy resources. You could choose to find out about: wind energy, solar energy for water heating, hydroelectricity, biomass energy, geothermal, tidal energy, wave energy. Find out if any of these methods are used in the UK. How much energy do they produce? Do they have any advantages? What problems are there in using them as our main source?

It is estimated that the core of the Earth is about 6650 °C. It is cooling down very slowly. It is thought to be cooling at the rate of about 300 °C in 3000 million years. Geothermal energy makes use of the energy that is stored in the Earth's crust. There is nothing new about this form of energy. It is used in France for urban heating. Chaudes-Aigues has had a district heating system since the fourteenth century. Chaudes-Aigues is a town in the Cantal region of Central France. It uses the hot water coming from over 30 springs to provide heating to houses and other buildings. The town owns five of the sources, the rest are privately owned. The smallest spring is used to heat just five houses. The largest one heats the majority of the houses. From the hottest spring the water comes out of the ground at 82 °C, the hottest in Europe. The coolest of the springs is around 50 °C. The water cannot be used directly in the houses for hot water or central heating – it is used in a **heat exchanger**.

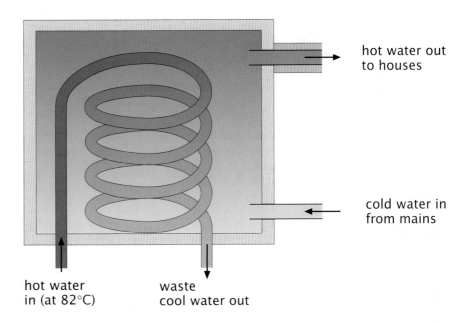

hot water out to houses

cold water in from mains

hot water in (at 82°C)

waste cool water out

A heat exchanger is used to transfer the hot water from the source to heat a separate tank of cold water. The hot water passes in a pipe through the tank and it heats the surrounding water. It is this water that is then used in the houses. One of the reasons for this is that the spring water contains lots of dissolved materials and over just a couple of years they form solids that build up in the pipes.

This is very similar to the 'fur' you get in a kettle. Because of this build up, the pipes have to be replaced often.

In the UK, at present, the only operating geothermal plant is at Southampton where several municipal buildings are heated. The energy is only available in a very local area. There are no fuels required like gas, coal or wood to provide the source of heat. It is a renewable source of energy.

8 Water coming from the springs has been heated. Where is this water heated?

9 Why is the water from the springs not connected directly to the hot taps in homes?

10 The diagram on page 241 shows a heat exchanger. Write a sentence to explain how it works.

11 Write a sentence to explain the term geothermal energy.

Energy from the Sun

Most of our energy comes from the Sun.

Energy resource	Process	Renewable or non-renewable	Advantages and disadvantages
wood logs	the Sun shines, the trees grow, the the trees are cut down and stored. When the winter comes they are burnt to keep us warm.	renewable	when wood burns it produces large amounts of carbon dioxide. However it does not produce many other pollutants like sulphur. Generally it is not burnt in power stations to generate electricity.
coal	the Sun shines, the trees and other plants grow, they die and over millions of years they are compressed and eventually turn into coal. We burn the coal at a power station to produce electricity.	non-renewable	
hydroelectric power	the Sun shines, water evaporates, it forms clouds and then falls as rain. The water runs into streams and rivers. It is trapped by dams and then is used to turn the turbines to generate electricity.	renewable	overall dams are fairly low cost. They are easy to build. The only costs are the expenses of building and maintaining the power stations and dams. There are no fuel costs or transport costs. They can only be built in mountainous regions. They can destroy the habitat. The electricity needs to be transferred overland by cables.

12 Can you think of the advantages and disadvantages of using coal? Can you think of any other advantages or disadvantages of using hydroelectric power or wood logs.

13 Can you explain how the Sun is the source of energy for oil and wind?

14 Copy and complete the table by adding information on coal, oil, wind, tidal power, geothermal energy and biomass.

→ *Nuclear energy*

There is another fuel source that we use to produce electricity. This is **uranium**. It is used in **nuclear power** stations. Today there is a lot of discussion about whether or not nuclear power stations should continue to be built. Some people are worried about the possibility of **radioactive** materials escaping into the surrounding area. This happened on 25 April 1986 at Chernobyl in Russia. Others think that nuclear power stations are cleaner than those that burn fossil fuels, because when fossil fuels are burnt they do more damage to the environment. Fossil fuels give off sulphur dioxide, which produces acid rain. Also, fossil fuels are not very efficient. A small mass of uranium can be used to provide enormous amounts of energy. However the disposal of the radioactive waste materials is a problem. Another problem is what to do with a nuclear power station when it is no longer useful for generating electricity.

Research Use the internet to research the disaster at Chernobyl in 1986 and the one in the USA at Three Mile Island in 1979.

Time to think
- Coal is a fossil fuel, a primary fuel and a non-renewable fuel. Explain what each of these three descriptions means.
- Design a poster to show whether you agree or disagree with nuclear power stations. Make sure that you use text as well as pictures to convey your ideas. Study the posters produced by others in the class. Draw up a table explaining each side of the argument about nuclear power stations.

→ *Electricity*

As we have already seen electricity is not a primary fuel but it is a very clean and convenient source of energy for the home. There are many things in the home that work with electricity. In the UK the production of electricity is about 350 000 GWh for a population of about 60 million people. This means each person uses on average 6 MWh. We need to be able to generate at least 50 million kilowatts. Of course we don't use the same amount of electricity throughout the day.

15 Do we need more energy in summer or winter? At what time of day will there be least demand for electricity?

16 Look at the graph below showing the demand for electricity during 24 hours in December.
   Look how the demand had sudden surges. At what times did they occur? These corresponded to the adverts after particular TV programmes. Can you explain why this might be?

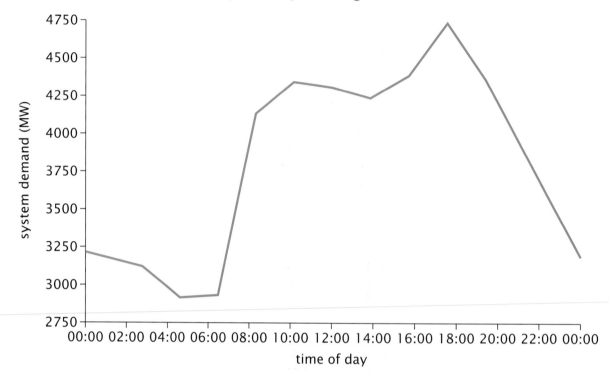

Generating electricity

Electricity is produced from many different types of power station. The graph below shows the amount of energy produced from different energy resources in the UK in 1990 and 2000.

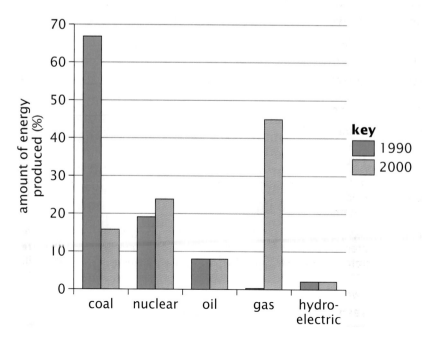

17 Can you explain the main changes between the information for 1990 and for 2000?
   What would you predict the trend would be over the next 10 years? 50 years? Give reasons for your predictions.

Information processing *Different energy resources*

The energy production in France in 1994 is shown in the table below.

Fuel	1994 (%)
coal	16
nuclear	50
oil	1
gas	4
hydroelectric	25
geothermal	4

1 Use a spreadsheet to produce a bar chart to show these results.
2 Table **Y** lists different resources for generating electricity. Table **Z** gives some of the advantages and disadvantages of these resources. Match the description to the energy resource and state whether it is renewable or non-renewable.

Y

	Energy resource
1	coal
2	biomass
3	oil
4	nuclear
5	gas
6	hydroelectric
7	wind
8	waves
9	solar
10	tides

Z

	Energy resource
A	No fuel is required. It is pollution free. Needs fine weather. A focusing collector is used to trap the Sun using mirrors which reflect onto a boiler that turns water into steam.
B	No fuel is required. It uses the gravitational forces of the Sun and Moon. Needs to be built by the sea where the tidal range is 7 m or more.
C	No fuel is required. The uneven heating of the Earth by the Sun causes differences in air pressure and produces wind. Electricity is only generated when the conditions are right. The initial cost of construction is high. It is noisy. Birds fly into the rotor blades.
D	Fission is a process in which a heavy nucleus splits into two nuclei. It releases large amounts of energy. It produces radioactive waste.
E	No fuel is required. It uses the energy from the ocean. There are various types. The oscillating water column and the Salter Duck are two. It is only suitable close to the ocean where you expect there to be many large waves.
F	Very convenient. Easily piped around the country. Very efficient when used to generate electricity in the latest power stations.
G	This uses energy stored in organic matter. It includes wood, crops and animal waste. It burns to produce large amounts of carbon dioxide. Trees can be grown to replace ones that are used.
H	This comes from the fossilised remains of plants. Mines are dug to bring the fuel to the surface. When it burns it produces carbon dioxide and other pollutants like sulphur dioxide.
I	This comes from the remains of ocean creatures living millions of years ago. It can be transported through pipes. When burnt it produces pollutants. It is a very useful raw material for industry.
J	A dam usually has to be built to create a difference in water levels. This gives a difference in water pressure that is used to generate the electricity. There are no fuel costs. Generators can be started quickly. Flooding of land can destroy habitats.

3 Why do we need to generate more electricity from renewable energy resources? What may happen if we don't?

➡ *Energy in industry*

Industry is also very concerned with reducing energy consumption and its impact on the environment.

Look at the chart produced by Wolverhampton and Dudley Breweries showing their fuel sources over a period of 20 years.

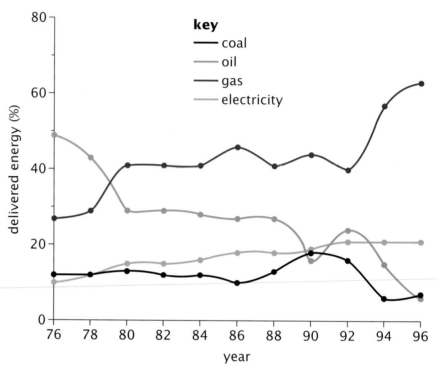

18 Use a spreadsheet to produce a pie chart showing the relative fuel consumption for 1976 compared to 1996. Explain whether the charts give any information about how the overall energy consumption has changed.

➡ *Food*

Plants and crops use energy from the Sun to grow. Animals eat these crops. Our fuel source is the food we eat. Some foods are better fuels than others. Energy is measured in joules (J). The sides of food packets and tins often contain a lot of information. A few examples are shown:

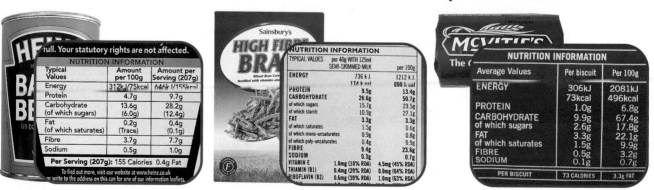

HEINZ BAKED BEANS

NUTRITION INFORMATION		
Typical Values	Amount per 100g	Amount per Serving (207g)
Energy	312kJ/75kcal	646k J/155kcal
Protein	4.7g	9.7g
Carbohydrate (of which sugars)	13.6g (6.0g)	28.2g (12.4g)
Fat (of which saturates)	0.2g (Trace)	0.4g (0.1g)
Fibre	3.7g	7.7g
Sodium	0.5g	1.0g
Per Serving (207g): 155 Calories 0.4g Fat		

To find out more, visit our website at www.heinz.co.uk or write to the address on this can for one of our information leaflets.

Sainsbury's HIGH FIBRE BRAN

NUTRITION INFORMATION		
TYPICAL VALUES	per 40g WITH 125ml SEMI-SKIMMED MILK	per 100g
ENERGY	736 k J. 174 k cal	1212 k J. 800 k cal
PROTEIN	9.5g	13.4g
CARBOHYDRATE	26.6g	50.7g
of which sugars	15.7g	23.5g
of which starch	10.9g	27.1g
FAT	3.3g	3.3g
of which saturates	1.5g	0.6g
of which mono-unsaturates	0.9g	0.8g
of which poly-unsaturates	0.4g	0.9g
FIBRE	9.4g	23.6g
SODIUM	0.3g	0.7g
VITAMIN E	1.8mg (18% RDA)	4.5mg (45% RDA)
THIAMIN (B1)	0.4mg (29% RDA)	0.9mg (64% RDA)
RIBOFLAVIN (B2)	0.6mg (39% RDA)	1.0mg (63% RDA)

McVITIE'S

NUTRITION INFORMATION		
Average Values	Per biscuit	Per 100g
ENERGY	306kJ 73kcal	2081kJ 496kcal
PROTEIN	1.0g	6.8g
CARBOHYDRATE of which sugars	9.9g 2.6g	67.4g 17.8g
FAT of which saturates	3.3g 1.5g	22.1g 9.9g
FIBRE	0.5g	3.2g
SODIUM	0.1g	0.7g
PER BISCUIT	73 CALORIES	3.3g FAT

Country	Average daily intake of food (MJ)
Afghanistan	7200
Australia	13500
Bangladesh	8800
China	11400
Germany	14800
India	9400
Japan	12400
Kenya	9100
New Zealand	14100
Nigeria	9700
Russia	13900
USA	13200
UK	15400

As you can see your breakfast cereal supplies you with a good source of fuel to start the day.

19 The amount of food we need depends on many factors. Can you think of some?

The food energy needs of a typical man is 10500 MJ and a typical woman is 8400 MJ.

The map below and the table on the left show two different ways of presenting data about food energy intake in countries throughout the world. The World Health Organization (WHO) recommends a minimum of 11000 MJ per day. A person is starving when their daily intake is less than 7140 MJ.

20 Present the information given in the table in a suitable chart.

Worldwide food consumption per person

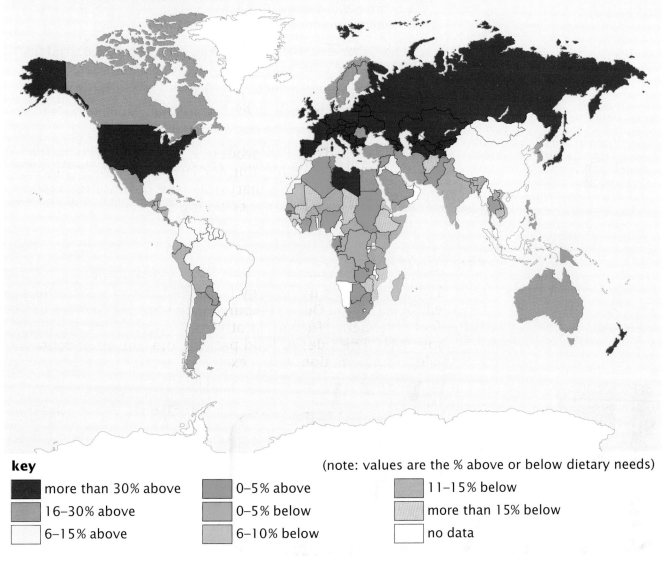

key

(note: values are the % above or below dietary needs)

■ more than 30% above	▨ 0–5% above	▨ 11–15% below
▨ 16–30% above	▨ 0–5% below	▨ more than 15% below
□ 6–15% above	▨ 6–10% below	□ no data

Information processing *Energy from food*

Use a spreadsheet to keep a record of what you eat during one day. The spreadsheet will give you the energy value of all the items of food that you eat and calculate your total energy intake.

1 How does your total energy intake compare to your energy requirements?

2 Does one meal give you enough energy for the day?

3 Which meal gives you the most energy? Is it the same for everyone in the class?

4 Which food gives you the most energy? Is this the same as others in the class?

Time to think

- By now you should have found out a lot about energy. Can you produce an energy leaflet? It could be on one of the following.

    what are fossil fuels
    renewable energy resources
    energy and food

    or another area that interests you. When completed, read the leaflets that other pupils have created to check your knowledge on this topic.

- Write a letter to your MP explaining what you think the Government should be doing about different fuels for generating electricity. You may think that we should be using less fossil fuels for example. You might find this writing frame useful.

Dear...

I would like to explain why...

The main reason for this is...

Another reason is...

The possible effects on the environment...

A further effect may be...

So I believe that the best fuel...

Index